9/10

HOW TO KEEP
KOSHER

HOW TO KEEP

KOSHER

A Comprehensive Guide
to Understanding
Jewish Dietary Laws

LISË STERN

WILLIAM MORROW

An Imprint of HarperCollinsPublishers

HarperCollins books may be purchased for educational, business, or sales promotional use. For information please write: Special Markets Department, HarperCollins Publishers Inc., 10 East 53rd Street, New York, NY 10022.

FIRST EDITION

DESIGNED BY SARAH MAYA GUBKIN

Printed on acid-free paper

Library of Congress Cataloging-in-Publication Data

Stern, Lisë.
    How to keep Kosher : a comprehensive guide to understanding Jewish dietary laws / Lisë Stern.—1st ed.
        p. cm.
    Includes bibliographical references and index.
    ISBN 0-06-051500-7
    1. Kosher food.   2. Jews—Dietary laws.   3. Jewish law.   I. Title.

BM710.S74 2004
296.7'3—dc22
                                                            2003066615

04   05   06   07   08   WBC/RRD   10   9   8   7   6   5   4   3   2   1

For my family:

Jeffrey, love of my life
Scientific, inventive Gabriel
Artistic, creative Eitan
Joyous, imaginative Shoshanna

CONTENTS

ACKNOWLEDGMENTS

SO MUCH GOES INTO CREATING A BOOK, and there are so many people to thank for this project coming into being. But before people, I feel I first need to thank God for opening this door. My Judaism, my faith, is an integral part of me, and I have always enjoyed studying Torah and learning more about my people and our history.

The opportunity to write this book gave me a chance to study in a way I hadn't in a very long time, giving me further insight into the history and range of ideologies that fall under the general category of Judaism and what it means to be Jewish. Kashrut is such an integral part of Judaism; whether or not you keep kosher, it is still a defining element of Jewish observance. I thank God for giving me this opportunity.

That said, there were several people who made *How to Keep Kosher* possible. My editor, Harriet Bell, conceived of the idea and saw a need for a general book on kashrut. She contacted my agent Doe Coover, who served as matchmaker between us. I thank both Doe and Harriet for making sure *How to Keep Kosher* happened. I would also like to thank the team at William Morrow: copy editor Sonia Greenbaum, senior production editor Ann Cahn, publicist Carrie Bachman, and editorial assistant (and general organizer) Lucy Baker.

This book would not have been possible without the support of my family. My husband, Jeffrey, has been infinitely encouraging throughout, from proposal through manuscript through final copy, and I thank him for his ongoing love, respect, and encouragement. I thank my wonderful children, Gabriel, Eitan, and Shoshanna, for their infinite patience during a very long summer when I disappeared for days at a time. My in-laws, Donald and Esther Robbins, always help make life easier for all of us.

My parents, Joyce and Michael Stern, gave me a strong Jewish foundation upon which to build my life. They helped make me particularly aware of the significance of keeping kosher when I was a child, and of the joys of studying Torah and the minute details of Jewish texts. All were elements essential to the creation of this book. A special thank you to my father for reading the manuscript and checking all the fine points of textual references and assertions, often under deadline pressure.

There were many scholars and rabbis, far more versed in the field of biblical studies than I, who helped me understand the minutiae of kashrut particulars. I am a Conservative Jew, and I present both Conservative and Orthodox points of view regarding kashrut. There is a conflict here since, for some Orthodox Jews, the Conservative interpretation of halacha cannot coexist with the Orthodox interpretation of halacha. For this reason, some rabbis I spoke with did not want their names to appear in this book. That said, they were still extremely respectful of my work, and incredibly helpful in explaining the finer points of concepts such as *basar b'chalav*, preparing food for Shabbat, and more general details. I am grateful to them for sharing their knowledge so willingly and so clearly.

Those at the "Big Four" kashrut certifying agencies were all very helpful, notably: Dr. Avrom Pollak and Rabbi Mayer Kurcfeld of Star-K Kosher Certification; Rabbi Dovid Steigman and Rabbi Levi Garelik of Organized Kashrus Laboratories (a.k.a. OK Kosher Certification); Rabbi Moshe Elefant of the Orthodox Union; and Rabbi Yehuda Rosenbaum of Kof K Supervision Organization.

There are several other rabbis whom I wish to thank for the time and expertise they shared with me. Rabbi Ari Z. Zivotofsky, Ph.D., is a lecturer in the brain science program at Bar Ilan University in Israel. He is also an expert in explaining the fine details and history of kashrut of various animals, and he has written brilliant essays on turkey, bison, birds, and more. He not only is extremely knowledgeable but his writing style makes complex and obscure issues of kashrut accessible.

Some of the issues dealt with in this book have been discussed with Rabbi Aaron Tendler, a member of the faculty of Ner Israel Rabbinical College in Baltimore, Maryland, and I thank him.

Rabbi Paul Plotkin, author of *The Lord Is My Shepherd, Why Do I Still Want?*, is also chairman of the Kashrut Subcommittee of the Committee on Jewish Law and Standards of the Rabbinical Assembly. He explained details of Conservative kashrut halacha and brought me up to date with the latest Responsa on controversial issues.

I thank the following rabbis for their insight: Rabbi Elliot Dorff, Rabbi Professor David Golinkin, Rabbi Richard Levy, Rabbi Victor Reinstein, our cousin Rabbi Mark Robbins, Rabbi Harry Sinoff, Rabbi David Starr, and Rabbi Shawn Zevit.

Joseph M. Regenstein, professor of food science at Cornell University, and Temple Grandin, associate professor of animal science at Colorado State University, are authorities on the treatment of animals during the slaughtering process, including those undergoing *shechita*. I thank them for their time explaining these details. Dr. James W. Atz, emeritus curator of the American Museum of Natural History, Ichthyology Department, is a leading authority on which species of fish are kosher and which are not (debated species notwithstanding), and I thank him for his expertise. Dr. Joseph Stern, Assistant Professor of Hebrew Law at Hebrew College, and Dr. Joseph Lowin, author of *Hebrewspeak*, provided the etymological information.

This book involved much research. I am a library junkie, and am fortunate enough to live near Hebrew College in Newton, Massachusetts, which has an extensive Judaica library, with dozens of essential volumes not available anywhere else. The staff at the library was extremely helpful, and I want to thank them for their help and knowledge: Mimi Mazor, Frankie Snyder, Suzan Rothschild Hirsch, Harvey Sukenic, and Robert Listernick. In addition, thank you to Helene Tuckman at the Temple Emanuel Library.

Several people shared recipes with me, and I'd like to thank Gabriel and Ted Kaptchuk, Barbara Model, Esty Oppenheimer, my aunt Judy Robbins, Deb Shapiro, Gregg Stern, my aunt Raya Stern, Elizabeth Sternberg, and my cousin Ittamar Weissbrem, plus my mother and mother-in-law.

Thanks to Anne Lynch, for providing expert childcare. I would also like to thank a circle of supportive friends, including Katherine Ellin, Kim Mayone, Jill and David Segal, Caroline and Steve Kaufer, and Carolyn Faye Fox, with her witty suggestions for chapter titles. And a special thank you to my grandmothers, Grandlady and Omi (z"l), who always encouraged me to do my best and follow my heart.

HOW TO KEEP
KOSHER

INTRODUCTION

KEEPING KOSHER IS A MULTIFACETED CONCEPT, one that brings to my mind the classic journalistic questions, the five Ws—who, what, where, when, why—plus how. Because all these questions apply when considering kashrut, the act of observing the Jewish dietary laws. There are short answers, and there are in-depth answers.

The short answers: **Who** keeps kosher? Jews. **What** is kashrut? Specific rules that guide how we eat. **Where** do we keep kosher? Wherever we eat. **When**? Whenever we eat. **How** is it observed? By learning the rules of kashrut and following them. And finally, **why** keep kosher? Because God says so.

Loaded questions, really, and short answers raise more questions, spark a desire for real explanations. So for longer answers—read on, as I answer the questions, not necessarily in the above order. As for *how*—there's a longer short answer here in the introduction. But the step-by-step explanation of how to follow the Jewish dietary laws comprises the body of this book.

What Is Kashrut?

Daily life is filled with routines. Some are universal and we do them almost without thought. We wake up, eat breakfast, go to work. We eat lunch, come home, eat dinner, and go to bed. Other routines are more thoughtful, more personal, and involve choices. We stick with one brand of shampoo or hand cream for years because of its particular scent; we make special dishes for certain holidays; or we read a story to our child every night before bed. Traditional Judaism injects sanctification into the ordinary habits of everyday life, adding a mindfulness to otherwise automatic actions. There are blessings that can cause us to consider any activity we do, such as blessings for getting dressed, for washing, for different kinds of food.

Food is one of the most pervasive elements of day-to-day living—we have to eat, our day is structured around meals. And it is pretty easy not to think about those meals, to grab a bite without considering what we're doing. Kashrut, the practice of keeping kosher, includes a series of biblically based rules that govern what and how we eat. Keeping kosher helps us pause and think about what we eat, and how we eat it, and elevates the act of eating into a spiritual as well as a physical activity.

How, When, and *Where* to Keep Kosher

When you decide to keep a kosher home, it will significantly change the way you live. Eating is an integral part of each day, and we all establish meal habits, from the favorite cereal we might buy to the bowl we choose to eat it from. When you go kosher, that may change. You may need new dishes. A preferred bread, a favorite soup, a treasured recipe may not be kosher. You'll find yourself reading ingredients like never before, checking packages for the *hechsher*, the symbol that indicates if the product is kosher. You'll develop a new vocabulary. The words "dairy" and "meat" will take on new significance.

Ask a dozen Jews why they keep kosher, and you'll probably get two dozen answers. Ask them *how* they keep kosher, and you'll get another dozen responses. But there are three core basics:

- No "forbidden" meat, fowl, or seafood (the list includes pork, birds of prey, and shellfish).

- No milk and meat together—they are not eaten together, and there are separate dishes, cookware, and utensils for milk and meat items.
- Meat consumed must be kosher meat.

The rest, to paraphrase the sage Hillel, is commentary.

Your Jewish community, who you entertain, can determine how you keep kosher in your home. An Orthodox Jew has stricter criteria for kashrut observance than a Reform Jew, and a strictly observant Orthodox Jew will not eat food prepared in a kitchen with a dishwasher used for mixed meat and dairy loads, or in a kitchen with nonapproved foods in the cupboards, or food that's been cooked on Shabbat, for example. If you will be entertaining strictly observant Jews in your home, you will want to keep a more strictly kosher kitchen. If your community is less strict, if the friends you entertain will eat items that are "ingredient kosher" rather than certified, that might indicate the best level of kashrut for you. The chapters that follow explore these differences.

As for *when* and *where*, start at home. Mealtime is the when. If you observe kashrut, you'll be keeping kosher whenever you eat. And this gets tied into *where* you keep kosher. People use the phrase "keeping kosher in, keeping kosher out." "In" refers to your home. "Out" refers to places you eat outside of your home, such as restaurants. There are some Jews who keep a kosher home, but when they go out to eat, they do not observe kashrut. It depends on the level at which you keep kosher. People who are most observant eat only in kosher restaurants and homes. Others may eat in a restaurant that serves unkosher food, but only consume a cold salad or fruit plate. Some eat fish or vegetarian dishes, but no meat. Others eat meat, but no pork or shellfish. And others eat anything. Where you keep kosher is a decision you will make when choosing *how* you'll keep kosher.

My husband grew up in a kosher home, but when his family went out to restaurants, they ate everything. The line became fuzzy for him when he went to college. His dorm cafeteria now was, effectively, "home," but he wasn't preparing the food. Was dorm food "in" or "out"? Ultimately, he realized, all meals he was eating now were, effectively, out, so he decided to follow basic laws of kashrut wherever he ate, eschewing meat for fish and vegetarian food in restaurants and in the dorm cafeteria.

Where Do These Kosher Laws Come From, Anyway?

The laws of kashrut come from historical sources, but what are they?

Let's start with the sources for what defines Judaism in the first place: the **Tanach**, the Bible, called by non-Jews the Old Testament. The Tanach consists of three parts, and the word *TaNaCh* is an acronym for those three parts: **Torah**, the Law, also called the *Chumash*, or the Pentateuch, the Five Books of Moses; **Nevi'im**, Prophets, which includes the books of various prophets, such as Joshua, Isaiah, and Samuel; and **Ketuvim**, Writings, including the Books of Psalms, Ruth, and Lamentations.

The laws and ordinances and commandments we follow are based on the text in the five books of the Torah, supplemented by the rest of the Tanach. This is called the **Written Law** or the **Written Torah**. But there are obscurities in this text, mysterious instructions that are not immediately clear. And so the debates began.

How to interpret properly God's words? For example, what constitutes forbidden work on the Sabbath? What birds are acceptable to eat? How should we build a sukkah? These are the kinds of questions Jewish sages have tried to answer to establish some sort of standard, the ultimate goal always being to fulfill God's commandments in the way God intended. The initial ongoing debates, which lasted hundreds of years, are referred to as *Torah She'ba'al Peh*, the **Oral Law** or the **Oral Torah**. This Oral Law was ultimately written down in the **Talmud,** starting around the third century. (Yes, Oral Law can be written down, it just refers to all Jewish law written down since the Tanach.)

The Talmud is not exactly linear text, and is known for discussions on particular issues that branch off into tangents upon tangents. It's sort of like the Internet, with Web pages linked to other Web pages linked to still more Web pages. . . . But it does have a rough organization. It consists of two parts, the **Mishnah** and the **Gemara**.

Rabbi Akiva, a second-century sage, hero, and, ultimately, martyr (murdered by the Romans for not renouncing his faith), laid the groundwork for the teachings found in the Mishnah, the first written-down text that categorizes the various issues of observance. The Mishnah was organized by Rabbi Judah the Prince at the end of the second century C.E.

The rabbinic debates about Jewish law did not end when the Mishnah was written down. The discussions in the Land of Israel eventually became the *Jerusalem Talmud*, while the discussions in Babylonia became the *Babylonian Talmud*. The word "Talmud" generally refers to the Babylonian Talmud. This Talmud was composed from about the third through the sixth centuries. The Talmud incorporates the Mishnah, and is organized in a similar way.

However, Jewish law is not based solely on the Tanach or on the Talmud, but on still more commentary by sages through the ages. Many of these scholars are known not by their birth names, but by honorary acronyms. Some of the most influential include **Rashi**, Rabbi Shlomo Yitzchaki, from eleventh-century France, who wrote commentary on all the Tanach and the Talmud, and most printed Talmuds today include his commentary as part of each page, as well as other commentary.

Rambam, the name of honor given to Rabbi Moshe ben Maimon, also called Maimonides, was a twelfth-century scholar and physician who lived in Cairo.

Rambam is most known for his fourteen-volume *Mishneh Torah*. *Mishneh Torah* can mean "Repetition of the Torah"; his work incorporates both the written and the oral Torah. In the *Mishneh-Torah*, Rambam compiled a list of the 613 *Mitzvot*, "Commandments," from the Torah, and then set forth the details of the Mitzvot. The 613 Mitzvot are part of the core of Judaism, and are dealt with in various parts of the Talmud, but Rambam organized his code of Jewish law into easy-to-read categories. Yes, the Ten Commandments are the *core* core of Judaism, but the 613 Mitzvot cover all aspects of day-to-day life, such as laws of character (not to embarrass others), study (learn Torah), and acquisition (don't overcharge or underpay). Rambam organized the 613 Mitzvot into fourteen categories—but he didn't just list them, he explained them in great detail.

Four hundred years later, Joseph Caro, a Sephardic rabbi living in Sfat (Safad), Israel, wrote the ***Shulchan Aruch***, which literally means "Prepared Table," but is translated as "Code of Law." Caro, called the **Mechaber** (literally, "author"), wrote this four-volume set over several decades, and published it in 1565—printed on a press. This made it easier to revise it, which became necessary, as Caro's work reflected only Sephardic practices and there were Ashkenazic practices that differed and were followed by many Eastern European Jews. The Polish Rabbi Moses Isserles, known as **Rama**, contributed Ashkenazic commentary to Caro's, called the *Mapa*, or "Tablecloth," which was incorporated into the revised Shulchan Aruch published in 1569, and is still regarded as standard Code of Jewish Law today.

"Sephardic" comes from the Hebrew word *S'farad*, Spain. Today, it ref scendants of Jews from Spain, Portugal, North Africa, and other Middle Ea countries.

"Ashkenazic" comes from *Ashkenaz*, a Hebrew word for Germany from Germany, Eastern Europe, and other northern European countries. The majority of Jews in the United States are Ashkenazic. Sephardic traditions are largely Orthodox, while those of Ashkenazi Jews fall under many different movements in the United States.

While the sixteenth-century Shulchan Aruch is still regarded as the standard code of Jewish law today, the world has seen many changes in the past four hundred years that affect Jewish observances, such as the advent of electricity and gas-powered ovens. Because the way we eat is dynamic, the way we keep kosher has to keep up with changes. New foods are introduced, new types of preparation. Rabbinical authorities write additional commentary rendering decisions on all topics (not just kashrut), and these are called **Responsa** or *Tshuvot*, answers. Responsa written by central authorities in different Jewish movements continue through today in determining issues of Jewish observance.

The Torah, the Talmud, the Shulchan Aruch, Responsa—all comprise what is called *halacha*. Halacha means "law" in Hebrew, but it also can mean "the way" or "path"; the root word *heh-lamed-chaf* means "go" or "walk." It describes the way the laws of the Torah apply to everyday living. When something is referred to as "halachically correct," it means that a particular act coincides with Jewish law as determined by the cumulative sources. Halacha covers all aspects of Jewish life, from prayers to holidays to how to dress and how to eat—that is, kashrut.

It has always been the desire of observant Jews to fulfill God's commandments to the absolute best of their abilities. If a commandment leaves room for doubt, rabbis through the ages have devised what is called "a fence around the law." The commandment might say, "Don't do X." That's specific. But there may be actions that are similar to but not the same as X. Are they permissible? Just in case, rabbis agreed on various stipulations to expand on that original commandment so we are at no risk of violating the commandment. So, "Don't do X" becomes "Don't do X or stuff that is like X in any way that someone could have thought possible. Therefore there is no chance you might inadvertently do X."

In summary, the laws of kashrut as observed today fall under three categories:

- Laws that come directly from the Torah
- Expansions of those laws by rabbis
- Laws determined by rabbis independent of the Torah

In addition, Jewish observance includes *minhag*, or custom, also called *mesorah*—the "Tradition!" of *Fiddler on the Roof* fame. This is a sort of an "unofficial" law that becomes official. If there is a certain practice that is not covered explicitly by halacha, but it has been a tradition to do it, it becomes like a law. Wearing a *kipa*, or yarmulke (skullcap), is an example, as is eating apples and honey on Rosh Hashanah or the amount of time you wait between eating a meat meal and a dairy meal.

Who Keeps Kosher? Jewish Affiliations

What is the proper way to keep kosher, based on the textual sources described above? Jews keep kosher, yes, but the rules of kashrut can vary, depending on your Jewish affiliation and level of observance. And even within the dictates of a particular affiliation, there are many ways you can choose to keep kosher.

There are several affiliations in Judaism, notably **Orthodox, Conservative, Reform,** and **Reconstructionist.** These are the American terms for these movements; elsewhere in the world they go by different names. Of the 5.2 million Jews in the United States, according to the 1990 National Jewish Population Survey, 7 percent of American Jews identify themselves as Orthodox, 38 percent as Conservative, 42 percent as Reform, and 1 percent as Reconstructionist. The remaining Jews either identify with smaller movements or are unaffiliated.

The 2000–01 Survey revamped the questions. Rather than categorize affiliations in terms of Jewish movements, respondents are categorized as "unaffiliated" (44 percent, no membership in a synagogue or Jewish organization), "moderately affiliated" (28 percent, membership in one such organization), and "highly affiliated" (28 percent, membership in two or more such organizations), with a breakdown indicating observances such as keeping kosher and observing Shabbat.

The differences between the official stand on kashrut in each affiliation varies. Bear in mind these are not hard-and-fast rules, and I am sure there are those who would disagree with whatever description I give to each—that seems to be the nature of Judaism, after all, without which we wouldn't have the Talmud. Further, while these are the four largest Jewish movements, there are others, and movements within movements as well. I shall try to describe the differences, while standing on one foot.

How each movement determines the proper way to observe kashrut is based on its fundamentals of how to be Jewish in general. What makes us Jewish? This age-old question has ever-evolving and countless answers.

The **Orthodox** view is that all of the Torah, both written and oral, was given to us by

God. Orthodoxy defines Judaism as following all the laws and traditions of halacha. Core halachic observances are the same throughout Orthodoxy, but Orthodoxy has several branches that have their variations. Chassidism, which has its own subgroups, is one such branch. Different groups follow the teachings of different rabbinic authorities.

Orthodoxy has several rabbinic authorities. One of the most well known is the Union of Orthodox Jewish Congregations, or the Orthodox Union (OU), and the Rabbinical Council of America (RCA), and there are several rabbinical schools.

A fundamental difference between Orthodoxy and all other movements is that in Orthodoxy, men and women have clearly defined and distinctly different roles. For example, men and women pray separately, and women cannot become rabbis or be counted as part of a *minyan*, the group of ten people needed in order to recite certain group prayers. Women are admitted to the rabbinical schools for the Conservative, Reform, and Reconstructionist movements.

Orthodoxy follows kashrut according to halacha and represents the most strict version of kashrut observance described in this book.

Conservative Judaism believes in the divine source for the Torah, but also believes in human contributions to all the commentary. There are others in the Conservative movement who believe that the Torah may have been divinely inspired, rather than revealed by God to Moses.

In his preface to *A Guide to Jewish Religious Practice*, Rabbi Isaac Klein writes that the philosophy of the Conservative movement "takes into consideration the historical and sociological factors, both past and present, operating in the development of the Halakha." The Committee on Jewish Law and Standards (CJLS) is the central halachic authority for the Conservative movement. The United Synagogue of Conservative Judaism (USCJ) is the central synagogue organization, and the Jewish Theological Seminary (JTS) in Manhattan is the main institution for Conservative rabbinical study.

The Conservative view on kashrut is similar in many ways to that of Orthodoxy but with some flexibility and some differences in halachic decisions concerning particular foods. As Rabbi David Starr, dean of the Me'ah study program at Hebrew College in Newton, Massachusetts, says, "Both movements are committed to kashrut as a core Jewish practice, integral to any serious approach to Jewish law."

The **Reform** movement, when it first began in Germany in the nineteenth century, rejected much of the historical practices of religious Judaism, asserting that it was possible to retain a Jewish identity while assimilating the local culture. Regarding kashrut, the 1885 Pittsburgh Platform, a Statement of Reform Principles, declared, "We hold that all such Mosaic and rabbinical laws that regulate diet, priestly purity, and dress originated in ages and under the influence of ideas altogether foreign to our present mental and spiritual state."

The movement acknowledges that adaptation can go both ways. Less observance was not always successful in helping Jews retain a Jewish identity; in recent years, the Reform movement has encouraged a more active study of Judaism. The Reform umbrella group, the Union for Reform Judaism (URJ), previously known as the Union of American Hebrew Congregations (UAHC), states on its website, "Reform Jews accept the Torah as the foundation of Jewish life containing God's ongoing revelation to our people and the record of our people's ongoing relationship with God. We see the Torah as God inspired, a living document that enables us to confront the timeless and timely challenges of our everyday lives."

The official Reform platform has been modified three times since 1885, most recently in 1999. This "Statement of Principles for Reform Judaism" went through several drafts, some of which explicitly encouraged kashrut, although this is still controversial within the movement. There are Reform Jews who actively believe kashrut should *not* be encouraged. The final version reads, "We are committed to the ongoing study of the whole array of *mitzvot* and to the fulfillment of those that address us as individuals and as a community. Some of these *mitzvot*, sacred obligations, have long been observed by Reform Jews; others, both ancient and modern, demand renewed attention as the result of the unique context of our own times." As with all things Jewish, the Statement of Principles has commentary, which elaborates the position on kashrut more explicitly: "The Third Draft of the Principles specifically mentioned *kashrut, tallit, tefillin,* and *mikveh* (ritual immersion) to demonstrate the principle that there is no *mitzvah* barred to Reform Jews, even as the Reform movement does not compel the observance of any *mitzvot*."

Kashrut, according to Reform principles, can include traditional halachic kashrut. The principles also advocate what some call "ethical" kashrut, or "eco-kashrut," which includes such concerns as the labor conditions of the workers who produced a particular product, the environmental friendliness of the packaging used, and the treatment of the animals before being slaughtered.

The other central organizations for the Reform movement are the Central Conference of American Rabbis (CCAR) and the Hebrew Union College (HUC) rabbinical school, with locations in Cincinnati, New York, Los Angeles, and Jerusalem.

The **Reconstructionist** movement was started by Mordechai Kaplan, a Conservative rabbi, in the 1930s. The central organization for the movement is the Jewish Reconstructionist Federation (JRF), with the Reconstructionist Rabbinical Association (RRC). According to the JRF, "Reconstructionism does not view Judaism as a total and immutable revelation from God to Moses at Sinai that is essentially unchanged through all generations. We see Judaism as the ever-evolving product of history, an ongoing attempt to forge a society based on holy values." Reconstructionism does not accept halacha as an obligatory authority, although it does appreciate the traditions it imparts.

Regarding kashrut, Reconstructionism examines traditional issues of kashrut and, effectively, reconstructs them. They follow similar lines as those of the Conservative movement, yet add other thoughts. In *A Guide to Jewish Practice*, Rabbi David A. Teutsch describes kashrut as the sanctification of food, and writes that we should examine where our food comes from, exploring, as with the Reform movement, "eco-kashrut."

It should be noted that most certifying agencies, organizations that supervise the production of kosher foods, are Orthodox. This falls under the lowest-common-denominator category. Kashrut observers of less strict movements will eat food that is acceptable to Orthodoxy, but an observant Orthodox Jew may not eat food that might be acceptable to other movements.

Why Keep Kosher?

Why do Jews around the world keep kosher? Keeping kosher is considered a mitzvah, the fulfillment of commandments from God. If you're Orthodox or Conservative, that alone is an answer. In **Deuteronomy 14:2–3,** God says, *"For you are a holy people unto the Lord your God, and the Lord has chosen you to be His own treasure out of all peoples that are upon the face of the earth. You shall not eat any abominable thing."*

Rabbi Victor Reinstein, the rabbi at my children's Solomon Schechter School in Newton, Massachusetts, explains, "What the Torah says is, be holy. That is the reason for kashrut. That is the starting point, the essential reason. It's part of our relationship, our covenant with God. It is a spiritual discipline which has been given us to create the framework for holiness. You be holy like I am holy—that is the purpose of kashrut—to be holy, to be separate from that which denies holiness, that which denies life."

But "why" can cover two areas. Why follow these laws, yes, but also why did God make these particular rules? Why no pork? Why should animals be killed in a certain way? and so on.

For naturally curious human beings, "Because I said so" is not always a satisfactory response, even if it is the true answer. Rambam wrote, "Although the statutes in the Law [Torah] are all of them divine edicts . . . yet it is proper to ponder over them and to give a reason for them, so far as we are able to give them a reason." Rambam himself offered a few reasons for the dietary mitzvot: that God, in making the laws, was considering both our moral and physical beings. In his *Guide to the Perplexed*, Rambam wrote that kashrut "trains us to master our appetites; to accustom us to restrain our desires; and to avoid considering the pleasure of eating and drinking as the goal of man's existence." Rambam also popularized the idea that the laws of kashrut were concerned with our health. In the *Sefer HaHinuch* (Book of Education) volume of his *Mishneh Torah*, he wrote, "God knows that in all foods prohibited to the chosen people, elements injurious to the body are found. For this reason, God removed us from them so that the souls can do their function."

Observing kashrut for health has been a popular explanation—pork was a source of various parasitic diseases, after all. But this reason doesn't fully explain all the rules of kashrut. Others describe the symbolic characteristics of forbidden food. For example, Dayan Dr. I. Grunfeld writes in *The Jewish Dietary Laws*, ". . . carnivorous animals, such as beasts and birds of prey, would be forbidden because with the consumption of their flesh, their cruel habits might enter the human being."

The reasons for the particular laws can be subject of a never-ending debate. The reason people keep kosher is one of individual choice. In researching this book, I spoke with people who observe some aspect of kashrut in manners ranging from the bare minimum of simply not eating pork and shellfish to those adhering to the most Orthodox interpretation of halacha.

Deciding to keep kosher, and *how* you keep kosher, is a personal choice. For me, keeping kosher reminds me of my Jewish beliefs, and God, every time I eat. It makes me consider what I am eating, and helps me appreciate it. I enjoy keeping kosher. I did not think I would, however, when I was nine.

That was the year my parents decided we were going to start keeping kosher. Neither of my parents had grown up in a kosher household, but they were gradually becoming more observant and had enrolled my brother and me in a parochial Jewish school in Washington, D.C.

I remember when my mother broke the news. I was familiar with kosher as a concept (it came up in conversation at my school, where we were not allowed to bring meat for lunch), but it was not a practice I particularly wanted to follow. I was a picky eater, and what I liked, I liked, and I liked bacon. And I loved Campbell's chicken noodle soup with a glass of milk. "No more Campbell's?" I asked my mother.

"No—but there is kosher chicken soup."

"But I can't have it with milk," I pouted. My pouting was short-lived, as I soon got caught up in the excitement of converting our kitchen. Boiling silverware, scrubbing out cupboards, lining shelves, buying new dishes, pots, pans—it was like a game, though I later realized immense planning went into that "game."

Making a kitchen kosher is a daunting undertaking at the outset, but once the groundwork is laid, the rest is easy. My mother remembers feeling initially overwhelmed. "I didn't have the background," she told me. "I was shocked when I found out you had to have two of *everything*, not just dishes, but pots and pans and even silverware. Learning about keeping kosher was like peeling an onion. I thought to myself, this is really involved."

Involved, challenging, but important for our family. My parents made the decision to keep kosher during the early 1970s, a time of upheaval and social change. They felt that kashrut would offer order and serenity in the house, helping to make it a refuge from the turbulence going on in the world. My father also sees kashrut as part of the bigger picture of how to live life as a better person. "Keeping kosher is one of the many things we do that gives meaning to most of what we do," he says. "It's perfectly possible for a person to act completely morally without any ritual element at all. But for human beings, being who they are, it's easier if it's part of a whole life pattern, in all kinds of contexts. I don't think kashrut all by itself would do it, but since eating is such an important and integral part of life, you're frequently brought back to thinking about what you're doing from a religious point of view. It gives you a structure within which you can focus your attempts to be a better human being."

Kashrut was a structured way of eating rooted in the laws of the Torah set out thousands of years before. By becoming more formally Jewish, my parents were allying our family with Jews who honored and practiced ways of life that had characterized the Jewish people for countless generations.

My mother-in-law, Esther Robbins, a Providence, Rhode Island, native, also started keeping kosher as an adult, after she met her husband, who hailed from the small town of Woonsocket, Rhode Island. The oft-told story in our family is how when my father-in-law, Don, proposed to Esther, he asked if she'd keep kosher. She said sure—as long as she didn't have to live in Woonsocket! The deal was struck, but Esther had little familiarity with kashrut. "I thought you had three sets of dishes," she says. "One for milk, one for meat, and one for treif." Treif refers to unkosher food. "I didn't know. I was raised with clams and oysters and pork. It was difficult at first. I learned by winging it. But after setting up the kitchen, it was no big deal. It became a way of life. It's not just religion. It's a way of maintaining our ties with Judaism, going back, something we do that sets us apart and makes eating special. It's nice for your children, your family."

Many Jews who keep kosher today did not keep kosher growing up, yet feel attracted to the concept of kashrut. Rabbi Harry Sinoff, dean of faculty at the Gann Academy, a Jewish high school in Waltham, Massachusetts, grew up in northern Florida, the only Jew in his community. "We were very assimilated," he says. A scholarship to the Conservative-affiliated Camp Ramah when he was fourteen changed that. He came home keeping kosher, except his parents did not keep a kosher home. Sinoff did the opposite of what many Jews do. He kept kosher *outside* of his home. "Out of respect for my parents," he says, "I ate the food they prepared at home," which included meat. In restaurants, however, he did not eat meat and observed the laws of kashrut to the best of his ability. The following year, when he came home from camp, his parents had converted the kitchen to a kosher kitchen, acknowledging that this might not be "just a phase."

As an adult, Sinoff says, "I realized I was more comfortable in Orthodox settings than Conservative settings." For Sinoff, this means being part of a decidedly Jewish community where he knows everyone is observing kashrut in a similar manner, where the dishwasher and oven are used according to the Orthodox interpretation of halacha, where all products that come into the house are marked with a kosher certification, where everyone observes the Sabbath. "As a Jew, my job is to live out life to conform to halacha," Sinoff says. "You can know what I'll eat by looking at halacha. I like keeping kosher; it fundamentally fits me, aesthetically, emotionally, intellectually—I'm happy. I am doing something that is good and ought to be done and is part of something greater than me: Torah. What you have when you live this way is a sense of the past and the future that is very vivid. It gives meaning to my life every day, with everything I do."

My cousin, Rabbi Benyomin Simpson, who is in his twenties, grew up keeping kosher according to the strict Orthodox principles of Lubavitch Chassidism. To him, keeping kosher is a fundamental part of Judaism. "I keep kosher because that is what HaShem wants," he says. "This is one of the mitzvot in the Torah, that's what we do." Although he lives in a community surrounded by fellow Lubavitchers, my cousin asserts that for him, kashrut is more than community. "Even if I was in a community where nobody was keeping kosher, I would definitely keep kosher," he says. "I have a firm belief in Torah and in the laws of Torah that go all the way down to the Shulchan Aruch."

My friend Jill Segal grew up in an Orthodox environment, but found the flexibility of

Conservative Judaism suited her better. Keeping kosher was always a given for her. "To me it's about mindfulness, taking something that's very mundane but integral to my day and making it holy," she says.

"I think becoming kosher is a wonderful step in terms of people's evolution Jewishly. I think it's very important," says Rabbi David Starr. Starr grew up "Reform if anything," but became friendly with observant Jews when he was in high school in Minneapolis. "As I was looking to grow Jewishly, I think I felt a sense that kashrut is a core practice. That notion of hey—you are what you eat. It's an incredibly basic marker of daily identity. I wanted to do something that was going to make me feel Jewish in a deep, palpable way, and it just felt like the right thing to do. By now it feels hard-wired into me. It's a basic building block of a committed Jewish life. We are a culture, a people, a history, laws, and those things are about difference. Kashrut is a core aspect of that culture. There's something magical about making that kind of commitment."

Rabbi Victor Reinstein found that kashrut led him naturally to vegetarianism, because of the message it teaches about respecting animal life. "As a discipline, kashrut creates a framework of acknowledging the holiness of all facets of life," Reinstein says. "To me, a major part of kashrut is a spiritual discipline that helps create a reverence for life. I really felt a sense of trying to feel and express and honor a harmony of life forms, feeling that being a vegetarian was a reminder of living with a greater sense of reverence for life. Kashrut is a beautiful, delicate way of reminding us not to just consume, not to just grab whatever we like. The hope would be that we can then transfer that discipline to much wider realms of life, which ultimately would make the world a much healthier place."

Both historical ideas and contemporary thought contribute to Rabbi Shawn Zevit's reasons for observing kashrut. Zevit, the director of Outreach and Community Development and Congregational Services for the Jewish Reconstructionist Federation, says, "Kashrut creates distinctions. The rabbis built on the idea of separation, pure and impure, clean and unclean. Contemporarily, that can mean taking that into ethical and ecological categories. What does kashrut ask us to pay attention to? The conduct that comes out from us. The food that we bring into us becomes who we are. The actions we do, define who we are in the world."

Social action is one element of kashrut that appeals to Rabbi Richard Levy, director of the School of Rabbinic Studies at the Hebrew Union College, Jewish Institute of Religion in Los Angeles, and former president of the Central Conference of American Rabbis. "In a world where many more people in general are concerned with having their values coincide with what they eat—vegetarians, vegans, health consciousness—this is a propitious time to reopen the question Does God care what we eat? The Torah says yes. I think an increasing number of Jews are saying that part of religious life should be a concern for what goes into our mouths, what our bodies do, how we behave toward other people, how we behave toward God. As Reform Jews, this feeling that issues of justice need to play a role in our dietary habits is also affecting things. We can use diet to lessen oppression of farm workers. See what products are supportive of just conditions, which products are not."

Levy also finds that kashrut is an important element of being Jewish. "When I was wrestling with the role that food should play in my life, I wanted to take on more acts that made me aware of what God wanted us to do," he says. "I think kashrut has a changing and growing role. On the one hand, all of us tend to think of kashrut as a single element, a single mitzvah, but in fact it's made up of a lot of discrete parts. A colleague said kashrut exists on a spectrum, and I think if we understand that kashrut is a series of steps, you would find a number of Reform Jews who do keep kosher. Whatever the degrees of kashrut one keeps, it gives one more in common with other Jews."

The Next Step

There you have it. Longer answers to short questions, a foundation of what keeping kosher is all about. The pages that follow give further explanations, offering a background of how the kashrut of today came to be, what foods are kosher, how to kosherize your kitchen, and the role of dietary laws in Shabbat, Pesach, and other Jewish holidays. I top it all off with recipes, because all discussions of food-related ideas should include recipes. As the Talmud says, *"Room can always be found in one's stomach for sweet things."*

You may choose to start keeping kosher gradually, by simply eliminating forbidden foods from your house. Then you may start buying only kosher meat. Eventually, you may take the more major step of obtaining separate dishes for meat and milk consumption, or you may choose to go cold turkey and make the changes all at once.

In *How to Keep Kosher* I discuss the steps you can take to do this—how to make do with dishes you already have, what can be made kosher, what must be sold or given away. Whatever you choose to do, kashrut is a connection, a tie; keeping kosher is a special experience that will connect you to me, to Moses and Miriam, to Ruth and Solomon, to Rashi and Rambam, to all Jews everywhere, who care about this important element of Jewish life.

KASHROOTS

I HAVE BEEN KEEPING KOSHER since I was about nine years old. That's when my family made the switch, and I remember the elaborate changes that I objected to initially, changes that evolved into personally meaningful practices. As I was a child at the time I began keeping kosher, I just accepted the various laws of kashrut at face value, without questioning the source and reason—this is just what we do. No pork, no meat with milk, only "kosher" meat—meat that has been slaughtered according to the laws of *shechita*. Chicken, which many general cookbooks categorize separately from meat, is as *fleishig* as beef under Jewish dietary laws. Fish, however, is considered *pareve*, neither meat or dairy. Fish could be served *before* meat, but it couldn't be served *with* meat. And eggs, which come from chickens, are also pareve, and *can* be served with meat.

Yes, it is confusing, but I just filed away the rules and followed them. Later, however, I wanted to understand these dietary laws; I thought, it may be easier to understand the various laws of kashrut if I had a better sense of where they came from.

I wanted to understand why the laws are what they are—not the philosophical or spiritual reasons, but the practical reasons. The *why* I was seeking was not really the logic or justification of kashrut, but the historical roots. I was curious about the sources for the laws of kashrut. What were the origins of the basic laws of kashrut (not to mention the wealth of detail) that we observe today? What exactly does it say to do in the Torah, the Talmud, the Shulchan Aruch, and other writings of Jewish sages over the millennia and beyond, and how did that all evolve into the way kashrut is observed today, in the twenty-first century?

Regardless of the whys, I appreciate kashrut as a way of sanctifying meals, but understanding the sources helps give a sense of the bigger picture, of how kashrut has been a part of Judaism since the time of the Torah. The biblical verses that set down the basic laws of kashrut provide a fascinating glimpse into our own history as a people. To think that we have maintained some observance in how we eat for thousands of years—it is a *kesher*, a tie, a connection between our ancestors and us as Jews living and eating and working in the twenty-first century.

K.Sh.R

Let's start with the word itself, *kosher*. It debuted in Webster's English-language dictionary in 1851, which traces its etymology to Yiddish and Hebrew. Indeed, *kosher* is a Hebrew word and goes back much further than the nineteenth century, though not as far back as one might think.

In Hebrew most words are variations based on a three-letter root. The Hebrew root *kaf-shin-resh* (*K.Sh.R*) is the basis for both the words *kashrut* and *kosher*, which literally mean "fit," "proper," or "worthy."

The word *kosher* is used to refer to a variety of concerns in Jewish laws, anything that has to be made or done according to certain halachic regulations, such as the proper way to tie the fringes when making a *tallit* (prayer shawl), or the correct production of *tefillin* (phylacteries, worn during weekday prayers), or the way a Torah scroll is written. If the object or activity meets halachic specifications, it is fit, proper for use, kosher.

While kosher *can* refer to more than just food, in general, the laws of kashrut refer specifically to the dietary laws. When people talk about keeping kosher, they are usually talking about food.

Surprisingly, however, the word *kosher* does not appear in the Torah, in the Five Books of Moses, where the Jewish dietary laws are introduced. A word using the *K.Sh.R* root appears just three times in later biblical texts, but not in reference to food: twice in the Book of Ecclesiastes, where it means "succeed"; and once in the Book of Esther, where it means "appropriate"—close to the current meaning.

Hebrew dictionaries attribute the *K.Sh.R* root to postbiblical Hebrew. Linguist Gabriel Birnbaum, a lecturer at the Department of Hebrew and Semitic Languages at Bar Ilan University in Israel, says, "The word *kasher* (and the root *K.Sh.R*) is a late word, probably a loan from Aramaic. It has its cognates in Akkadian and in Ugaritic. One of its meanings in Mishnaic (Rabbinic) Hebrew is 'ritually, legally fit or permitted.' It is used— among other contexts—in reference to dietary laws, e.g, Chullin 3,2: '*Ve'elu ksherot babehemot . . .* ' ('The following [defects] in animals are [still] kasher . . . '). From usage like this it came to be used mainly in reference to food. But this specific usage of the word is quite late: According to the dictionaries of Ben Yehuda and Even Shoshan it is later than the Middle Ages."

My cousin, a Lubavitch rabbi, theorizes on the choice of this word, "We can't eat the animals as they are. Even animals that are not unclean, we have to examine. There are defects that could render the animal unfit, and we have to verify that it is fit. It could be that the word came in to indicate that now the meat is finally proper, fit."

Early usage of the word *kasher* in the Talmud is invariably in reference to the fitness of the animal after being slaughtered.

If the word *kosher* isn't in the Torah, how do we know that certain foods are or are not, well, kosher? Because the Torah does use particular words when discussing food that is fit or forbidden.

After describing which animals are permitted and which are not, God concludes the instructions in **Leviticus 11:46–47,** saying, *"This is the law of the beast, and of the bird, and of every living creature that swarms in the waters, and of every creature that teems upon the earth; to make a difference between the* **unclean** *and the* **clean***, and between the living thing that may be eaten and the living thing that may not be eaten."* (Boldface is my emphasis.)

The word for "unclean" is *tamei* or *tumah*; and the word for "clean" is *tahara* or *tahor*. These are the words the Torah uses for unkosher and kosher food—and for a few other concerns, which imbue added significance to these particular words when used in reference to dietary laws. Contact with a dead body is considered *tamei*, which also is translated as ritually "impure" or "defiled." A woman who has just given birth is *tamei*, and, according to traditional Judaism, women are also *tamei* when they are menstruating. Touching someone with the mysterious biblical disease called *tsaraat* (generally translated as "leprosy," but different from the disease called leprosy today) was also *tamei*. When you become *tamei*, you perform a special cleansing involving a *mikvah*, a ritual bath, in order to become *tahor*, ritually clean.

In the case of eating and *tamei*, it is simply a matter of not eating the foods that are forbidden to us. A second word is also used to describe unkosher foods: *sheketz*, "detestable." Foods not to be eaten are either "unclean" or "detestable."

In the Beginning

All laws of kashrut are based on a few verses in the Torah. Over thousands of years, Jewish scholars have done their best to interpret how the basics outlined in the Torah should be applied to daily life. The few sentences outlining dietary laws in the Torah have evolved into hundreds of thousands of words discussing the true meaning of that outline.

In the beginning, we were instructed to be vegetarians. As stated in **Genesis 1:29**, *"And God said: 'Behold, I have given you every herb yielding seed, which is upon the face of all the earth, and every tree, in which is the fruit of a tree yielding seed; to you it shall be for food.'"* The rabbis interpret this to mean that initially people were meant to eat plant-based foods only. Rabbi Victor Reinstein points out, "It is significant to notice that at the time of Gan Eden, animals and people were to eat the same diet, the vegetarian diet."

But human nature intervened. Eight chapters later, after the flood, God expands the list of acceptable foods, telling Noah, in **Genesis 9:2–3**, *"And the fear of you and the dread of you shall be upon every beast of the earth, and upon every bird of the heavens, in everything that swarms on land, and in all the fishes of the sea: into your hand are they delivered. Every moving thing that lives shall be food for you; as the green herb have I given you all."* Reinstein comments, "Only following the flood, when human violence had risen in the world, was the eating of meat allowed. Ultimately, it was an effort to channel human aggression."

This implies that, up to this point, God preferred that we not eat meat. As Rabbi Dayan Grunfeld wrote in *The Jewish Dietary Laws*, "It must be assumed that after the flood, man's nature changed. . . . The duration of his allotted span of life was decreased. . . . The shorter lifetime was bound to intensify and concentrate the process of life, which is perhaps the reason why a food more vitalizing than vegetables became necessary."

Notice that, at this point, people can eat "every moving thing." It is not until the Jews are given the Ten Commandments in Exodus that specific animals are forbidden. However, there are still some important dietary stipulations given in Genesis.

Ever Min Hachai

Immediately after telling Noah that people can now eat animals, God says, in **Genesis 9:4,** *"Only flesh, with its soul its blood you shall not eat."*

This sentence yields two laws of kashrut, and is known by the Hebrew phrase *ever min hachai,* literally, "flesh torn from a living body." First, we cannot eat flesh or limbs from a live animal. Second, we cannot drink blood from a live animal. This law is considered so important that it is one of the Seven Laws of Noah, laws given by God before the Ten Commandments. The Talmud determined that these are Universal Laws, laws not only for Jews, but laws to be followed by all people. It is also an example of *tza'ar ba'alei chayim,* laws in the Torah of minimizing animal suffering.

Commentary states that by forbidding a certain action, the Torah implies that such a thing was a common practice at the time. So while the concept of cutting off a leg from a live cow but not killing the animal may seem appalling, it was likely not such a foreign concept in ancient Israel.

This law is also the first time the prohibition against eating blood is mentioned, which I will discuss further.

There is a less obvious question that *ever min hachai* raises: What about milk and eggs? These are items taken from a live animal (indeed, a reason why vegans don't eat either item), so do they count as *ever min hachai,* as flesh taken from a live animal? Or are they prohibited because eating a live animal is prohibited, according to the rule described in the Talmud, "That which comes from the unclean is unclean; from the clean, clean." Because a live animal is forbidden as food, is anything that comes from a live animal therefore forbidden?

On the first point, milk and eggs don't count as "flesh torn from a live animal" because, well, they're not. Milking an animal, taking a bird's eggs do not harm the animal in any way. And regarding the second point, the Talmud determined that actually we can eat milk, and eggs, even though they come from live animals because the Torah refers to both of them. Regarding eggs, in **Deuteronomy 22:6–7,** we are instructed, *"If a bird's nest happens to be before you on the path, in any tree or on the ground, with young ones or eggs, and the mother sitting upon the young, or upon the eggs, you shall not take the mother with the young; you shall surely send the mother away, and take the young for yourself."* This implies that eggs are acceptable; it also is an example of *tza'ar ba'alei chayim,* in that you are instructed to spare the mother animal the pain of seeing her young, or eggs, removed from the nest.

As for milk, Israel is described as a land flowing with milk and honey. Milk would not be used as part of this positive metaphor if it were not permissible to eat it.

Similarly, honey is permissible, in part for the same reason. Honey comes from a bee, which is a forbidden creature, but the rabbis determined that the honey was not technically a secretion from a bee; rather, the bee acts as a carrier for the nectar that becomes honey. As Rambam says, "Bees' and hornets' honey is permitted, since it is not exuded from their bodies; rather they collect it from the flowers into their mouths and then regurgitate it into the hive, in order that they may have it available for food during the winter." Therefore, eggs, honey, and milk are all permissible foods, although milk and eggs from unkosher animals are not permissible.

Gid Hanasheh

The next dietary law comes several generations later. It is a highly symbolic law, and very specific. Jacob, after years of a less-than-amicable separation from his brother Esau, is preparing to meet him again. The night before the meeting is to take place, a mysterious stranger fights with Jacob, but is unable to overpower him. **Genesis 32:26** describes the situation, *"And when he saw that he prevailed not against him, he touched the hollow of his thigh; and the hollow of Jacob's thigh was strained, as he wrestled with him."* He asks Jacob to let him go; Jacob does so in exchange for a blessing. This is when the stranger, an angel, gives Jacob (in Hebrew, *Ya'acov*, "held by the heel") a new name, Israel (*Yisrael*, "wrestled with God"). From this period on, Jacob's descendants, including those who wandered in the desert, are called *B'nai Yisrael*, the Children of Israel.

To honor Jacob, and to commemorate this event, we do not eat the sciatic nerve of any animal, as this is thought to be the wound that Jacob received from the angel. Lest there be any doubt, **Genesis 32:33** spells it out for us: *"Therefore the Children of Israel eat not the sinew of the thigh-vein which is upon the hollow of the thigh, unto this day; because he touched the hollow of Jacob's thigh, even in the sinew of the thigh-vein."* The "sinew of the thigh-vein" is called in Hebrew *gid hanasheh*. The sciatic nerve is located in the hind legs of mammals. It can be removed, but in general we do not eat from the hindquarters of animals.

These are the only dietary laws until the Exodus, when the Children of Israel are given the Ten Commandments and then the Torah.

Forbidden and Permitted Animals

The laws concerning forbidden and permitted animals are explained in great detail in **Leviticus 11.** The same rules are repeated, with slight variations, in **Deuteronomy 14.**

Animals are divided into categories. Four-legged mammals fall under two subcategories: animals (*chaya*) or beasts (*behema*). *Chaya* is also translated as "living things," as it has the same Hebrew root as the word for "life." Other categories are "all that are in the waters," or seafood; birds (*off* or *tzipor*); and "swarming things" (*sheretz*).

Creatures and Beasts

Of beasts, the list of *tahara*, or permitted, animals is a short one: animals who have *both* cloven hooves and chew their cud. Regarding animals, in **Leviticus 11:2–3,** God says, *"These are the creatures that you may eat from among all the animals that are upon the earth. Everything among the animals that has a split hoof, which is completely separated into double hooves, and that brings up its cud—that one you may eat."* The Torah then gives four examples of animals that might appear to meet the criteria but do not. The first three—*shafan*, translated as rock-badger or hyrax; *arnevet*, translated as hare; and camels—*"chew the cud but part not the hoof."* Note: The cud-chewing abilities of the hyrax and hare have been subject to lengthy and heated debate because they are not actually ruminants in the same way that camels or cows are. Could God have made a mistake? some ask. In fact, although they are not ruminants, they do digest food through a process called "reflection," or redigestion. To get technical, they excrete food in two ways. One is regular excrement, the second is soft pellets that the animals then re-eat. The way they chew also gives the appearance of chewing cud. On the other hand, "hyrax" and "hare" are modern interpretations of biblical terms; for all we know, *shafan* and *arnevet* could be referring to now-extinct animals.

The fourth animal, pigs, on the other hand, have cloven hooves but do *not* chew their cud. Therefore, they too are forbidden. As for nonhoofed beasts, in **Leviticus 11:27,** God says, *"And all that walk on its paws, among all animals that go on all fours, they are unclean unto you."*

Why, given how many animals are not permitted (horses, dogs, elephants), have pigs become the quintessential symbol for unkosherness? For a number of reasons, the most likely being availability. Unlike camels or donkeys, which served another useful purpose (transportation and portation—they carried stuff), pigs existed solely as a source for food, and peoples all around the Israelites ate pork. Pigs became a way to torture Jews, as in the example of Hannah during the Maccabbean revolts. Hannah and her sons died rather than submit to eating pork. Further, pigs are symbolically unappealing, known for eating anything and everything—unselectively eating garbage, the opposite of kashrut, where we are aware of every aspect of what we eat. And pigs wallow in their own filth.

The pig is symbolic in another way. Cud-chewing is a subtle, internal trait, whereas a cloven hoof is something you see right away. Despite the cud-chewing, you can look at a camel and know immediately that it is not kosher; its hooves are not split. A pig, on the other hand, has a cloven hoof but doesn't chew its cud. In an article for the Business Ethics Center of Jerusalem, Rabbi Yoel Domb writes, "The pig is the archetypal hypocrite, since it displays its kosher sign for all to see, claiming that it is kosher while it conceals the fact that it does not chew the cud and is technically not kosher."

In **Deuteronomy 14:4–5,** animals that are permissible are actually listed: *"These are the beasts which you may eat: the ox, the sheep, and the goat, the hart, and the gazelle, and the roebuck, and the wild goat, and the pygarg, and the antelope, and the mountain-sheep."* However, because we are given the criteria of what makes these animals kosher, we are able to apply the same criteria to other animals not mentioned. Giraffe, moose, buffalo, and bison have all been determined to be kosher.

There is a distinction between wild and domesticated beasts. There are wild animals, such as deer, that are permissible; they just have to be slaughtered correctly, which can be a challenge. There are now farms where "wild" animals, such as venison and bison, are domesticated.

Seafood

In **Leviticus 11:9–12,** God says, *"This may you eat from everything that is in the water: everything that has fins and scales in the water, in the seas, and in the streams, those may you eat. And everything that does not have fins and scales in the waters and in the streams—from all that teems in the water, and from all living creatures in the water—they are an abomination to you."* This means that shellfish are out, eel are out; so are octopus, catfish, squid—if it doesn't have scales and fins, it isn't kosher. This point is repeated in **Deuteronomy 14:9–10.**

This might seem fairly straightforward, but there are a number of seemingly fin-and-scale fish that don't quite meet the criteria. A few fish types are controversial, and are considered kosher by Conservatives but not by the Orthodox. I discuss these in detail in the chapter "Kosher Foods."

Birds

When it comes to birds, the Torah is both more and less specific than it is with other species. With mammals and seafood, God specifies the characteristics that make each type kosher. With birds, however, God simply lists the unkosher birds. In **Leviticus 11:13,** God says, *"These shall you abominate from among the birds, they may not be eaten—they are an abomination,"* and proceeds to list twenty forbidden birds, without describing any criteria for what makes them an abomination, or criteria for which other birds are acceptable.

Again, in **Deuteronomy 14:11,** God says, *"Every clean bird you may eat,"* then lists twenty-one birds that are forbidden, without explanation. In all, the Talmud states, there are twenty-four forbidden birds. According to Rambam, the forbidden birds are great vulture, bearded vulture, osprey, kite, falcon, a second species of falcon, raven, starling, ostrich, nighthawk, seamew, hawk, a second species of hawk, little owl, cormorant, great owl, horned owl, pelican, carrion vulture, stork, heron, a second species of heron, hoopoe, and bat. The "second species" of certain birds comes from the biblical phrase "after its kind" that is repeated after certain birds, indicating that there is more than one type of this particular bird that is forbidden. So, even though we are not certain that the Hebrew word *bat haya'anah* actually meant ostrich, it is commonly accepted that ostrich are not kosher. Ostrich are, after all, native to Africa, so it is not impossible that they might have been seen in ancient Egypt (for example, the Egyptian goddess Ma'at was depicted wearing an ostrich feather in her hair).

Because no criteria are given to indicate what constitutes an acceptable bird, the rabbis determined that all birds *except* those on the list are acceptable. The problem is that even by Talmudic times the identity of the birds on the list was uncertain. While all the listed bird names can be found in Hebrew dictionaries today, the original biblical meaning is not certain, even for those bird names that have been in seemingly continuous use. Like the "hyrax" and the "hare," we don't *know* if they are the same, but the Rambam's list is the traditionally accepted one.

Mindful that we not inadvertently eat any forbidden birds, the rabbis decided that specific criteria were needed to determine which birds were kosher to eat and which were not. They looked at what characteristics those forbidden birds had in common. They determined that the birds listed are birds of prey, *dores* in Hebrew. What exactly is a "bird of prey"? Birds, such as owls or eagles, that hunt and kill their food. Also vultures and buzzards, birds that eat carrion. Therefore, all birds of prey are forbidden.

To determine the other indicators of forbidden birds, the rabbis looked at a clean bird as an example of what was acceptable to eat. The *tur*, turtle dove, is a bird used often for sacrifices outlined in the Torah, so that was the bird chosen to exemplify a *tahor* bird. *"The characteristics of Birds are not stated,"* the Mishnah determines, then describes four criteria based on research: *"But the Sages have said, every bird that seizes its prey is unclean. Every bird that has an extra toe, a crop, and a gizzard that can be peeled, is clean. R. Eliezer, son of R. Zadok, says, every bird that parts its toes is unclean."* Clear?

Well, not exactly. What does "extra toe" mean, since almost all birds, with the exception of a few varieties of chickens, have four toes? It refers to the division of those toes: Three toes are in front and one is behind, the hallux, the innermost digit. (Since many birds of prey have this characteristic as well, the Talmud reiterates one point several times: Clean birds must have *all four* characteristics. If a bird has only three, it is forbidden.)

"Crop" refers to a rounded part of a bird's gullet or esophagus, an area where the bird effectively "chews" its food before the food continues into the stomach. Finally, the "gizzard that can be peeled" refers to the part of a bird's alimentary canal that helps grind food. Gizzards have a lining; on kosher birds, this lining can easily be peeled by hand, while unkosher bird gizzards require a knife.

These are the rabbinically established characteristics for kosher birds, but birds still have provided something of a controversy through the ages, as people encountered different species of birds, and every new bird needs to be examined and analyzed. Some rabbis added an egg test as well. The egg of a kosher bird must be shaped like a chicken egg—wider and rounded at one end, narrower and pointed at the other.

Many birds that are eaten today are considered kosher because of *mesorah*, a tradition or custom. Because of the ambiguity of what is acceptable, birds, more than any other kosher creatures, are more subject to the *mesorah* rule. The establishment of customs is a little fuzzy, but if a community has a tradition of eating a particular bird that seems to meet the Talmudically established criteria, it is acceptably kosher. If not, even if it meets the criteria, it may not be considered kosher.

Rabbi Ari Z. Zivotofsky, Ph.D., lecturer in the brain science program at Bar Ilan University, Israel, has trained as a *shochet*, ritual slaughterer. He has written extensively on the subject of birds, animals, and kashrut, including turkey. Turkey is a New World bird, and there are those who argue that, when the bird was first introduced in Europe five hundred years ago, there couldn't have been a *mesorah* of eating turkey, since there were no Jews in the New World at the time of the Talmud. In an article, "Is Turkey Kosher?," Zivotofsky writes, "When the turkey question was posed it often took the form of 'why is it eaten?' rather than 'may it be eaten?' . . . The turkey is no longer new and its kosher status has been addressed by both the great and not-so-great Jewish minds over the last 250 years and has received near-universal endorsement."

Zivotofsky didn't stop at turkey; in 2002, he and his study partner, Dr. Ari Greenspan, researched several species of birds, searching through Israel to find some-one, *anyone* who met qualifications of authority (e.g., a religious Jew, preferably a community rabbi or *shochet*) who could vouch for a tradition of eating various more obscure birds. If the pair could themselves witness the *shechita* of these birds, they would count as part of a new generation participating in the tradition of eating the particular species. "In order to stem the loss of traditions," Zivotofsky and Greenspan write in the December 2002 *Jewish Observer*, "We decided to organize a dinner in which we would serve all known kosher birds and as many types of animals as possible." Ultimately, the dinner featured thirteen species of birds, including mallard, pigeon, dove, sparrow, partridge, quail, and guinea fowl.

Sheretz, Swarming Things

Finally, **Leviticus** describes other forbidden creatures, *sheretz*, "swarming things." While some *sheretz* are specifically described, there are also vague descriptions of others, so we rely on Talmudic interpretations to understand fully what *sheretz* are considered forbidden. **Leviticus 11:20** is subject to some interpretation: *"Every winged swarming thing that walks on all fours are a detestable thing unto you."* Rashi gives as examples flies and hornets. Part of the debate here is the reference of "four" legs, when we know insects have six. Since determining the kashrut of various animals has to do with appearances, some commentators suggest that insects appear to walk with four legs, and to use the additional two legs for jumping.

There are also insects that are kosher, as described in **Leviticus 11:21–22:** *"Yet these may you eat of all winged swarming things that go upon all fours, which have jointed legs above their feet, with which to leap upon the earth. You may eat these from among them: the locust after its kind, and the bald locust after its kind, and the cricket after its kind, and the* *grasshopper after its kind."* Not that the average person might want to rush out and chow down some crickets, but this indicates that there have been kosher insects. But, even though Rambam describes acceptable insects, rabbis have since determined that we can't *really* know the meaning of the Hebrew names of these kosher locusts, crickets, and grasshoppers, so it is better to avoid insects, unless one has a tradition to identify the kosher types. Convenient rationalization, perhaps? Rabbi Zivotofsky told me, however, when he was preparing for his *mesorah* dinner, he did find Yemenite and Moroccan Jews with a generations-old tradition of eating *chegavim*, a kind of grasshopper. Although a bevy of rabbinical experts, called *posekim*, gave mixed decisions as to whether the *chegavim* could be included at the dinner, there were those who gave their approval, and so they were served, roasted and boiled. "Surprisingly, many more of the participants actually tried them than we expected," Greenspan and Zivotofsky write. (I'll stick with popcorn myself.)

Winged insects are one kind of swarming thing, but there are other *sheretz* that are forbidden. In **Leviticus 11:29–30,** God says, *"And these are they which are unclean unto you among the swarming things that swarm upon the earth: the weasel, and the mouse, and the great lizard after its kind, and the gecko, and the land-crocodile, and the lizard, and the sand-lizard, and the chameleon."* **Verses 41–42** elaborate, *"And every swarming thing that swarms upon the earth is a detestable thing; it shall not be eaten. Everything that creeps on the belly, and everything that goes upon all fours, or everything that has many feet, even all swarming things that swarm upon the earth, you shall not eat them, for they are a detestable thing."* These include rodents, snakes, worms, maggots, centipedes—you know, all those creepy crawly things that just make your mouth water. Lest there be any doubt, we are *commanded* not to eat such things.

Deuteronomy 14:19 is briefer on this topic, saying simply, *"And all winged swarming things are unclean unto you; they shall not be eaten."*

No Blood

The blood of any mammal or bird is prohibited. The prohibition against the consumption of blood is the one dietary law that is repeated most often in the Torah, more than half a dozen times, beginning in Genesis, before any other dietary laws have been given. In **Leviticus 17:14,** God says, *"You shall not consume the blood of any creature; for the* *life of any creature is its blood, whoever consumes it will be cut off."* Forbidden foods such as pork or shrimp are unclean, but consuming blood leads to virtual excommunication, as in **Leviticus 7:27,** *"Any person who eats any blood, that soul shall be cut off from his people."* Grunfeld writes that this is "the severest and most dreaded punishment for a believing Jew because it means the loss of everlasting life."

This commandment is repeated several times, especially in Leviticus and Deuteronomy, where most of the dietary laws are described. The injunction against eating blood determined both how animals are to be slaughtered, and how the meat is then to be prepared before it can be cooked.

Fish do not carry the same status as animals and birds. In the Torah, fish are never used as a sacrifice, whereas animals and birds are, and sprinkling their blood is often part of the sacrificial ceremony. Fish do not have to be killed in any special way, and fish blood is not prohibited. However, the Shulchan Aruch states that if fish blood has collected in a container, it should not be consumed because it may look as if you are eating the blood of an animal.

Forbidden Fat

In addition to blood and the sciatic nerve, a certain kind of fat is also prohibited. There are two words for fat, *shuman,* which is acceptable, and *chelev,* which is not; *chelev* includes suet. (On an etymological note, *chelev* has the same root letters as *chalav,* the word for milk. This is because *chelev* is creamy and white in color, like milk.) **Leviticus 3:17** states, *"It shall be a perpetual statute throughout your generations in all your dwellings, you may not eat any fat or any blood."* The forbidden *chelev* is used specifically for sacrificial offerings, and **Leviticus 3:3-4** elaborates with some technical anatomical detail, *"The fat that covers the innards, and all the fat that is upon the innards, and the two kidneys and the fat that is on them, which is by the loins, and the lobe above the liver, which he shall take away hard by the kidneys."* The Talmud explains that forbidden *chelev* is distinguishable from acceptable *shuman* in that it forms a separate layer, easily removed from the meat, as opposed to the *shuman,* which is intermingled with the flesh.

Today, *chelev* is removed from animals after they have been ritually slaughtered, and then discarded.

The prohibition against eating *chelev* carries the same weight as the prohibition against eating blood, as stated in **Leviticus 7:25**, *"For anyone who eats the fat of the beast, from which one may present a fire offering to the Lord, the soul that eats it will be cut off from his people."*

Neveilah and *Treif*

Neveilah literally means "carcass" or "corpse," and refers to animals that can be kosher but have not died according to the laws of *shechita*, ritual slaughter. This includes animals that have died naturally, or animals in which the *shechita* was done improperly. In **Deuteronomy 14:21,** God says, *"You shall not eat of any carcass; you may give it to the stranger that is within your gates, that he may eat it; or you may sell it to a foreigner; for you are a holy people unto the Lord your God."*

From this comes the rule of not eating hunted meat. To be kosher, an animal may only be killed according to the rules of *shechita*; shooting it with a bullet or an arrow in the woods would violate this commandment. Further, we can't eat an animal found dead or killed by a wild beast or other causes.

We also cannot eat wounded animals. An animal may be potentially kosher, but if it is wounded in any way, it is not acceptable for *shechita*. **Exodus 22:30** states, *"You shall not eat flesh of an animal that was torn in the field."* The Hebrew word for "torn" is *treifah*, which has come to be shortened to *treif*.

The rabbis interpreted this commandment to mean that we cannot eat meat from an animal that was injured before dying. The Mishnah and the Talmud determined that such injuries could be internal or external, but are injuries that would lead to an animal's death within a year. The Talmud enumerates eight defects; a few hundred years later, Rambam went into further detail, outlining seventy different ways an animal could be considered treif.

Sometimes the wound is apparent—the animal may walk with a limp or have surface cuts. Other times the imperfection cannot be discovered until after the animal is slaughtered, such as a pneumatic lung.

Just as *kosher* has become the de facto word referring to acceptable food under Jewish dietary laws, *treif*, with its myriad transliterated spellings, has become the generic word meaning blatantly unkosher. Is it treif? someone might ask, referring to a particular food product. Meaning, does it have any pork, shellfish, uncertified ingredients in it?

A technical differentiation between *neveilah* and treif: A dead animal is *neveilah* if it died in any manner other than a proper *shechita*. An animal is treif if it has injuries or imperfections but has otherwise been properly slaughtered. Both *neveilah* and treif animals are prohibited.

Meat Consumed Should Be Kosher Meat

Kosher meat refers to meat that has been ritually slaughtered and cleaned according to certain specifications. The existence of a ritual method for killing animals for food comes from a short phrase in **Deuteronomy 12:21**, *"You may slaughter from your cattle and from your flocks, which the Lord has given you, as I have commanded you."* The rabbis interpreted the phrase *"as I have commanded you"* as referring to a specific method by which animals are to be killed. However, God does not elaborate, at least not in writing. Tradition holds that God gave Moses instructions on how to kill an animal for food at Mount Sinai; these instructions were passed on orally, for many generations, until they were written down in the Talmud. The Talmud states that we know the rules of ritual slaughter "by tradition," which refers to the Oral Law.

The word for ritual slaughter is *shechita,* based on the Hebrew root letters *shin-chet-tet,* meaning "slaughter" or "kill." A *shochet* is the person who performs the ritual slaughter. An animal that has been properly killed has been *shechted.*

Unlike the word *kosher,* the root word *shechita* does appear in the Torah, in reference to sacrificial slaughter, as in **Leviticus 1:5**, *"And he shall kill the bullock before the Lord . . ."* The word for kill here is *shachat.* A second word for killing an animal, *zavach,* also appears in the Torah (and is the word used in **Deuteronomy 12:21**), but *shachat* evolved into the word used for ritual slaughter of meat for food. The reference to biblical sacrificial slaughter elevates the act of *shechita* for food.

Tza'ar ba'alei chayim, "prevention of cruelty to animals," is a basic tenet of Judaism, of which I have already given some examples. There are several biblical passages, not only in relation to food, that indicate the proper way to treat animals. For example, animals, like people, are commanded to rest on the Sabbath. *Shechita* follows this philosophy. Yes, the animal is being killed, but the method of slaughter should be as quick and painless as possible. The sages determined that cutting the animal's throat in one smooth, fast stroke, severing vital arteries, was the most merciful method of killing an animal.

The Chullin section of the Talmud deals with many of the laws of ritual slaughter.

The laws as they evolved in Talmudic times still govern the methods of *shechita* performed today.

The laws of *shechita* apply to both mammals and birds; they do not apply to fish. Both mammals and birds are used in ritual sacrifices described in the Torah; again, fish are not. There are no rules governing how fish are to be killed; the laws of *shechita* apply specifically to acceptable mammals and birds.

On Eating Dead Animals

Although many more people eat meat than not, the details of animal slaughter are often an uncomfortable topic for discussion. Most people prefer to purchase their meat packaged into pieces, making it easier to ignore the animal it once was.

Speaking with those involved in the kosher meat industry was a reality check for me. I am not a big meat eater, more for matters of taste than strong feelings about animals, but I will eat the turkey meatballs prepared by my mother-in-law, or savor the beefy cholent at a friend's Shabbat afternoon lunch, without giving much thought to the source of the flavors and textures of the meal. In considering *shechita* and the tremendous amount of thought that has gone into this ritual, I realized how important it is to understand where our meat comes from, and how we regard it through the laws of kashrut. So often we eat meat without thinking of the source, of the animal that gave its life in order for us to have sustenance.

I found myself greatly respecting the people who do the mitzvah of *shechita,* who perform the ritual slaughter. It is indeed a mitzvah, the execution of a job I know that few of us would want to do—who really wants to kill the evening's dinner?—yet most of us are nourished by these animals thanks to those who are, literally, doing the dirty work.

A slaughterhouse, by nature, is not a pretty place. Animals are killed there, and they bleed great amounts of blood, their internal organs must be examined to determine if the animal is kosher, they have hides—skin—that need to be removed from the flesh, or feathers that need to be plucked, inedible parts that need to be disposed of, and edible parts that need to be butchered and assembled into the appealing packages or cuts we see displayed at the butcher.

Rabbi Richard Levy makes this observation about the kosher market where he buys his meat. "There's a big picture of a steer," he says. "It's hard to forget that this comes from a real animal, a noble creature in life, whose purpose is to nurture other creatures, as ours is to nurture the earth. This is a living creature whose life we are using to strengthen our own lives. That itself suggests that we should be respectful both when we buy and when we eat."

The Art of Shechita

Who can be a *shochet*? Anyone, according to the Mishnah, except a deaf-mute; an "imbecile," meaning someone not of sound mind; and a minor. However, the Mishnah does stipulate that if *"others were standing over them, their slaughtering is valid."*

Rabbi Dovid Steigman, rabbinic coordinator with the OK kosher certification organization, trained and worked as a *shochet* early in his career, in Mexico. He notes that, in pre-Talmudic times, everyone slaughtered and butchered their own meat. But by the time of the Talmud, professional roles were more definitively delineated—a *shochet* was a *shochet*, a scribe, and so on, hence the discussion of who could qualify for the job. Over time, it evolved that each community had a *shochet*.

Could a woman be a *shochet*? I wondered. Rabbi Steigman confirmed that a woman could; however, he says, "At the time of the Talmud, women stopped. A couple of reasons are given. It was thought that the amount of blood in a *shechita* would cause a lot of women to become too nervous [to perform the *shechita* properly]. Also, if something would go wrong with the *shechita* and she wouldn't have supper ready when her husband came home, she might face the wrath of her husband." I found a 1937 pamphlet, published in London, that traces the opinions of various Jewish sages since the Talmud on this issue, and opinions seems to be split. Those who were against it had less than flattering reasons: Women are careless, lazy, couldn't learn the laws properly. There were others, such as Rambam, who disagreed. There are documented cases of female *shochetot*, but they usually *shechted* just chickens, for personal rather than public use. Ultimately, tradition today dictates that women do not perform *shechita*.

Today, a *shochet* must be an "observant" Jew; this generally means a Jew who follows Judaism according to Orthodox dictates. And the *shochet* must be "properly trained." Properly trained means the *shochet* is familiar both with the Talmudic laws related to *shechita* and treif (whatever would make an animal unkosher) and has actual hands-on experience. Once trained, a *shochet* receives a *kabbalah*, a certificate, from an administering rabbi indicating that he has met all training requirements.

Before beginning a session of *shechita* (usually lasting several hours, during which hundreds of cattle or chickens might be killed), the *shochet* recites a blessing, *"Blessed are you, Lord our God, who has commanded us to fulfill the mitzvah of shechita."*

The *shochet* must use the proper instrument, a special knife called a *chalef*. *Chalef* comes from the Hebrew root *chet-lamed-feh*, which literally means "change," so called because this knife is the instrument of change for an animal, from life to death. The *chalef* must be twice the length of an animal's neck, made of finely honed metal, with no nicks, nothing that could catch on the animal's fur and give anything less than an absolutely smooth, clean cut. The *shochet* must correctly execute the animal with a single, fast stroke.

After each slaughter, either the acting *shochet* or a second *shochet* must check the smoothness of the blade by running the back of a fingernail up, then down, along each side and on the front of the blade, for a total of six times.

For a mammal, the cut must sever both the trachea and the esophagus; for the smaller necks of fowl, one or the other must be cut. This ensures that the jugular veins and carotid arteries will also be cut. Cutting these major blood vessels that lead to and from the brain serves a dual purpose. First, it immediately cuts off the blood supply to the animal's brain, rendering it unconscious within seconds. It also begins the process of draining blood from the body; kosher meat must be free of blood.

The Talmud outlines five acts that would render a *shechita* invalid. They are:

1. *Shehiah*, "pausing," "hesitation." The knife stroke must be direct, quick, and smooth, without stopping. If the *shochet* pauses, he cannot restart; the animal is *neveilah*.
2. *Drasa*, "pressing," "pushing down." The *shochet* may not press down as he cuts, which would be like chopping; it must be a back-and-forth stroke, not a chop, which can be more painful.
3. *Chalada*, "thrusting." The blade cannot be thrust into the neck, hiding it; the *chalef* must always be visible.
4. *Hagramah*, "deflecting," "deviating." There is a specific area of the animal's neck, from which the *shochet* cannot deviate. It should be below the first ring of the trachea. The ring itself is hard and can nick the knife, negatively affecting the required smooth stroke. Too low, and the thick chest muscles interfere with the smooth stroke.
5. *Ikur*, "tearing." The cut must be a smooth cut, not a tearing laceration, which can cause the animal pain. The blade of the *chalef* must be checked to ensure there are no nicks; a nick in the knife implies that the blade would catch and tear, again rendering the animal *neveilah*.

Blood drains from the animal for a minute or two before the next step, examination, or *bedikah*. A second *shochet* acts as a *bodek*. The word *bodek* means "check" or "inspect," and the *bodek* inspects the internal organs of the *shechted* (slaughtered) animal for abnormalities. The Shulchan Aruch outlines all the possible abnormalities that can be present in an animal that can be discovered during a postslaughter examination, from "perforation of the brain and its membranes" to "dislocation and fracture of forelimbs."

The first thing a *bodek* checks are the lungs. If the lungs are smooth and free of adhesions, they are called *glatt*, Yiddish for "smooth" (*chalak* in Hebrew). Certain kinds of adhesions immediately render the animal treif. But there are some minor adhesions that make the animal acceptable to eat—it would be "regular" kosher, rather than glatt kosher.

However, says Rabbi Mayer Kurcfeld, assistant director of supervision and a *shochet* at Star-K Kosher Certification, "We don't bother with that. It's too time-consuming." Many kosher slaughterers only approve glatt kosher meat, he says, because the decision about glatt can be made fairly quickly. If a *bodek* determines that an animal is not glatt, but could possibly be "regular" kosher, he must proceed with several more examinations, which takes a while. Kurcfeld adds, "Because of the pressures and environment of production, we have to move too quickly to make that determination. It can be too complicated to do a thorough job, and the pressure is on." There are some larger kosher slaughterhouses that do use "regular" kosher meat. If the meat is glatt kosher, this will be indicated on the package. Some Jews prefer to eat only glatt kosher meat, so the labels distinguish between the two.

In the 1970s, glatt kosher became more universally important. This was when the word *glatt* started to transcend its literal meaning of "smooth," used only in reference to meat. Producers of kosher goods began to label even nonmeat products as "glatt" kosher; glatt came to imply that a product was extra-kosher, somehow more carefully examined than "regular" kosher. This is not, however, an official stance by any kosher certification organization, but it seems to have become a *mesorah*.

Because of the work involved in kosher slaughter, and because today all meat is slaughtered on a large scale, there are no slaughterhouses in the United States devoted exclusively to kosher slaughter, though there are those that slaughter only animals that *can* be kosher (steer, lamb, calves, poultry). Rabbi Kurcfeld notes that of one hundred cattle slaughtered, about forty qualify as glatt kosher. All animals are also examined by United States Department of Agriculture (USDA) inspectors after slaughter. The remaining animals that are not kosher may be determined acceptable by the USDA inspectors; they are kept in a separate area from the kosher meat.

The cattle that is deemed unkosher is then sold to nonkosher butchers. The hindquarters of ruminants (cows, lambs, calves) are not kosher, and are sold to nonkosher meat distributors. The reason for this is twofold. First, as mentioned previously, the sciatic nerve of all animals is not kosher, and it is located in the hindquarters. Second, the hindquarters are riddled with *chelev*, the kind of fat that is unkosher. Cuts such as sirloin and flank are located in the hindquarters, and can be made kosher, but the labor-intensive process of removing the *chelev* and various veins—a process called *nikkur* in Hebrew, *treiboring* in Yiddish, or *porging*—makes this not financially worthwhile for a meat processor. The procedure is so particular that it has not been practiced in the United States for decades. Forequarters also need to be *porged*, but there are fewer veins and less *chelev* in this part of the animal, and it does not take as much time or training.

With kosher slaughter, if any part of the animal is found to be treif, the entire animal is deemed unkosher. This is not the case with USDA inspections. They may find a cancerous liver, for example, but will determine that the rest of the steer is unaffected and therefore safe for consumption. Unkosher animals can still have inspection-acceptable parts; but as Rabbi Kurcfeld says, "There are no such thing as kosher *parts*."

Once an animal or bird has passed the *bedikah* and is deemed to be kosher, it must be *kashered. Kashering* is the procedure used to extract all blood from the meat, as blood is forbidden. This must be done within seventy-two hours of the animal being slaughtered; if more time passes, the blood can congeal in the meat, thereby making it impossible to remove the blood properly. Meat may not be ground for hamburger until it has been kashered. There are two methods of kashering: soaking and salting, or broiling.

For soaking and salting, the meat is first rinsed of any surface blood. It is then soaked in tepid water for thirty minutes. If the water is too cold, it can hinder the release of blood. Soaking opens the pores of the meat to make it more receptive for the next step, salting, which helps draw out the blood from the meat.

The meat must be sprinkled with medium salt. The type of salt that is used matters. The so-called kosher salt that you see in the supermarket really refers to what the salt is used for, rather than to the salt itself being kosher (which it is). Salt that is too fine would just dissolve; too coarse salt might fall off the meat. The salt-coated meat rests on special draining boards for one hour. It is then rinsed thoroughly three times, and can now be cooked.

Liver, because it is so heavy with blood, is kashered by broiling, which cooks off the blood. Soaking and salting alone will not remove all the blood. The liver must be placed on a perforated surface so the blood can drain while it broils. It should be lightly sprinkled with salt. As it broils, the blood drips away, and the liver can then be cooked further.

During our grandparents' time, forty or fifty years ago, the meat you bought at the kosher butcher had not yet been kashered. It usually had been through the soaking process, but had not yet been salted. Even thirty years ago, when my family began keeping kosher, and it is true today as well, most meat goes from the slaughterhouse to a meat processor or butcher, who immediately kashers the meat completely. Meat that you buy at a kosher butcher today is usually completely kashered and ready to cook as soon as you buy it. Kashered meat may be frozen, as the blood has been removed.

Shechita Then and Now

The entry for *Shechita* in the 1906 *Jewish Encyclopedia* features an eighteenth-century etching of a German-Jewish slaughtering yard. Two men are depicted holding down a steer whose legs are bound, as a third administers a fatal stroke with a *chalef*; blood pours from the wound onto the ground. Elsewhere, a beheaded, split carcass hangs from a rail as another *shochet* reaches his hand into the carcass, presumably to inspect the organs.

Today, much has changed in the world of meat slaughter, but in the world of *shechita*, some aspects have not changed at all. Animals are still killed with the same kind of *chalef* that was used 250 years ago, and a *bodek* still reaches into the carcass to check the animal's organs for defects by hand.

Most commercially available meat, kosher and nonkosher, that we buy in the United States, is slaughtered in large slaughterhouses located close to the source of the meat (i.e., Iowa, Wisconsin, South America), with hundreds of animals processed over the course of an hour. Much has been done over the last century to ensure that conditions of slaughterhouses are as clean and well maintained as possible.

No Milk and Meat Together

One of the defining principles of kashrut is the injunction against combining dairy and meat, called *basar b'chalav*, literally, "meat in milk." The entire setup of your kosher kitchen is shaped by this law, and this is one of the ongoing challenges of maintaining a kosher home. Unless you are a vegetarian, you most likely have both dairy and meat products in your home, and keeping them distinct and separate while you cook, clean, store, and eat will define the way you manage food in your home.

This concept is based on a passage that appears identically three separate times in the Torah: *"You shall not cook a kid in the milk of its mother."* In **Exodus 23:19,** the passage occurs in a paragraph that discusses the Three Pilgrimage Festivals (Pesach, Shavuot, and Sukkot). The law is prefaced by the sentence *"The choicest first-fruits of your land you shall bring into the house of the Lord your God."*

Eleven chapters later, in **Exodus 34:26,** the same two-part verse occurs verbatim, this time in a chapter in which God commands Moses to replace the two stone tablets of the Ten Commandments, which he had broken upon witnessing the incident of the golden calf. This is a significant, moving passage, for this is the time when God renews His covenant with the Israelites. *Immediately* following the commandment about a kid and its mother's milk, God says to Moses, *"Write you these words, for according to these words I have sealed a covenant with you and with Israel."* To me, this underlines the importance of the commandment against eating milk and meat together.

The third time *basar b'chalav* appears is in **Deuteronomy 14:21.** Unlike the two chapters in Exodus, this chapter deals specifically with dietary laws. The verses leading up to this one describe kosher and unkosher animals, concluding with a list of forbidden birds and the injunction against swarming things. Verse 21 also contains the commandment regarding *neveilah.*

What does it mean, to cook a kid in its mother's milk? There is the obvious meaning—don't milk a goat, kill its kid, then cook it in its own mother's milk—certainly a cruel image. But what about other animals, such as cows and sheep? The rabbis determined that the word *kid* represents all acceptable meat. The rabbis further determined that meat, or flesh, included fowl as well as beast, but did not include fish or acceptable locusts. Milk includes all milk products as well, namely cheese and butter.

Technically, poultry is pareve, since birds don't produce milk, but birds came to be considered meat because visually the flesh resembles meat. If the rules about poultry were different from those regarding red meat, it could potentially be confusing. A piece of beef might resemble poultry (such as dark meat) and one might inadvertently eat the meat with milk, thinking the piece of meat was a piece of chicken. To ensure that no one might accidentally transgress the commandment of eating meat with milk, the sages determined that the rules that apply to red meat also apply to poultry. Also, I think it is significant that one of the three mentions of *basar b'chalav* comes at the end of the list of forbidden birds; to me, this implies that birds are included as meat.

Rabbi Reinstein finds the commandment momentous. "There is something much more universal in terms of life forces, in separating milk and meat," he says. "Milk is that which nurtures and sustains life, meat represents a life that's been taken. To combine these is an insult."

Stylistically, nothing in the Torah is random, so the triple mention of this law is significant. Injunctions against *neveilah* and treif, and the commandment that leads to the laws of *shechita*, occur only once. But *basar b'chalav* occurs three times. In the Talmud, the rabbis conclude that the three mentions represent three aspects of the rule: It is forbidden to *cook* meat and milk together; to *eat* meat and milk together; and to *derive any benefit from* meat and milk together. This includes preparing a meat and milk dish for a non-Jew, or giving a pet food that contains dairy and meat products, even if the meat is unkosher meat.

KOSHER FOODS

I WALK INTO THE BUTCHERIE, my local kosher market, and peruse the aisles—pasta, salsa, jams, cake mixes, cereals, snack foods, kashered chicken, deli meats, packaged knishes, cheeses from France and Israel, Kiddush wines, fine Merlot. How easy it is, in the twenty-first century, to obtain kosher goods. Even supermarket shelves are crammed with certified kosher goods. This abundance is a relatively recent phenomenon. Integrated Marketing Communications, a firm that tracks trends in the kosher industry, estimates that in 2003 there were more than eighty thousand certified kosher products in the United States. This compares to some sixteen thousand in 1986.

"Ingredient Kosher" and Kosher Certification

What makes a packaged product kosher? There are two ways to check: Read the ingredients or look on the package for a *hechsher,* a symbol indicating that a certifying organization has supervised the production and that all ingredients used are kosher.

Some Jews, more often those who identify as Conservative, Reconstructionist, or Reform, observe what is referred to as **"ingredient kosher."** To check the kashrut of any packaged product, you must read the ingredients. If the item contains any animal products (e.g., beef fat, chicken stock), you can't eat it. This was the form of kashrut my family observed when we began keeping kosher when I was a kid, and it is how I keep kosher today. Over the past thirty years, ingredients labels have become more explicit, making label reading an easier task. Perhaps because the Food and Drug Administration (FDA) labeling regulations have become more stringent, the ingredients manufacturers use tend to be more appealing as well.

For example, in the early 1970s, there were several products—cake mixes, cookies, crackers—we couldn't buy because the label listed "shortening" as an ingredient. Shortening could mean any kind of fat, from vegetable oil to lard. Since it was a general, catchall term, and we couldn't be sure, we did not purchase those products.

Then, in the mid-1970s, FDA regulations required ingredients lists on labels to be more precise, and the truth came out. "Shortening" suddenly became "animal and/or vegetable shortening." A documented no-no if you keep kosher. It still meant that we couldn't purchase those products, but it also meant that we now knew for sure what a company was using. Further labeling laws required listing the *kind* of animal shortening (beef fat or lard) and the *kind* of vegetable shortening (soybean oil, partially hydrogenated cottonseed oil, etc.). Hydrogenated oils and cholesterol-laden animal fats became a negative selling point, and most products that had used animal shortening switched to vegetable shortening, with manufacturers touting this as a benefit on their packaging with bright labels on the front of the box. It is now rare to find a product, at least one manufactured in the United States, that contains animal shortening.

Even with more detailed ingredients descriptions, there are a few potential problems with keeping "ingredient kosher," and again it is something to consider when you determine at what level you wish to keep kosher. Most commercially produced packaged goods contain some kind of additive. Additives are ingredients not usually used in home cooking that are necessary for prolonging the shelf life of packaged goods. Commercial products need to maintain their integrity while being shipped around the country and while sitting on grocery shelves. Additives affect the food's appearance, texture, color, flavor, shelf life, and stability. Many additives can be derived from either animal or plant sources, such as glycerin and "natural flavors," and FDA labeling does not require that the source information be included on the label.

Further, a dairy or vegetarian product may be prepared using the same equipment that is used to prepare meat. For example, a canned vegetable soup might be prepared in the same pots used to prepare a beef broth. Again, these concerns may not be a problem for you, depending on how you choose to observe kashrut.

But if you wish to observe a stricter level of kashrut, how can you be certain that the packaged goods you're eating are truly kosher? If you know who's making the food and how they're doing it, that's one way. I spoke with an Orthodox rabbi in Baltimore who patronizes a local deli that has been around for decades. No one certifies the establishment, but everyone who goes there knows it is kosher. However, the same rules don't work regarding a box of cereal packaged 1,700 miles away. Therefore, kosher certification agencies are necessary.

Hechsher History

Even if you haven't kept kosher, you may have noticed little symbols on various products you've purchased. Products that are certified kosher bear a symbol that represents the organization that does the certifying. Examples of such symbols are a *U* in a circle (OU) and a *K* in a star (Star-K). Such a symbol is called a *hechsher*, which means "ritual permit," and comes from the same Hebrew root as "kosher." A hechsher appears on a given product indicating that a kosher certification organization has supervised the production of that item and guarantees that all ingredients used and all equipment used to produce it are kosher. Such supervision is called *hashgacha* (literally, "supervision"), a word that is sometimes used synonymously for the word *hechsher*. The word *hechsher* has also been vowel-ized; for example, a product is *hechshered*, meaning it has been supervised and has a hechsher.

Now, what does it mean to certify that a product is kosher? If the ingredients are all acceptable, isn't that enough? Can't the company basically say, hey—we're kosher? Perhaps in a perfect world, but in the real world, we need a system of checks and balances, hence the development of kashrut certifying agencies.

In the multimillennial history of kashrut, certification organizations are relatively new, and relatively American. But then, modern food production is relatively new, and the development of modern kashrut parallels the development of industrialized food production as well as the development of modern Judaism in the United States.

For Jews, nineteenth-century United States delivered religious freedom unlike in any previous era. This freedom yielded multiple results. It gave Jews the ability to be *less* observant—hence the rise of the Reform movement. It also gave more observant Jews the chance to practice their religion with the support, rather than the opposition, of the government. For example, *shechita,* ritual slaughter, has always been permitted in the United States, without question. (*Shechita* is forbidden in some European countries.)

Jews from communities all over Europe began to immigrate to the United States in earnest in the nineteenth century. They came from cities and villages, from all over Europe—Germany, Russia, Poland. Since they came from different places, they brought with them different traditions. There were similarities, to be sure, since religious Jews all followed halacha according to the Shulchan Aruch, but there were certain practical differences, which led to clashes and power struggles. In Europe communities tended to be clustered together, and Jewish law was under the guidance of the local rabbi, but the communal structure was different in the United States.

As the population grew, so did the conflicts. This was especially apparent in New York City, where the greatest number of Jewish immigrants settled. In the decade between 1880 and 1890, the Jewish population there more than doubled, from 60,000 in 1880 to 135,000 in 1890. Joseph Adler writes in *Jewish Frontier* magazine, "Old-World religious authoritarianism could not easily be transferred wholesale to the New-World. In the new environment with its congregational polity and voluntaristic character, the automatic leadership of the rabbinate was not accepted without question." Neither was the supervision of *shechita* and of kosher food production.

When food first began to be mass-produced in America, fraud was unfortunately part of the system (sawdust in flour, dirt in cocoa, who knows what in canned meat), which inspired the creation of the Food and Drug Administration (FDA). There were also fallacies perpetuated in the kosher food market. Individual rabbis might be assigned to supervise the kashrut practices of a given store or butcher, but they were employed by the same store or butcher. Not exactly an incentive for objectivity: If they questioned the kashrut practices too stringently, they might lose their jobs. "The only possibility of controlling supervision was to create a cohesive community of Jews who would be willing to live according to one basic set of standards," writes Harold P. Gastwirt in *Fraud, Corruption, and Holiness: The Controversy Over the Supervision of Jewish Dietary Practice in New York City 1881–1940.*

Establishing such a cohesive community proved to be an elusive task that would take many decades. Because at the same time, Judaism in general was going through a period of major upheaval. The antitradition Reform movement and the middle-of-the-road

Conservative movement have their roots in this period, as do the delineations among different Orthodox factions. Ultimately, there would be no "one set of basic standards," although a form of controlling supervision was eventually established.

The Union of Orthodox Jewish Congregations of America (UOJC) was established in 1898. This organization became the Orthodox Union of today. In 1923, the UOJC started their Kosher Certification Service and contacted larger food producers, requesting that they consider making some of their products kosher, under supervision, with a certification symbol on the label. One of the first certified-kosher products was Heinz baked beans. In negotiating with the company, the UOJC also designed their own hechsher, still used today. "One of the problems that had to be overcome was the possibility that the Gentile consumer would object to the word kosher that appeared on the label," Gastwirt writes. "An agreement was reached to drop the word kosher and to use, instead, the symbol of a capital U in a circle." This set a precedent for kosher certifiers through today. (Unfortunately, fringe hate groups also see this as fuel for anti-Semitism; I came across rambling tirades that ascribed the symbol to malevolent Jewish forces seeking secretly to tax unwitting consumers. In truth, manufacturers have found that kashrut certification has helped sales, both from Jewish and non-Jewish clientele, since it indicates an extra level of inspection.)

Jewish organizations also began to look to state governments for support, and several states have kosher laws to help thwart fraud in the kashrut industry.

Hechshers Today

In the mid-1930s, the Orthodox Union was joined by other organizations, including Organized Kashrus Laboratories, with an OK—*K* in a circle—symbol. The 1960s saw a surge in kashrut supervision agencies. Today, the Orthodox Union, usually called simply "OU," is the largest kashrut certifier in the country, but it is by no means the only one. Both the number of certifiers and the number of certified products have increased.

There are several kosher certification organizations around the world, primarily in the United States. *Kashrus Magazine* compiles an annual list of kosher certifiers worldwide, and listed more than six hundred for 2004. Of course, with so many organizations, reliability can sometimes be a question.

The six hundred plus kashrut organizations include many small companies—sometimes a single rabbi—that oversee primarily the kashrut of local establishments such as restaurants. This is not to say they are not as valid as larger organizations, but if a certifying agency is less well known, you may need to research it to verify its credentials—check its references, as it were. Some synagogues publish annual lists of certifiers that are acceptable to their community.

Kashrut supervision organizations are almost exclusively Orthodox, including those that supervise manufactured goods. This is due in part to the "lowest common denominator" reality. Conservative, Reform, and Reconstructionist Jews eat foods supervised by an Orthodox authority, but the stricter Orthodox only eat foods supervised by an Orthodox authority—and even then, not every hechsher is acceptable to every Orthodox Jew.

There are different types of certifying procedures for different types of institutions: manufacturers and food service. Manufacturers are companies that produce raw ingredients, such as additives, as well as those that make packaged goods, such as canned sauces or boxes of crackers. Food service includes restaurants, bakeries, hotels, nursing homes, and hospitals, places where food is prepared and served.

Smaller, local certifiers tend to supervise food-service establishments. Manufactured food is the type of food you will be most concerned about regarding how you keep your kitchen kosher. The larger organizations certify thousands of products throughout the world. Products that meet the certification requirements are stamped with the hechsher that is unique to each certifying organization. The four largest organizations (sometimes called "the Big Four") are the following:

Orthodox Union ⓤ, based in New York City

The Organized Kashrus Laboratories ⓚ (OK, also called Circle K), based in Brooklyn

Star-K Kosher Certification ☆, based in Baltimore

Kof-K Supervision Organization ⬝, based in New Jersey

Hechshers are often accompanied by letters or words that offer more detail. If the food is pareve (contains no meat or dairy products) the label may say so, as with Star-K and the word *pareve* that appears in tiny letters under the star. For the Orthodox Union, a plain OU indicates the product is pareve. A *D* next to the hechsher indicates that it is dairy. *DE* means the product may be pareve, but was manufactured using dairy equipment. An *M* may indicate meat. These hechsher subclassifications are relatively new and are still evolving; an industry standard has yet to be set in stone. The letter *P* usually indicates a product that is kosher for Pesach, but it sometimes can mean the product is pareve. To be sure if a product is pareve or not, you still need to read the ingredients label.

One symbol that can cause more confusion than reassurance is a little letter *K* that appears on some products, including Kellogg's cereals. Just a plain *K*—no star around it, no circle, *kaf*, nada. Technically, this could mean anything. It is not a registered trademark, unlike other hechshers. It *can* mean that the company is asserting that, although unsupervised, their product is kosher. It can also mean that the product is actually supervised. Some companies opt for a "generic K," as it is sometimes called, to give themselves the option to change kashrut supervision without having to alter the packaging. If they go from OU to Star-K and back, they don't have to make a new package bearing the new hechsher each time they switch. Kellogg's is one such major company that is certified, yet retains the generic K as its hechsher.

If you see a generic K on the package of a product you are interested in purchasing, you need to contact the company to verify if the product is indeed certified. Rabbi Paul Plotkin, chairman of the kashrut subcommittee of the Committee on Jewish Law and Standards of the Rabbinical Assembly, recounts this anecdote: "A meat-packing company in Kansas City, non-Jewish, nonkosher, was canning meat and put a K on the product. When they were approached by people asking why they put a K on it, they responded, 'We were told by a marketing company that if you put a K on a product it sells better in the Northeast.'" This is not to say that all products bearing a K are not kosher; you just need to check with the company before using the product. And read the ingredients to double-check.

While kosher certification organizations exist abroad, the system is primarily used in the United States. Packaged foods in England, for example, do not necessarily carry hechshers; rather, you can obtain a booklet listing all certified kosher products sold in that country. Products from Israel imported to the United States do carry hechshers.

The Certification Process

Integrated Marketing Communications counted eighty thousand packaged kosher products in 2003. But packaged products contain many raw ingredients, each of which has to be certified in order for the final product to be considered kosher. The "Big Four" companies alone certify close to half a million items, including raw ingredients such as vitamins, flavorings, emulsifiers, and stabilizers.

What does it mean to be certified? There are those who describe the meaning of certification by saying it is food blessed by a rabbi. This is inaccurate. The **hechsher** you notice on your breakfast cereal is a symbol indicating that the production of a product has been supervised by a **mashgiach,** literally, "inspector." The *mashgiach,* who is not necessarily a rabbi, does not bless the food. He merely ensures that it is produced according to the laws of kashrut. (Even a *shochet,* when performing ritual slaughter, is not blessing the meat; rather, he is blessing the act of *shechita.* Blessing food is reserved for when the food is eaten.) A *mashgiach* operates under the auspices of a kosher certifying organization, checking that all ingredients used in the production of a product are kosher, and that the organization follows all necessary kosher regulations.

A *mashgiach* does not need to be a rabbi, and can even be a woman (though most are men), but must meet specific criteria. The certifying agencies I spoke with all described the position in a similar manner. The *mashgiach* must be an observant Jew, that is, an Orthodox Jew who follows all of the Torah's mitzvot, which means he/she keeps strictly kosher and observes Shabbat. *Mashgichim* need to know the laws of kashrut, and must be intelligent and perceptive, since whenever they are assigned to a new plant, they must learn and understand new procedures. Today, knowledge of food technology is also useful.

Rabbi Moshe Elefant, executive rabbinic coordinator for the Orthodox Union, emphasizes the importance of familiarity with food technology in the twenty-first century. "A factory is a very complex area," he says. "There is a lot of different machinery, a lot of different types of ingredients than you would use at home. There has to be an appreciation and understanding of that." Some companies, including Nabisco, produce both kosher and nonkosher items, and the *mashgiach* needs to ensure that no unkosher ingredients contaminate the kosher areas.

Different organizations have slightly different systems, but the larger agencies have a hierarchy of *mashgichim.* There is the field *mashgiach,* who is on the site inspecting, whether full time or periodic. He has a supervisor, to whom he reports if anything is amiss. In an attempt to avoid conflict of interest, the *mashgiach*'s employers are the supervising agency, not the company where he works. So if there's a kashrut issue, he first contacts his superiors back at the main office, who offer advice on how to proceed accordingly.

How does a *mashgiach* supervise? Some companies don't technically need certification, but opt to have it anyway. Facilities such as a water bottling plant do not need daily monitoring to make sure the plant is following the kashrut specifications. For these, the *mashgiach* makes periodic visits to ensure that everything is as kosher as it should be. Other facilities, especially those producing meat products, including a butcher, need constant monitoring, because there is such a high possibility that something unkosher could happen. These facilities have a full-time *mashgiach* assigned to supervise production. Facilities that prepare fresh food daily, such as restaurants and bakeries, must also have full-time *mashgichim.*

How Does a Product Get a Hechsher?

When a company like Nabisco decides it wants to have a certain product, such as Oreos, certified kosher, it contacts a kosher supervision organization. Supervisors are assigned to oversee the kosherizing process ("kosherize" is a real word in the world of kosher supervision, used to describe the process of turning an unkosher facility into a kosher one). The company must submit a list of all ingredients used in the production of a product. All ingredients must also be certified. If, for example, cocoa is used, it must come from a kosher facility. If an unkosher ingredient is used in the current, uncertified version of the product, it must be replaced with a kosher equivalent, or that ingredient, too, must be certified if possible. This can get tricky when it comes to flavorings and preservatives, if the company relies on particular flavorings as essential to its formula.

Equipment must also be kosherized. The procedure used to kosherize equipment is not unlike the procedure you'll use at home (see Spiritual Renovation: Kashering Your Kitchen, page 79), but on a much, much larger scale. When it comes to kosherization, the basic rule of thumb is, whatever made it unkosher, that's what can make it kosher. For example, a commercial oven needs to be heated, to a temperature of 900 to 1,000 degrees, to the point where it is red hot. Baking pans must be heated similarly; some materials, such as aluminum, cannot be heated to that point without being ruined; in such cases, new equipment must be purchased.

Once a plant passes all the initial inspections of the kosherization, it must be overseen periodically by the *mashgiach,* who checks that the facility remains up to kosher code.

There is a fee that a company must pay to be kosher. Although certifying agencies are nonprofit institutions, the employees still have to make a living doing what they do. One certifier I spoke with said, "Companies see a payoff by becoming kosher. They get asked more frequently if a product is kosher, and if they can say yes, a sale will often go through that much more quickly."

Another certifier said, "Overall, in terms of their budget, what a company spends on certification is a fraction of the budget they spend on advertising, certainly with a larger company."

Inadvertent and intentional misuses of the system are inevitable. Larger organizations publish annual lists of the products they supervise, with periodic "kosher alerts," published in magazines and on their websites, such as the following:

KOSHER ALERT: Please be advised that **Peanut Butter Chips** manufactured by Kargher Corp., Hatfield, PA, are now **KOF-K DAIRY**.

Sysco Classic Bleu Cheese Dressing (single size serving), Sysco Corp., Houston, TX, mistakenly bears on **OU symbol** and is not kosher. The product is being recalled.

Kosher Gourmet Hors D'oeuvres Kosher Assorted Quiche Pack, distributed by Kosher Gourmet, Chicago, IL, is pareve even though whey is listed in the ingredient panel in error. The labels are being corrected. This product is certified **Star-K kosher pareve.**

Kashrut Basics

Basar b'Chalav: Milk and Meat

Kosher foods fall under three basic categories: **Meat** (*basar* in Hebrew, *fleishig* in Yiddish), **Dairy** (*chalavi* in Hebrew, *milchig* in Yiddish), and **Pareve,** meaning neutral, neither meat or milk. Fish and eggs are pareve.

The word *pareve*, incidentally, has an intriguingly indeterminate etymology. It seems to have been popularized by Eastern Yiddish speakers, possibly coming from Slavic roots, perhaps, according to *The Language and Culture Atlas of Ashkenazic Jewry, Volume III*, from the Czech word *parovy*, which means "dual purpose." Western Yiddish speakers initially used the word *min[i]ç* to mean "containing neither milk nor meat." The *Atlas* sites the etymology for *min[i]ç* as either Vulgar Latin *münich*, meaning "castrated horse," or German *munch,* meaning monk; both images of a kind of neutrality. Premier Yiddish Linguist Max Weinreich writes in his *History of the Yiddish Language*, "Up to now I have seen no satisfactory etymology of [the word] párev(e)." The modern Hebrew word for pareve is *stam*, which can mean "vagueness."

As explained previously, dairy and meat products are incompatible in kashrut; they cannot be eaten together or cooked together, nor can you derive any benefit from the combination. For example, you can't sell cheeseburgers to non-Jews. You can't even give your dog pet food containing dairy and meat.

Pareve foods, such as green beans or rice, can be eaten with either meat or milk, with the exception of fish, which, according to Orthodox kashrut, cannot be eaten with meat. All kashrut rules regarding meat and milk are called **basar b'chalav,** literally, "meat in milk."

Bitul/Nullification: All About Flavor

Even the flavor of milk cannot be mixed with the flavor of meat, the basic premise of the *basar b'chalav* prohibition. Similarly, unkosher food cannot be used to flavor kosher food, even if you don't actually eat the flavoring agent. This concept is called **ta'am k'ikar,** "taste is like the essence." You can't stick a piece of bacon in a pot of baked beans, then remove it and eat just the beans, for example. The rabbis discussed and determined the many different ways in which the flavor of one item can permeate and infuse flavors into a second item. For this reason, we have separate dishes, pots, pans, and silverware for meat and dairy foods. As the Talmudic discussions indicate, accidents regarding meat and milk, and treif and kosher food, occur frequently. In a kosher kitchen, inadvertently mixing dairy and meat is the issue most likely to occur in kosher food preparation. It is less likely that you'll have many treif ingredients in your kosher kitchen, so *basar b'chalav* is the more common situation. The rabbis determined various ways that such inadvertent milk and meat encounters and kosher and treif accidental trysts could or could not be nullified.

Bitul (also called *batel*) is the word for nullification, and it is used with other words to describe the conditions that warrant nullification.

The concept of *bitul* is quite complex. The descriptions below can give you a rough idea of situations in which it could apply, but this writing should *not* be used as the definitive word on how such a situation must be dealt with, if it arises in your kosher kitchen. If you have questions about kashrut situations, always contact a rabbi who can understand the exact situation and direct you as to the proper way to proceed. As long as you understand this, continue to read.

The primary way in which flavor is transferred is through heat, by cooking. If a cold piece of meat touches a cold dairy plate, all you need to do is remove the meat from the plate and wash both the meat and the plate. If a hot piece of meat touches even a cold dairy plate, that plate and the meat become treif. If you were heating milk in a pot on the stovetop, for example, and a piece of meat inadvertently fell in, it could flavor the milk with its meatiness. There are different ways to ascertain if the amount of meat that fell into the pot is enough to contaminate it.

Bitul b'shishim means "nullification in sixty," that is, if the ratio of the two substances is at least 60:1—or if the proportion of the larger substances is 60 times more than the secondary substance—the rabbis determined that at such a ratio the two flavors would not affect each other. *Bitul b'shishim* is the method used to judge nullification when there are two dissimilar substances—such as milk and a piece of meat. In the preceding example, as soon as you notice the meat that fell in the pot, you should remove it. If the meat is less than one-sixtieth proportionately to the amount of liquid, everything is fine, continue cooking. If it is not, you need to discard the contents of the pot—and the pot needs to be kashered.

This method of nullification is valid only if the mixture of substances was accidental. You cannot deliberately add forbidden substances together and have them then be nullified. This is why unkosher flavorings may not be used in commercial products. Even though the added extract may be as small as one one-thousandth of the item in question, it is added intentionally. Also, it is a flavoring, so it will directly affect the flavor because, as the name implies, that's what flavoring is all about.

Bitul b'rov means "nullification in a majority," and is used when two similar substances are inadvertently mixed together—say, a piece of unkosher beef somehow falls into a pot containing kosher beef. The kosher food simply has to be in larger quantity than the unkosher food—some say two to one. This is based on the principle that in the Torah, a decision is made by majority rule. Even if there is a piece of unkosher meat in the pot, the whole pot is considered acceptable, although there is some variation in opinion on how it should be eaten. Again, *bitul* cannot happen if the unkosher meat was added intentionally.

The concern is always about flavor: Can the two different substances—milk, meat, kosher, unkosher—affect each other flavorwise? If they can, the substance cannot be eaten. This is the underlying principle of **kavush k'mevushal,** literally, "preserved as if it were cooked," also referred to as simply *kavush.* The idea is that something soaking in a liquid absorbs its flavors after twenty-four hours. So, if you had cold milk in a cold meat pot and left it for twenty-four hours, that pot would need to be kashered because it would have absorbed the flavors of the milk. Similarly, if you left a piece of cold meat on a dairy plate overnight, both would become unkosher.

There is a flip side to this rule, called **ben yomo,** "of that day," and **eino ben yomo,** "not of the day." This refers to when a pot was last used. As mentioned, we are to have separate pots for meat and dairy cooking. The belief is that, whatever material the pot is made of, invariably some amount of flavor is infused therein, so that meat foods could give dairy foods a meat taste, and vice versa—or treif foods, if the pot had been used for treif. However, any flavor left in a pot that has not been used for twenty-four hours will have spoiled. If the flavor that a vessel might impart to your kosher food would be unappealing, then it is not considered unkosher. However, it should be noted that *ben yomo* is not a substitute for kashering pots and dishes. That is, you can't not use any item in your kitchen for a day and then declare it kosher.

This leads to another rule, called **noten ta'am lifgam**, "gives a bad taste." If an unkosher food might give a disgusting taste to the kosher food, then it is not considered unkosher. A rabbi I spoke with cited an example of a mouse falling into a pot of cholent. Not that you'd *want* to eat this cholent, but this is an example of *noten ta'am lifgam,* and the cholent would not be rendered unkosher (you couldn't eat the mouse, however—it still would be treif). If the food that fell in the pot were, say, a piece of unkosher beef, something that a non-Jew could eat, then the cholent would be unkosher. However, if it were something inedible for the non-Jew, such as a mouse, then the kashrut of the cholent is not compromised.

So, while it is unlikely that a pot not used for a day or more would actually impart a truly spoiled flavor to whatever food you were cooking in it, it would be acceptable to use. But not on a regular basis.

The preceding descriptions give you an idea of how foods can be nullified in unkosher situations, but there are many exceptions to those rules, and many more details as well. As always, whenever you have a question about a kashrut situation, check with a rabbi.

Waiting Between Meals

We've established that you cannot eat meat and dairy foods together. This means that a meal is either a meat meal or a dairy meal (or a pareve meal, for that matter). You cannot even have meat and dairy at the same table; that is, one person can't eat a bagel with cream cheese at the same table where someone is eating fried chicken. To clarify further, you can't have a piece of steak on one plate, prepared without any dairy, then turn to a second plate and chomp down on a piece of cheese—even if you've swallowed the steak. To ensure that meat and milk not be eaten together in any way, it is customary to wait a certain amount of time between meals. After eating meat, the wait time varies, but the generally accepted amount of time to wait is six hours.

Different traditions developed as to the exact amount of time that must pass between meat and dairy meals. Wait time is required because of the nature of meat. In *The Laws of Kashrus*, Binyomin Forst explains that the sages give two primary reasons: Meat leaves behind a fatty residue in the throat, and particles of meat might remain between your teeth. Time is necessary for the digestive powers of saliva to break down both that fatty residue and the meat particles.

For Orthodox Jews, the most common wait time is six hours. According to Sephardic tradition, six hours is not merely tradition, but halacha, required by Jewish law. Ashkenazic tradition says that more lenient options are also halachically correct. Most agree that the meat meal should be concluded with appropriate blessings, signifying the meal is over. You should then clean and rinse your mouth and wash your hands. Some say one hour is sufficient time, and this has been the accepted tradition of Dutch Jews. German Jews follow a tradition of waiting three hours. Forst says this may be based on the idea that in winter the time between meals is shorter; therefore, it is acceptable to wait a shorter amount of time year round.

These are three generally accepted wait-time traditions. However, even today, I've encountered people who've developed their own traditions within their communities. Some wait four hours after eating chicken, five hours after meat. Some start counting the wait time after saying blessings, some start counting as soon as they've swallowed the last bite of meat.

With dairy foods, the wait time between dairy and meat is minimal. This is based on **Chullin 105a,** where it says, *"How long must one wait between cheese and flesh? And he replied, Nothing at all."* Still, you should eat something like bread to effectively wipe your mouth of any milky taste, and you should rinse your mouth and wash your hands.

Hard cheese, described as cheese that has aged over six months, such as Swiss cheese, has a stronger flavor and is thought to leave a fatty residue, so it requires a six-hour wait.

Bishual Akum and Bishul Yisrael

Another issue in Orthodox kashrut observance involves food preparation and non-Jews. According to the Talmud and the Shulchan Aruch, there are certain foods that can only be kosher when prepared by a Jew. Foods prepared by non-Jews are called *akum*, which is an acronym for the Hebrew phrase *ovdei kochavim umazalot,* literally, "servant of the stars and constellations"; in other words, pagans or idolators. There are four types of food that according to Orthodox kashrut cannot be made by non-Jews: milk and cheese, which I discuss in the dairy section under kosher foods (see page 59); bread, discussed under bread (see page 65); and wine, discussed under grapes in the section on produce (see page 70).

A final concern is meals prepared by non-Jews, called **bishul akum,** literally, "pagan cooking." We need to look at the social conditions under which these laws were formulated. During much of the past two thousand years, conditions for Jews in the world historically have not been exactly friendly. Jews were ghettoized, denied citizenship, often not allowed to own land, and so on. A big fear was intermarriage and assimilation. Jews were not encouraged to share meals with non-Jews, as sharing a meal is a popular way of socializing, and socializing can lead to friendship, which can lead to intermarriage, which can lead to the end of that particular family practicing Judaism. If non-Jews were overly involved in food preparation for Jews, again intermarriage might result.

At the time this law was made, most people ate food they prepared in their homes. Wealthier Jews might have non-Jewish servants. A stipulation was made in the Shulchan Aruch that if a Jew lit the fire, or even "raked the fire while the cooking was done," the food could be kosher and would count as **bishul Yisrael,** "Jewish cooking." The rules of *bishul akum* actually apply to only a small percentage of prepared food. Specifically, it applies to "food that is fit to be served at the table of a king." So it does not apply to mundane delicacies such as canned beans or mashed potatoes. In fact, there is a such a lengthy list of prepared foods to which *bishul akum* does *not* apply that it can be confusing to determine exactly when the laws should be applied.

The instance of *bishul akum* most likely to be an issue for those observing kashrut according to Orthodox dictates is in the home. Rabbi Yaakov Luban, senior rabbinic coordinator of the Orthodox Union, Kashrut Division, wrote in the November 1994 issue of *Jewish Action*, "Rav Moshe Feinstein, zt"l, ruled that there is no prohibition of bishul akum in a factory that uses specialized equipment for the following reason . . . if the food is processed in equipment which is completely different than normal household cooking utensils, bishul akum does not apply."

At home, however, if you have a cook or babysitter who might be preparing food, this employee is subject to the laws of *bishul akum*. If the employee is using your pots and pans, you, as a Jew, must turn on the stove or oven—even if the employee is making food for only him or herself, and all the ingredients are kosher. Otherwise, according to the laws of *bishul akum*, the food they make and the cookware they use will be considered treif.

The Conservative and other movements do not subscribe to the tenet of *bishul Yisrael or bishul akum*. "It is not something we have ever been concerned with," says Rabbi Paul Plotkin of the kashrut subcommittee of the Committee on Jewish Law and Standards.

Understanding Kosher Foods

If you choose to keep "hechsher kosher," some foods require supervision and some do not. All meat does. Other foods may or may not require a hechsher, and I will mention what does in each section on food. You should also check with a rabbi, as not all communities necessarily accept the same hechshers. This is especially true for smaller supervising agencies.

Meat and Poultry

If you buy meat at a kosher butcher, there should be a certificate of supervision on display. Packaged meats, such as chicken, should have a *plumba*, a metal tag attached to the bird indicating it has been under constant supervision. The package should also bear a hechsher.

Meat and poultry need to be properly kashered, that is, soaked and salted to remove all blood, before you can cook them. Most butchers today do the kashering, but you should double-check that the meat you buy is indeed already kashered.

While relatively exotic animals such as goat, buffalo, and ibex are technically kosher, you're not apt to find them at your local kosher butcher. Beef, veal, and lamb are what you're likely to find. There are kosher buffalo and venison farms in the United States, although most of their business right now is by mail order (see Sources).

Not all cuts of beef, veal, and lamb are kosher; kosher butchers carry only those cuts that are. There are several veins and sections of fat that have to be removed from meat before it can be kashered. The hindquarters have many more such veins and fat deposits; so much so that in the United States the hindquarters of a kosher animal are immediately sold to nonkosher butchers and meat processors.

The front quarters of a steer are divided into seven sections, and cuts from those sections are all acceptable. The unkosher cuts in the hindquarters include filet mignon and sirloin. Following are the kosher sections, with sample cuts of beef from each section:

Chuck (above the shoulder, between the neck and ribs)—chuck roast, French roast, T-bone (not to be confused with a nonkosher cut from the hindquarters, also called a T-bone)

Rib—Chateaubriand, pot roast, spareribs

Shoulder—minute steak, London broil

Brisket—(from behind the foreleg) brisket, of course

The **foreshank, neck,** and **short plate** (located on the animal's underside) are sources for tougher cuts, namely stewing beef, which needs long, slow cooking, and ground beef. In addition, the liver (after proper kashering), tongue, and sweetbreads (thymus glands) are kosher.

For **veal,** a.k.a. baby cow, the forequarters are divided into five sections:

Neck and **foreshanks**—ground veal and stewing veal

Shoulder—veal cutlet, shoulder roast

Rib—rib roast, veal chops

Breast—spareribs, breast

Veal has its own particular issues because of how the animal is raised for meat. Veal calves, which are slaughtered when they are four to five months old, spend their short lives in tiny crates that prevent movement and are force-fed in order that their meat be as tender as possible, and they are raised with little light to keep them anemic, so that their meat will be whiter. This is called "factory farming." It is not the only way veal calves are raised, but it is the most common. The issue here is one of *tza'ar ba'alei chayim*, not causing an animal to suffer.

The Orthodox Rabbi Moshe Feinstein ruled in 1982 that Jews could not raise a calf in this way; further, he asserted that calves raised in such a way were more likely to be treif when examined after *shechita*. Feinstein recommended against eating such veal, but did not say that veal itself is not kosher, so the Orthodox stand today is that veal is kosher.

The Conservative movement has debated this issue extensively. While not forbidding veal as unkosher, the movement does not recommend eating factory-farmed veal. In a

Forum in the Winter 2000 issue of *JTS Magazine*, Rabbi Arthur Lavinsky writes, "[I]f we are to guarantee that the meat that we consume is truly fit, or kosher, we must be sure that the animals we consume live and die humanely." On how veal calves are raised and if that should affect their kashrut status, Lavinsky asserts, "In fact, when animals are treated inhumanely, the meat from those animals should not be deemed kosher under any circumstances."

In the same Forum, Rabbi Paul Plotkin acknowledges that the way veal calves are raised may be inhumane, but says it is *not* an issue of kashrut. "It is clear that there is a strong biblical foundation for *tza'ar ba'alei chayim*. Nevertheless, neither the Torah nor the rabbis ever associated this commandment with kashrut. The two exist independently, and a violation of one has no effect on the other," he writes. "The halakhic system includes cases where an action is prohibited, yet the result of the prohibited act is permitted. . . . Violating *tza'ar ba'alei chayim* is forbidden, but the animals are not treif."

Conclusion? Veal is kosher, but proceed with caution and consideration.

Lamb is also divided into five parts:

Neck—stewing meat
Shoulder—lamb chop, shoulder roast
Rib—rack of lamb, crown roast
Shank (foreleg)—shank of lamb (often used on the Seder plate at Pesach)
Breast—lamb skirt, lamb breast

The head can also be kosher, with special preparation (it is traditionally eaten on Rosh Hashanah in some Sephardic households).

In the Torah, birds are considered pareve because they do not produce milk; however, the Talmud determined that birds are to be treated as meat, to avoid confusion. Kosher birds found in most markets include chicken, turkey, and duck. Goose and squab (pigeon) are also kosher, but finding them can be a challenge. Chicken comes in several forms. Capon is a castrated rooster (no, the castration does not render the bird treif, since it is not a mortal injury). It is older than standard broiler-fryers, and is therefore larger, weighing four to ten pounds, which makes it good for roasting. Cornish hens are a small breed of chicken, sold young (one to two months old), and weigh less than two pounds.

Foie gras, which can be difficult to kasher because of the blood in liver, has issues similar to those regarding veal. In order to turn their livers into foie gras and not just potential chopped liver, duck and geese are force-fed, which can cause internal injuries, making them treif. This treatment is also considered inhumane, and is an issue of *tza'ar ba'alei chayim*.

Eggs

Because eggs come from birds, which in the Torah are not meat, eggs are considered pareve and can be cooked with meat or dairy foods.

However (and there's always a however), there are some exceptions. An egg that is found in a *shechted* chicken is considered to be meat. This is not a situation that arises very often these days, with chickens slaughtered by the thousands per hour, and chickens bred for meat aren't usually egg layers, but in the days of smaller, local butchers, an egg found in a *shechted* chicken was actually considered something of a delicacy. These eggs, a rarity today, are called *ova*, or unborn eggs.

Eggs must come from kosher birds. This means, if you can find them, duck, turkey, and goose eggs are kosher, as well as those from chickens. Ostrich eggs are not. As for eggs from farm-raised quail, it depends on who you ask. Some find quail on the list of acceptable birds, others do not; it is a check-with-your-rabbi issue. Pasteurized egg products, such as egg substitutes and powdered egg whites, do need certification, as heat is involved in their preparations.

Whole eggs do not have to be hechshered. However, there are packaged eggs with a hechsher, and sometimes each individual egg has a little inspection stamp on it. I spoke to a certifier who said that some companies want the hechsher, although it is not necessary; it indicates that no unkosher wash is used on the eggs. The hechsher does not guarantee that the eggs will have no blood spots, however.

Before being sold, eggs are "candled," that is, illuminated with a bright light to determine if there are blood spots in them. Eggs found with blood spots are discarded. Some eggs with spots do slip by this process.

When cooking with eggs, break each one individually into a glass beforehand, to check for blood spots. Eggs that have a blood spot on the yolk are not kosher and must be discarded. There are two possibilities here. One, the egg could be fertilized, so the blood spot could be indicative of a just barely developing chicken, which turns the egg into meat, improperly slaughtered. This is an unlikely scenario these days, since most chickens are not put into situations where their eggs could be fertilized. That is, the hens are raised without a rooster around. In recent years, though, natural-food stores sell fertile eggs, and these cannot be kosher.

A blood spot on the yolk more likely is a tiny burst blood vessel that occurred as the egg was being formed. Since blood is forbidden, such eggs are off-limits. There was a debate in the Talmud about such eggs that had blood spots but were known to come from chickens raised without a rooster nearby and the possibility of fertilization. Would the whole egg have to be discarded? Or just the spot of blood removed? While the latter was considered acceptable, the preferred choice is to discard the whole egg.

Is there a difference between brown eggs and white eggs? Not in taste, certainly. But based solely on my personal experience in the Boston area, brown eggs, including the standard supermarket brand, the pricey organic brand, and the certified kosher brand, tend to have many more blood spots per dozen than white eggs. Rarely do I find a blood spot when I buy white eggs. I have rarely bought a carton of brown eggs that did not have at least one egg with a blood spot, more often two or three. I have yet to find an explanation for this phenomenon. (So why buy brown eggs? you might wonder. Two reasons: Sometimes that is all a market has. And the Happy Hen eggs that are free-range and organic really do make better-tasting scrambled eggs.)

How do you check for blood spots when making roasted or hard-boiled eggs, whole, in the shell? The Shulchan Aruch determined that it is acceptable to eat such eggs, unchecked, since most eggs do not contain a blood spot.

Dairy

Dairy foods include any product containing milk. Milk, cream, butter, cheese, whey, milk powder are all dairy, as is anything containing them. Casein (described in Additives, page 74) is also dairy, as it is milk protein. If a product includes any form of milk, it is dairy and cannot be eaten with meat.

Milk itself has particular kashrut issues.

Determining the kashrut of dairy products can get surprisingly complex. Milk is milk, yes—fairly straightforward, right? Not necessarily. The milk we drink must come from a kosher animal, which practically means cow, goat, or sheep, in terms of what's generally available. Before the U.S. Department of Agriculture (USDA), which oversees dairy production, set up stringent standards of inspection in the United States, a more recent development, milk carried with it a Talmudic commandment—Jews could drink only ***chalav Yisrael*** (literally, "milk of Israel"), milk that had been supervised from milking to bottling by a Jew. The concern was that milk from a nonkosher animal (such as a camel or a pig) might be mixed with the milk from a kosher animal, thereby rendering it unkosher. Milk that has not been supervised by a Jew through the entire process is called *chalav akum*.

But in the United States, and several other countries, the dairy industry is carefully monitored by a federal institution such as the USDA. Only cow's milk is allowed in containers that are labeled "cow's milk." A dairy would incur heavy fines and could lose its license as a dairy if it attempted to dilute the cow's milk with milk from another animal. (And anyway, since dairies are set up for cows, milking another animal with a quite different body shape, such as a horse or a pig, would likely only increase the dairy's expenses.) Because of the strict government regulations, the late Rabbi Moshe Feinstein, one of the leading Orthodox halachic authorities of the twentieth century, wrote a Responsum regarding milk. He determined that, in the United States, the production of milk was thoroughly supervised; fear of government fines and other repercussions would ensure that only cow's milk is used, and thus Jews could drink milk that was not constantly supervised by a Jew. Feinstein determined that such government-regulated milk was a separate category, *chalav stam,* "neutral milk." Feinstein's Responsum applies only to milk from commercially regulated dairies, not small, local farms. However, Feinstein did say that, if possible, it is still preferable to drink *chalav Yisrael*, when it is available. There are many observant Jews who do not choose the more lenient option and prefer to consume *chalav Yisrael* products. This means that anything containing dairy products must use *chalav Yisrael*, such as milk chocolate, cream soups, ice cream.

Cream and butter historically did not need a hechsher, nor did they need to be made from *chalav Yisrael,* because cream from a nonkosher animal will not easily separate from the milk, and it will not easily coagulate into butter through traditional methods of making butter and cream. But modern technology makes it possible to separate cream from milk of nonkosher animals, so there are some issues in butter production today. Also there are additives added to butter and cream that may have kashrut concerns, so you may want to stick with hechshered butter and cream.

Chalav stam does not generally need a hechsher. Vitamin D is added to all milk, to help with the body's absorption of the calcium. Vitamin D is usually produced synthetically, and is not a kashrut issue. However, there was a case of a large commercial dairy in the Boston area that was using shark oil for its vitamin D source. If the milk says "natural" on the label, you may need to check the source of the vitamins, since sharks are not kosher. Flavored milk does need a hechsher.

Conservative kashrut does not require milk to be *chalav Yisrael.*

Cheese

In ancient times, just as the Talmud indicated that Jews could only drink *chalav Yisrael,* cheese made by non-Jews was called **g'vinat akum,** "pagan cheese," and was also forbidden. Cheese could only be made by an observant Jew. *Chalav Yisrael* was not necessary for **g'vinat Yisrael,** because only milk from kosher animals actually coagulates into cheese. But the cheese production itself had to be supervised by a Jew. The rennet (discussed below), which causes cheese to coagulate (separate into solids and liquid), had to be from a kosher animal. Also, non-Jews sometimes rubbed the rind of cheese with lard.

There are two kinds of cheeses: soft, fresh cheese, such as cream cheese or cottage cheese, and hard, aged cheese, such as Cheddar or Swiss. Cheese starts to form when enzymes are added to milk, causing it to coagulate. Traditionally, the enzyme added is rennin, which comes from rennet, the lining of a calf's fourth stomach.

You have to wonder how they discovered this. I picture a bunch of people sitting around with a dead calf. "Hey Joe! Let's see what happens if we put this calf's stomach in this bucket of milk! Huh. Nothing. Try the next stomach."

Now, I would think the very method of cheesemaking—a calf's stomach, combined with milk—would not be unlike combining meat and milk. But cheese must have been a necessary enough product that the rabbis determined that, as long as the rennet came from a kosher animal that was properly slaughtered, the cheese could be kosher. The Shulchan Aruch states, "This is permitted inasmuch as it has become dry it became like a mere piece of wood and there is not any meat juice in it." Therefore, no meat *flavor* would be transferred to the milk. In the Talmud, in **Chullin 116b,** the rabbis determined that cheese made from the rennet of a *neveilah* animal—that is, an animal that was improperly slaughtered—was not kosher; however, cheese curdled from the *milk* in that stomach was acceptable, *"because the milk collected within is considered as dung.".*

Cheese made with kosher rennet is still considered kosher today, and it does need a hechsher. (Strict vegetarians will not eat cheese made with animal rennet.) According to the rabbis I spoke with from various certification organizations, no certified kosher cheese made in North America today is made with animal-based rennet. Kosher cheese made in this country invariably uses plant-based or microbial rennet, listed on food labels as vegetarian rennet or enzymes. If you are observing "ingredient kashrut," read the cheese label. If it says "rennet," this usually means the cheese was made using animal rennet. If the cheese is not certified, it likely means that the rennet would not be considered kosher because it came from animals that were not *shechted,* or ritually slaughtered. If the label says "enzymes," this usually means microbial rennet, which can be certified.

Cheese is a food where Conservative and Orthodox halacha diverge. It should be noted, too, that the Orthodox feel strongly that the Conservative opinion on such matters is invalid. If you are considering how you want to keep kosher, keep this in mind.

Isaac Klein, a Conservative rabbi who wrote many definitive Responsa, explored the issue of cheese extensively. "Now we have to explain why so many *posekim* [rabbinical authorities] have forbidden such cheeses," he writes. "To this I humbly submit the answer that first of all there is a general reluctance to permit anything that was once forbidden, even if the reason for forbidding it does not exist any longer."

Based on thorough research, Klein concludes that cheese using rennet from both *neveilah* and kosher animals is acceptable to eat and does not need a hechsher: "It is our considered opinion that commercial cheeses, all of them, including those in which rennet from any animal, kosher or nonkosher, is used as the curdling agent, should be permitted." Klein also acknowledges that there are rabbinic authorities who will not accept this *heter*, "permitted thing." He concludes saying, "We have decided that all the usual cheese on the market, that list the ingredients hard as well as soft, domestic as well as foreign, are kosher."

As Klein anticipated, the Orthodox stand says the opposite. All cheese does need a hechsher in order to be considered kosher—so assert the "Big Four" supervising agencies. Some say that the cheese must also be made from *chalav Yisrael*, but even if it is not, it must be certified Kosher. And to be kosher, it cannot use rennet derived from an unkosher animal. Rabbi Moshe Heinemann, the rabbinic administrator for Star-K Kosher Certification, writes in the company's publication, *Kashrus Kurrents*, "It makes no difference whether the rennet comes from a non-Kosher species, a non-ritually slaughtered or an improperly slaughtered Kosher species. If rennet comes from such an animal, the cheese made from this rennet is not Kosher. . . ." Heinemann reiterates that a *mashgiach* needs to be involved in the actual production of cheese, not just supervision of the cheesemaking process, in order that the cheese not be *g'vinat akum*. He continues, "Clearly, we see that the rennet source and its addition to the cheese is crucial in Kosher cheesemaking." As you can see, quite different opinions.

Fish

Kosher fish must have fins and scales. As it happens, all fish with scales also have fins, but the reverse is not the case (think eels). Shellfish such as shrimp, lobster, clams—those get ruled out easily. There are thousands of species of fin fish; many are kosher. There are also many that do not have scales or have questionable scales. Since there are different kinds of scales, the Talmud defined "scales," in **Chullin 66b:** "If it has no [fins and scales] now but grows them later on . . . it is permitted; if it has them now but sheds them when drawn out of the water . . . it is permitted." (The ellipses here represent different fish types given as examples; translations vary. Interestingly, the Soncino translation of the Talmud lists the controversial swordfish among those in the second example.

The Talmud determined that scales of kosher fish should be easily removed without tearing the fish's skin. Ichthyologists list four types of scales: ctenoid and cycloid, which the Orthodox consider permissible, and ganoid and placoid, which they do not.

Sharks, which are definitively unkosher, have placoid scales, which are like tiny teeth. Catfish do not have scales at all. Neither do monkfish; instead of scales, they are covered with a coating of slime (that's an official fish term).

There are two fish that are controversial, with differing opinions in Orthodox and Conservative halacha: sturgeon and swordfish. Orthodox Jews say both are treif. Sturgeon, which have ganoid scales, are debated in the Conservative movement as well, and there is not an official Conservative Responsum. Some in the movement say sturgeon is acceptable, others do not. I contacted a well-known restaurant in New York City where sturgeon is offered. When I asked if sturgeon was kosher, they acknowledged it is controversial, and said, "You need to check with a rabbi." Caviar comes from sturgeon; if you follow the halacha that says sturgeon is not kosher, then caviar cannot be kosher. There is kosher fish roe (eggs), called "kosher caviar," which does not come from sturgeon.

Swordfish has perhaps been more hotly debated. Swordfish do have scales when they are young; they fall off by the time the fish reach maturity. Since this situation—having scales at one point and then not having them—is not discussed in the Talmud, an Orthodox Responsum by Rabbi Moshe Tendler emphatically asserts that swordfish cannot be kosher.

Rabbi Isaac Klein, after consulting with ichthyologists who confirmed that swordfish do have scales when young, wrote a Responsum in 1966 addressing Tendler's concerns. The official Conservative stand is that swordfish are kosher.

James W. Atz, Curator Emeritus, Department of Herpetology and Ichthyology of the American Museum of Natural History in New York, compiled a lengthy list of kosher and unkosher fish several years ago. His list has become the standard reference for fish and kashrut, and includes more than a hundred varieties. (On his list, sturgeon and swordfish are not kosher, incidentally.) Many of these fish are ones you're not likely to see unless you go fishing. I've shortened the list to include fish you might find at markets around the United States. Because of the differing opinions on swordfish and sturgeon, I do not include them on either list; check with your rabbi.

KOSHER

Amberjack	Mackerel	Smelts
Arctic Char	Mahi Mahi	Snapper
Barracuda	Mullet	Sole
Bass (Black, Chilean, Sea, Wild)	Perch	Sunfish
	Pollock	Tautog
Bluefish	Pomfret	Tilapia
Butterfish	Pompano	Tilefish
Carp	Porgies	Trout
Cod	Redfish	Tuna
Croaker/Drum	Rockfish	Turbot (some kinds are not kosher)
Flounder	Sablefish	
Grouper	Salmon	Whiting
Haddock	Sardine (Herring)	
Hake	Scrod (generic name; usually means cod or haddock)	
Halibut		
Herring		
Kingfish	Shad (Herring)	

UNKOSHER

Turbot (some kinds are kosher)	Dogfish	Ray
	Eel	Shark
Calamari (squid)	Marlin	Skate
Catfish	Monkfish	
Cusk	Octopus	

While some kosher markets sell fresh fish, it's more likely you'll buy fish at the supermarket or a fish market. If you are buying fresh fish at an establishment that also sells unkosher seafood, it is recommended that either you ask the fishmonger to wash the knife before cutting your fish or bring your own knife. You might also prefer to buy the fish whole and fillet it at home. Some rabbis recommend that you only select fish that you can see whole, to verify that they have the requisite scales. Some fish have distinctive coloring, such as salmon, so that you know they are acceptable, even if already cut.

Frozen fish fillets need a hechsher for the more observant, to be certain that the fish is what the packaging says it is. Canned fish and frozen prepared fish such as fish sticks or cod cakes also need a hechsher, as they have been cooked. Surimi is a Japanese fish product made from ground fin fish that has been flavored and formed to appear like various shellfish, including crab. It is usually made with pollock or whiting, but is sometimes flavored with an extract derived from shellfish, and it also needs a hechsher.

Fish and Meat Together

There are some foods that the Shulchan Aruch forbids because they were deemed in Talmudic times to be **sakanah,** "dangerous foods." Some rules are not really relevant, though they are still forbidden, such as the injunction against putting food or beverages under the bed "because an evil spirit descends upon them." The one relevant to kashrut today is the injunction against eating fish and meat together, even though fish is pareve. You can eat one before or after the other—note the traditional first course of gefilte fish followed by roast chicken on Shabbat—but not at the same time, and, according to Orthodox ruling, you should eat some bread or drink something between those courses. You also should not cook fish and meat in the oven at the same time.

Why was this considered dangerous? At the time, there was a belief that the combination of meat and fish could cause leprosy. This particular rule is only in the Shulchan Aruch—not in the Talmud or Rambam, according to Rabbi Plotkin. Plotkin wrote a Responsa on the matter of fish and meat in the 2000 issue of *JTS Magazine*, concluding, "Today we know that there is no *sakanah* affecting *tzara'at* (leprosy) by eating fish and meat together. Therefore, we would permit not only putting fish and meat on the same plate, but would allow them to be consumed together." Here again Conservative and Orthodox halacha differ. According to Orthodox ruling, fish and meat cannot be eaten together, period.

Bread

According to halacha, bread should be pareve. This is so you know that you can unquestioningly eat bread with any meal. There are exceptions. If you are going to make a dairy bread, it should be made in a shape that is different from standard bread, so you wouldn't mistake it for pareve bread. Also, if you make just enough bread for one meal, it is acceptable for it to be dairy (the most likely scenario—think buttery brioche or bread with cheese kneaded into it) or meat. Smaller breads, such as Danish and other pastries, can also be dairy. The fact that a bread is dairy or meat should be visibly obvious.

Bread is another food that Orthodox kashrut dictates must be made by a Jew; called **pat Yisrael** (the word for bread here is *pat, peh-taf* in Hebrew; some pronounce it *pas*). **Pat akum** is bread made by a Gentile, and again the reason for this rabbinic injunction was a measure taken against a situation that could lead to intermarriage. However, when this rule was made, not everyone had ovens in which they could easily bake their own bread, so eating only *pat Yisrael* was more difficult than obtaining *g'vinat Yisrael*. The rabbis agreed that supervised **pat palter,** "bakery bread," was acceptable. They reasoned that commercially produced bread would not invite the same kind of social interaction as sharing bread made by an individual.

Bread that needs to be *Yisrael* is only that which is made of one of the five grains mentioned in the Torah: wheat, rye, oats, spelt, and barley—the same grains that are forbidden on Pesach. Breads made exclusively with other grains, such as corn or millet, are not considered *akum*, although their production still needs to be supervised.

Orthodox ruling on *akum* versus *palter* varies. Some do not advocate *pat palter* if *pat Yisrael* is available. Bread can be *Yisrael* if a Jew is involved in the production even minimally, such as turning on the oven or adding an ingredient. But even *pat palter* needs to be supervised and needs a hechsher. Commercial breads often contain additives that can be dairy or unkosher. For example, one national chain bakery uses chicken stock in many of its breads.

SEPARATING CHALLAH

The word *challah* has two meanings in Jewish cuisine. The more well known is that it is the bread we eat on Shabbat. The second meaning for *challah* comes from the mitzvah *hafrashat challah*, "separating" or "taking" challah. This designation applies to any kind of bread that you purchase (not just challah) and, potentially, to bread you make at home. You may notice signs at kosher bakeries that say, "Challah has been taken." This is referring to the mitzvah of separating challah.

Traditionally, in Orthodox Judaism, this is a mitzvah a woman is to perform, although men can as well. The Lubavitch cookbook *Spice and Spirit* describes *hafrashat challah* as "symbolic of the entire practice of kashrut, with its element of elevating the physical and the mundane to the realm of holiness."

Separating challah is based on a biblical ordinance in which the Jews were instructed to give a portion of bread as an offering to the Levite priests, in **Numbers 15: 20-21,** *"Of the first of your dough you shall set apart a loaf as a portion; like the portion which is set apart of the threshing-floor, so shall you set it apart. Of the first of your dough you shall give unto the Lord a portion throughout your generations."* The word for "loaf" here is *challah.*

The portion that was separated for God was given to the Levite priests to eat. The mitzvah of separating challah recalls that ceremonial offering. Since we no longer have Levite priests, the separation of challah is symbolic, and no one may eat the portion, which is to be baked and burned separately from the rest of the bread you may make.

There are very precise rules involved in the separation of challah, concerning the amount of flour and liquid used. I am describing rough guidelines here, but if you want more exact details, check with your rabbi.

The requirement applies to bread or cake made with flour from one of the five biblical grains: wheat, rye, barley, oats, spelt. Breads made from other grains that do not include these five do not require separation of challah.

You also need to make a good-sized recipe in order to be required to separate challah. The rabbis determined that the amount of flour that warranted a separating of challah was based on an *omer*, a measurement used in the Torah. The exact weight of an *omer* has been debated (of course), but the net conclusion is that a recipe must use at least two and a half pounds (about ten cups) of flour to require separation of challah. You can make a number of good-sized loaves of bread with that much flour.

If you are, in fact, making those good-sized loaves, there are two methods of separating challah—with and without a blessing.

Recipes that use about ten to fourteen cups of flour (just over three and a half pounds) require separation without a blessing. Those using more flour than that do require the blessing below. This includes recipes for cakes and pastries, too, though they generally use less flour than bread recipes.

> *Baruch ata Adonai, Eloheinu melech ha'olam, asher kidshanu b'mitz votav vitzivanu lehafrish challah.*
> Praised are you, Lord our God, King of the universe, who has sanctified us with His commandments and commanded us to separate challah.

Separating challah is literally that. Separate a small portion of the dough, about one ounce, about half the size of an egg. Wrap it in aluminum foil and bake it until it burns. Do not bake any bread you'll be eating at the same time. When the separated challah is burned, symbolic of burnt offerings, you should discard it, still wrapped.

Produce

In general, all produce not from Israel is acceptable all the time. Israeli produce has some particular biblical issues which I'll discuss later on in this section.

In recent years, however, much attention has been given to the issue of insect infestation. We have always had to check produce for insects, since it is forbidden to eat them. More recently this has become a concern because of the banning of harmful pesticides—which is a good thing. It just means you need to check produce, especially leafy greens, very carefully. However, bugs that are so small you can't see them with your naked eye don't qualify.

Insect infestation has been somewhat controversial within the Orthodox community, with some groups insisting on more stringency than others. OK Laboratories, for example, on their website, lists a variety of produce and how to clean them properly to avoid insects. Some, such as asparagus tips, broccoli florets, and raspberries, they write, "may not be used due to heavy infestation. Avoid use." Star-K allows them to be used, just washed and inspected quite thoroughly.

My own feeling is that fruits and vegetables were eaten for thousands of years before DDT came along. What was the insect infestation situation like two thousand years ago? Nevertheless, this is an injunction of grave concern to many.

Once cleaned, most produce is fine to eat. Frozen vegetables do not need a hechsher, unless flavorings have been added. Vegetables that are canned in water alone do not need one either, but if they are mixed with anything else, such as spices, they do need a hechsher.

Canned fruit in syrup also needs a hechsher.

Canned beans are cooked, so they need a hechsher. Dry legumes and grains do not.

Dried fruit may need a hechsher, as it can be sprayed with oils or other additives to prevent sticking. If the ingredients include anything other than the fruit, the dried fruit may need a hechsher.

DAVAR HARIF

Certain types of produce, and a few other foods, fall under a separate category called *davar harif*, "hot thing." These are foods that are particularly flavorful or pungent, and heat alone is not necessary to transfer their flavor. Say a cold potato touches a cold piece of meat. You simply rinse the potato off and it stays pareve. But if a cold onion touched that same cold bit of meat, it would become meat. If a sliced onion were to touch an unkosher piece of meat, the onion would then be considered treif. Further, if you cut the onion with a meat knife, the onion would be considered meat. Foods that fall under this category, according to Binyomin Forst in *The Laws of Kashrus*, include:

Garlic	Certain spices (pepper, ginger)
Onions	Vinegar
Leeks	Whiskey
Olives	Olive oil
Sour fruit (lemon, *etrog*, sour apple, sour plum)	Wine
	Horseradish
Pickled fruits and vegetables	Radish
Brine	Salted herring
Sauerkraut	Chile peppers
Salted herring	

These items are still pareve, but their sharp flavor acts like heat in terms of imparting flavor to foods without actual heat. They can therefore become meat or dairy more easily than other foods.

JUICE AND OTHER BEVERAGES

Some organizations say that juice does not need a hechsher. Others say it does, because juice is often prepared on equipment that might be used to process dairy products. It also may contain grape juice or be colored from grape skins; grapes have particular halachic issues (see page 70).

Most nonalcoholic beverages (soda, fruit drinks) do need certification. Basically, anything other than plain, unflavored water usually needs certification.

GRAPES

Fresh grapes are fine. It is when grapes are in any other form that kashrut becomes an issue. In the supermarket, you may notice it is more difficult to find grape juice or grape drinks with a hechsher than other kinds of juice.

Grape products are a particular concern because of halacha with respect to wine. Wine is an essential beverage in Jewish ritual. Every festive occasion, from Shabbat through Pesach, is greeted with a blessing over wine—before bread or any other food. Because wine is made from grapes, it requires special supervision. According to the Orthodox laws of kashrut, wine must be made by a Jew. Conservative laws differ.

Yayin nesech, literally, "wine of libation," is a reference to wine used as part of pagan rituals, a concern at the time of the Torah. A Jew should not partake of any kind of wine used for Gentile rituals. Idolatry is not so much an issue these days, so the more applicable law regarding wine is that of *stam yaynam*, literally, "neutral wine," figuratively, wine made by a non-Jew for everyday use; it is also forbidden. As with the various *akum* prohibitions, the injunction against drinking the wine of non-Jews is based on the concern about intermarriage. As Dayan Grunfeld writes, "Our Sages . . . knew very well that nothing helps so much to drop the barrier between people and to create intimacy which may finally lead to intermarriage as the drinking of wine together." Even Jewish-made wine that has been *poured* by a non-Jew is forbidden.

Unlike, say, orange juice, the production of grape juice must be supervised by a Jew throughout the entire process in order to receive a hechsher. Other juices do not need a Jewish presence throughout. Taking it one step further, all products made from grapes must have a Jew *involved* in their production, not simply overseeing it. Grape-based products include jam, jelly, and other preserves (fruit juice–sweetened preserves are often made with a white grape juice concentrate); brandy, Cognac, wine vinegar, balsamic vinegar; grape skins, which are used as a colorant called *enocianina*; and cream of tartar, a by-product of winemaking used in baking (sometimes one of the ingredients in baking powder).

However, wine (or grape juice) that has been boiled or pasteurized, called *yayin mevushal* (cooked wine), does not carry the same restrictions, as such wine could not be used at the time of the Temple for sacrifices. Therefore, once the wine has been heated, it can be handled by non-Jews. The label should still have a hechsher, and should also have *yayin mevushal* written on the label.

The Conservative stand on wine is more lenient. The issue was addressed in a 1964 Responsum by Rabbi Israel Silverman, after conducting a study of American-produced wine sponsored by the CLSR. He determined that the winemaking process in the United States is automated; since no person actually *touched* the wine, it could be kosher. However, this was before the proliferation of small wineries in California and other states, which have more direct human involvement in the wine production.

Rabbi Klein writes, "Since it is a *mitswah* to support Israel, [Rabbi Silverman] suggested, we should give priority to wines imported from Israel, all of which are kosher according to the traditional standard, as indicated by the *hekhsher* they bear." Also, wine used for ceremonial purposes (Shabbat, Yom Tov), should have a hechsher, and wine used on Pesach should be kosher for Pesach.

A more recent Conservative Responsum, written in 2001 in *JTS Magazine* by Rabbi Elliot Dorff, mentions a few issues in wine production. Specifically, the process of "fining," in which stabilizers are added to wine to help it maintain its integrity through hot or cold storage. Gelatin and dairy derivatives might be used. Dorff cites an eighteenth-century Responsum from the Noda B'Yehuda regarding a fining procedure using unkosher fish in wine made by Jews in Germany and Poland, writing, "Because the intention is not to nullify but only to clarify," it was acceptable. However, Dorff writes, "Many respected rabbis have questioned such exceptions or severely restricted their use. So while there are grounds to permit all wines regardless of the fining used, the grounds are not beyond challenge." This is regarding wine made by Jews. As for wine made by Gentiles, Dorff asserts, "If I thought for one minute that prohibiting wine made by Gentiles would have the slightest effect on diminishing the number of mixed marriages, I would drop all other concerns and opt for prohibiting it on that basis alone. I frankly doubt, however, that prohibiting wine touched by non-Jews will have any effect whatsoever on eliminating or even mitigating that problem."

Dorff says that it has become common practice for Conservative Jews who keep kosher to drink Gentile-made wine. "Even if we decided that we wanted to maintain *stam yeinam* as part of the law, I doubt that it would be very high on our list of educational and halakhic priorities. We are better off acknowledging that this prohibition has fallen into disuse and letting it be." In synagogues and Jewish institutions, however, it is preferable to use only kosher wine. And Dorff reiterates Silverman's arguments regarding Israel and ceremonial uses of wine:

"In light of the questions raised about uncertified wine, however, it certainly should be a standard for our movement that only certified wines be used for sacramental purposes—kiddush, the seder, etc.—at home as well as in the synagogue. One should fulfill a mitzvah as elegantly as possible, and there is no reason to use wine about which there is some question. The Conservative movement is the only religious movement which has always been Zionistic and has never had an anti-Zionist wing. It is therefore fitting that this Conservative Responsum indicate that Israeli wines are especially appropriate for sacramental use."

PRODUCE FROM ISRAEL

Produce from Israel has its own set of concerns. There are various biblical laws regarding produce, and the rabbis determined that today these laws apply only to produce grown in Israel. **Orlah** refers to fruit that comes from a tree during its first three years, and is forbidden.

Produce from Israel is subject to tithes, **terumah** and **ma'asrot**. This derives from a biblical passage in **Deuteronomy**, in which the tribes were to set aside a portion of their produce for the Levites, who had no land. Today, the *terumah* portion is very small, since there are no pure Levites to consume it, so it is largely symbolic—but must be set aside; this is similar to taking challah. There are several symbolic procedures that must be done in order for this produce from Israel to be considered acceptable. They are procedures done commercially in Israel, not at home.

GENETICALLY MODIFIED ORGANISMS (GMOS)

GMOs are produce that has been genetically altered. At this writing, the jury is still out in terms of kashrut, although some rulings have been made. In "A Jewish Perspective on Genetic Engineering" on the website www.besr.org (Business Ethics Center of Jerusalem), Rabbi Akiva Wolff writes, "According to most authorities, genetic material from non-kosher species is not itself non-kosher and does not render the new host organism non-kosher." The Star-K website states, "If it looks like a tomato, smells like a tomato, feels like a tomato and tastes like a tomato, it's a tomato and it's kosher." The issue is still being debated, and it is of concern to many, especially those who are advocates of eco-kashrut.

Alcoholic Beverages

Wine, as indicated above, has its own set of rules. Orthodox kashrut has determined that several kinds of liquor do not need supervision, because of the method of production. Flavored alcohols, including sloe gin, which is flavored with the sloe berry, do need hechshers. Liquors that do not, include: bourbon, whiskey, rum (unflavored), gin (sloe gin needs a hechsher), scotch, rye, tequila (except for the kind with the unkosher worm in the bottle), and vodka (unflavored only).

Beer does not necessarily require a hechsher, but you should check with your rabbi about specific brands. Liqueurs, because of the cooking and flavoring process, do need *hashgacha*. As mentioned in the section on grapes, brandy and Cognac, made from wine, also need hechshers, as do sherry and port, which are also grape-based.

Raw Ingredients

Several raw-ingredient staples do not need certification, although many do have it. There is a term used in the industry, "group one ingredient," which refers to products that are a single ingredient, with no additives, which do not need supervision. This rule does not apply to all single-ingredient foods because of some of the issues of kashrut discussed in this chapter. Further, some seemingly single-ingredient foods sometimes have added ingredients.

Grains and flours do not usually need a hechsher, but there is another issue. Some Orthodox Jews may be concerned with *chadash*, a law of kashrut regarding when grain was planted. *Chadash*, "new" grain, is grain of the five species (wheat, oats, barley, rye, and spelt) that was planted during or after Pesach. This grain cannot be eaten until the following Pesach, when it is called *yashan*. Those who observe *chadash* do not eat any products containing grains planted during this time, including flour and baked goods.

The following generally do not need a hechsher, unless otherwise noted:

Flour, from any grain
Cornmeal, cornstarch
Whole grains, including rice, cracked wheat, wild rice, kasha (buckwheat), millet
Plain popcorn kernels (the microwave kind have added ingredients and need to be certified)
Sugar (brown, white, confectioners')
Honey
Maple syrup
Molasses
Spices (although some say that ground spices need supervision because treif anticaking additives may be added)

Coffee, plain. Flavored coffee does need a hechsher.

Tea, plain. Flavored tea does need a hechsher.

Nuts. Raw nuts do not need a hechsher. Roasted nuts, since they are cooked, do need hechshers.

Salt, baking powder, and baking soda need hechshers.

Oils usually do need hechshers, because of the refining process. Margarine needs a hechsher. You should also check that margarine is marked "pareve"; there are many margarines, including those marked "100 % corn oil" that have whey or other dairy ingredients added.

Additives

These include all those mysterious items you just gloss over as you read ingredients, labels—items such as emulsifiers, stabilizers, preservatives. Just chemicals, right? Well, chemicals come from somewhere, and many of these have animal, insect, or dairy sources. There are literally thousands of additives, if you count all the various vitamins, flavorings, and colors. There are some in particular that have kashrut issues.

ANIMAL-BASED ADDITIVES

Several additives can be derived from animal, plant, or mineral sources. If the product is certified, you know the additive is from a kosher source. Otherwise, you may need to call the company to learn the source. Rennet (discussed under Dairy) is one example. The most well-known and kosherly controversial animal-based additive is gelatin.

Gelatin is another substance on which Conservative and Orthodox rulings diverge. Gelatin has been around for thousands of years: it is made by boiling bones to produce a gelatinous substance. Added to a variety of goods, mainly sweets, it gives them a creamy, chewy, or bouncy texture. Its most well-known uses are in marshmallows and in Jell-O.

Gelatin began to be used and produced commercially in the eighteenth century. It was popularized in the United States at the end of the nineteenth century by Charles Knox, of Knox gelatin fame.

Gelatin is made from collagen, which comes from various animal parts, including bones, hides, tendons, and ligaments. According to the Gelatin Manufacturers Institute of America (GMIA), gelatin is used for three purposes: food, pharmaceuticals (such as gel caps), and photography. Cattle skins, left over from leather production, bones, and pork skins, usually obtained from slaughterhouses and meat-processing plants, go through a lengthy treatment process involving drying, boiling, and soaking in lime and caustic soda, to remove excess hair, soften the parts, and bring out the collagen.

So what is the concern? The Talmud, Rambam, the Shulchan Aruch all debate the status of bones, determining that, while *meat* is forbidden, *bones* are not. Therefore, could gelatin be kosher? And further, if kosher, is it pareve?

According to the GMIA, "Pork skin is currently the most significant raw material source for production of edible gelatin in North America." Both Orthodox and Conservative Responsa have fluctuated on the kashrut status of gelatin. Because of the stages it goes through, it could be considered a *davar chadash*, that is, a new substance that no longer resembles its origin—namely, an animal. Further, the treatment given to the animal parts renders them inedible at certain stages of production, which also could contribute to their acceptability in kashrut. For many years, the prevailing opinion for both Conservative and Orthodox was that gelatin was therefore both kosher and pareve.

One older Responsum by Rabbi Moshe Feinstein stated that, since gelatin is flavorless, it is acceptable, as long as it comes from kosher animals. Products made with gelatin are pareve. However, gelatin made from *shechted* animals is very expensive to make. Regular gelatin is made from discarded hides, bones, and such, and doesn't require special kashering procedures. Kosher gelatin does. The hides have to be soaked and salted to remove any blood. For many years, no one made kosher gelatin; at this writing, there is a kosher gelatin on the market called Kolatin.

Avram Pollock, president of Star-K, questions the pareve status of this gelatin. Originally, he says, the rabbis determined that gelatin derived from kosher animals could be considered both kosher and pareve because it was so far removed from the original product that it no longer had a meat flavor. According to Pollock, the way gelatin was made a century ago was from the dried-out hides and bones of *shechted* animals. However, today, gelatin is generally made from the collagen in hides before they are fully dried, and they may have a lingering meat flavor.

There are products imported from Israel containing "kosher gelatin." Certification of gelatin may be different in Israel. If you want to use such products (notably, marshmallows), check with your rabbi. I have read mixed opinions on both the kashrut and pareve status of kosher gelatin from Israel.

The Conservative ruling, based on Isaac Klein's 1969 Responsum, is that all gelatin is acceptable. Klein addresses the many issues involved at great length, and acknowledges that the issue will continue to be controversial.

The more I learn about gelatin, the less acceptably kosher it seems to me. Supposedly the substance is flavorless, but I have in the past used plain gelatin, and it has a definite strange, not altogether pleasant odor, although it does not seem to affect the flavor of whatever it is added to. There is a nonhalachic reason that I think supports not using any kind of gelatin, or at least not as a pareve ingredient. Ethical vegetarians, those who don't eat meat for ethical (as opposed to health) reasons, will not eat foods containing gelatin. An animal must be killed in order to make gelatin. That makes gelatin meat to me.

There are other forms of gelatin. Gelatin made from fish, called "isinglass," has its own issues because it can be made from sturgeon, a fish that is debatably unkosher. Also, there is the issue of mixing fish with meat. Agar, a vegetable gelatin that comes from seaweed, has no kashrut issues, but it doesn't cause foods to set as well as gelatin, which may be why we don't see marshmallows made with agar.

(For the record, Marshmallow Fluff contains no gelatin and is certified kosher.)

Following are other potentially animal-based additives. Some can be made synthetically or from plant sources. If they cannot be kosher, I indicate this:

Albumen is egg white. **Albumin** is the protein in egg whites, but it can also be found in animal blood. It is used in baked goods as a coagulant.

Ambergris (treif), from whales, used as a flavoring.

Aspartic acid can be animal or plant-based, and is found in sugarcane and molasses. It is the basis for aspartame, such as in NutraSweet.

Castoreum (treif), from beaver glands, used as a flavoring.

Carmine, or **cochineal** (treif), from the South American insect *Coccus cacti*, used as a pink or red food coloring. Also called **carminic acid**. Not an FDA red dye color.

Civet, absolute (treif), from cats, used as a flavoring.

L-cysteine, from hair (including human hair!) or feathers, or synthetic. Used as a dough conditioner, often in pizza and bagels.

Glycerides (mono-or di-), produced by causing glycerine to react with fat, either animal- or plant-based. Monoglycerides and diglycerides are used as stabilizers in many kinds of foods, including frozen French fries, salad dressings, ice cream, and bread. In a Responsum influenced by Isaac Klein's Responsum on gelatin, the Conservative movement has ruled that "mono-and di-glycerides, whatever their origin, are kosher and pareve." The Orthodox movement only certifies plant-based glycerides.

Glycerine (glycerol), a by-product of refined fat, animal- or plant-based. It is a humectant, which means it helps retain moisture, and is used to give a smooth texture to syrups and extracts. It also may be sprayed on dried fruit to prevent sticking.

Glycine (treif if you don't eat gelatin), a derivative of gelatin, used as a preservative.

Inosinic acid (inosinate), from yeast, fish, or animals, or synthetic. A flavor enhancer (like plant-based monosodium glutamate, MSG), used in imitation meat products, soup mixes, and spice mixes.

Lanolin (treif), found in sheep's wool. Used primarily in cosmetics, but also in some chewing gum.

Lipase (treif), an enzyme found in various cattle. Used as an artificial butter flavoring in, for example, microwave popcorn and margarine.

Oleic acid, from animal- or plant-based fats, used as defoamer.

Oxystearin, from glycerides and stearic acid, animal or plant sources, used to coat tablets and in vegetable oils.

Pepsin (treif), an enzyme from pig or cow stomachs. Used in antacids, as a coagulant for cheese, and as a flavoring for chewing gum.

Polysorbates, derived from animal- or plant-based fatty acids (including stearic). Used as emulsifiers, in dressings, ice cream, pickles, and other foods.

Resinous glaze (treif), also known as shellac, excreted from a Southeast Asian insect called *lac*, or *Tachardia lacca*. Used for candy coating.

Sodium guanylate (guanylic acid), can be synthetic or from yeast, or from animals or fish. A flavor enhancer; see Inosinic acid.

Stearic acid, derived from animal or vegetable fats. It is a lubricant used to coat tablets and to prevent caking in powdered goods. It is also used in combination to create other additives with similar functions, including **calcium stearate** and **magnesium stearate.**

Stearoyl lactylates, from stearic acid, used as a dough conditioner and a preservative for baked goods.

DAIRY-BASED ADDITIVES

Casein, milk protein. For many years, legislation (credited to the American dairy lobby) required casein and casein derivatives such as **sodium caseinate** to be classified as "nondairy." Many so-called nondairy creamers actually contain this dairy protein, as do "nondairy" cheeses. More recent labeling laws have changed that, so you may see some labels that clarify casein, explaining that it is a dairy derivative. Hydrolyzed casein is sometimes added to canned tuna, thereby making it a dairy product (read your labels!).

Lactic acid can be milk- or plant-based, or synthetic. Used in several foods as a preservative, including canned fruits, baked goods, and juice.

Lactose, milk sugar. Used as a sweetener and in baked goods, margarine, and other foods.

Phenylalanine, from proteins in eggs, milk, or grains; sometimes blood. Used in the artificial sweetener aspartame.

Proprionic acid, from milk or synthetic. Used as a preservative.

Whey, from milk. Used in cheese, breads, and other products.

There are certified kosher vitamins and medicines, but there are also many that are not, and those may be what you prefer or need for reasons of health. You should check with your rabbi regarding all issues concerning medications and kashrut.

SPIRITUAL RENOVATION: KASHERING YOUR KITCHEN

KASHERING YOUR KITCHEN MEANS converting it from one in which un-kosher food has been prepared into one in which only kosher food will be prepared. If you have not kept kosher before, there are several steps you will have to take to ready your kitchen for kosher food preparation.

When kashering your kitchen, you have to decide exactly *how* you want to keep kosher. What exactly does "keeping kosher" mean? Yes, it means following the laws of kashrut, as outlined in the chapter on Kosher Foods. But people define kashrut in different ways, and your Jewish affiliation—Orthodox, Conservative, Reform, Reconstructionist, other—may determine how you choose to keep kosher.

The Orthodox rules for kashrut are the strictest, followed by the Conservative rules. While there are variations among different Orthodox communities in terms of kashrut observance, there are several set interpretations of halacha they have in common. Those observing Orthodox kashrut are more likely to purchase only packaged goods marked with a hechsher, for example. Orthodoxy has fairly precise rules on how to kasher your kitchen, although there are certain areas of the modern kitchen that are debated inconclusively.

Conservative Judaism also has precise rules regarding kashering your kitchen. There are many areas upon which Orthodox and Conservative overlap, and some areas on which they have different rulings.

As mentioned in the introduction, kashrut observance is new to the Reform movement, so there are no official Reform rules regarding kashering your kitchen. The Reconstructionist movement is also fairly open-ended, but has preferred methods to follow, similar to Conservative. Because Conservative and Orthodox do have exacting rules regarding kashering your kitchen, those are the instructions I present here.

How you keep kosher is an individual decision, but it is also community-based. Who you entertain can determine how you keep kosher in your home. An Orthodox Jew has stricter criteria for kashrut observance than a Reform Jew, and a strictly observant Orthodox Jew might not eat food prepared in a kitchen whose cupboards contained foods without a hechsher. A strictly observant Conservative Jew might not eat foods prepared in a kitchen without separate dishes for dairy and meat foods, for example.

Even within Orthodox kashrut observation, there are stricter, *machmir,* and more lenient, *mekil,* practices that are both halachically acceptable. For example, some Jews only eat glatt kosher meat, but they may still eat nonmeat foods at the kosher home of someone who will prepare regular kosher meats.

Some people prefer to follow one level of observance more than the other. *Machmir* and *mekil* primarily refer to observance levels within Orthodox guidelines; they are not terms used in Conservative Judaism. Further, an Orthodox rabbi would not likely consider a Conservative ruling that differed from an Orthodox stand as a more lenient ruling on a particular issue.

Our cousin Rabbi Mark Robbins, a Conservative rabbi, reflects on the way many Conservative Jews observe kashrut. "Instead of necessarily doing all the details, they follow the general laws and some of the details in order to sufficiently affirm their Jewish identity," he says. "Their fear is not that breaking a detail of a law will get them punishment; I think their goal is to do a sufficient amount which makes them feel an integral part of a community and affirmed as a Jew. The spirit of the law is what is most important to them, as opposed to the letter. Whereas from a fully halachic perspective, both the detail and the spirit of the law are equally important."

An Orthodox rabbi I spoke with admitted he is not comfortable with the Conservative point of view. "To the best of my knowledge, Conservative is based on man's feeling of how halacha should adapt to society, when *we* should be adapting to halacha," he says. "It's a slippery slope you start going down once you use societal needs as a standard, versus halachic needs as a standard."

And this is where the individual decision of how to keep kashrut is made. You must decide who you are as a Jew, the kind of kashrut that is important to you, and choose that path.

You might choose a gradual path toward keeping a kosher home, and for some certain basics are enough. Some opt for simple changes, not quite going for full-fledged kashrut, but eliminating, for example, pork and shellfish from their home-cooking repertoire. Others purchase only kosher meat, although they might not have separate dishes for meat and dairy. Others might have separate dishes for dairy and meat, yet do not purchase kosher meat. All of these are steps toward kashrut, steps that might be considered acceptably kosher under the auspices of the Reform movement. Going for full-blown kashrut, according to the dictates of the Orthodox or Conservative movement, involves kashering your kitchen.

Why Kasher Your Kitchen?

Isn't it enough that you have decided to stop eating pork, mixing meat and milk, and buy only kosher meat? Why change the kitchen? Assuming you are choosing to keep kosher according to Orthodox or Conservative tenets, the actions you took are first steps, but it doesn't mean your kitchen is kosher. Your kitchen up to this point has been used to prepare treif foods, and the flavors of those unkosher foods may have permeated your oven, dishwasher, cutlery, and dishes. To make your kitchen truly kosher, you will need to eliminate all unkosher foods from your kitchen, and to follow various procedures to purge your kitchen equipment of treif flavors. This process is called *kashering* (or koshering, or kosherizing) your kitchen. (It is not necessary to kasher your whole house, unless you prepare food in areas other than the kitchen.)

IMPORTANT NOTE: This book is intended as a guide to kashrut, but to ensure that your kitchen is truly kosher, it is best to work with a rabbi and have the rabbi oversee the kitchen-kashering process. I am *not* a rabbinic authority, I do *not* have the authority to make any official decisions on kashrut. Therefore, it is imperative that you check everything with a rabbi. There are even Internet acronyms regarding issues of kashrut and Jewish law: CYLAH, *C*onsult *Y*our *L*ocal *A*uthority on *H*alacha; and AYLR, *A*sk *Y*our *L*ocal *R*abbi.

A rabbi will best be able to walk you through the kashering process. There can be a lot of ambiguity in kashrut, and a rabbi can help make various concerns more definitive.

Different communities have different practices in certain areas (such as whether or not plastic can be kashered), and the rabbi you choose to help you should be familiar with your community's practices.

When you are kashering your kitchen, there are many, many items that can be questionable; a rabbi will answer those questions or will be able to consult with others and know where to find the answers.

Some synagogues offer kosher-education classes, and some have a sort of "Kosher Corps," a group of people who will come to your house and assist you through the labor-intensive kashering process. Some may charge a set fee for this, some may not, or they may welcome donations. Chabad House, the outreach arm of the Lubavitch movement, is usually available for such a service in many places across the United States. While they represent one of the most *machmir* forms of Orthodox kashrut, they will kasher a kitchen regardless of your Jewish affiliation. Note that it is easier to go from a more strict level of kashrut to a less strict level when kashering your kitchen.

When to Kasher Your Kitchen

If you are planning to kasher your kitchen, you might want to do it just in time for Pesach. Kashering your kitchen for Pesach is almost as elaborate as kashering your kitchen for the first time. So, for one year, you can save yourself the extra work of kashering your kitchen for Pesach on top of kashering your kitchen for the first time. However, there is no reason to wait eleven more months to start keeping kosher. It is just a happy convenience if early spring is when you've started the kashering process.

Operation Kosher Kitchen

What's the Dish on Dairy and Meat?

Kitchens today come equipped with the usual basics: oven and cooktop (stove), refrigerator, cabinets, and running water in the form of a sink. Then there might be a dishwasher, microwave, toaster, blender, food processor, coffeemaker. Name the food preparation activity, and there is probably an electronic gadget to go with it: dishes—platters, saucers, plates in various sizes for dinner, salad, dessert; bowls for cereal, soup, mixing, fruit; drinking vessels—mugs, teacups, glasses. And cutlery for bread, butter, steak, chopping, paring, mincing, carving; spoons for tea, soup, mixing, serving; forks for dinner, tossing salad, dessert, to name a few. And everything must be examined when you kasher your kitchen.

The main criteria for designing the layout of your kosher kitchen concern dairy and meat, or the issue of *basar b'chalav*, literally, "meat in milk." Yes, there are various other dictates of kashrut (no pork, no blood). But in your kosher kitchen, presumably you are going to have kosher meat only and kosher foods. So the main issue of concern is to make sure that you do not mix meat and dairy together. Therefore, you must have separate dishes for eating dairy and meat foods and separate cookware for preparing each.

Using separate dishes and cookware is mentioned in the Talmud, as in **Chullin 111b,** in which the rabbis discuss concerns over transference of flavors, "*In a pot wherein meat had been cooked a person may not boil milk, and if he did boil* [milk] *therein* [it is forbidden] *if the pot imparts a flavor* [to the milk]."

I imagine that the two sets of dishes as we use them today are a more recent convention. Dishes were once much more costly than they are now; today they are practically a dime a dozen. Part of the dictates of kashrut changing with the times is that modern conveniences make it easier to keep dairy and meat separate because the cost is not what it once was.

Meat and dairy items are referred to interchangeably by their English, Hebrew (*basar, chalav*, respectively), and Yiddish (*fleishig, milchig,* respectively) nomenclatures. For simplicity's sake, and because this is often how the products are labeled with initials by certifying organizations in the United States, I'll use the English designations.

The issue of *basar b'chalav*, of mixing meat and dairy, is not likely to be an issue if you are vegetarian. The guidelines given here can be followed if you are a vegetarian; you just may not need two sets of everything, since you will not be cooking meat in your kitchen.

Kitchen Design

If money is no object, the ideal would be to have two separate kitchens, one for meat, one for dairy (and one more just for show, to paraphrase Tevye from *Fiddler on the Roof*). Both could be built from scratch—all new everything, including the shape of the rooms, appliances, cabinets, sinks, countertops, dishes, cookware.

And if your budget is generous, but not quite limitless, designing and installing one brand-new kitchen with two of all major appliances is the next alternative. There are several kitchen design firms that specialize in kosher-kitchen plans and can advise you on the best appliances for kashrut concerns, ideal food prep areas, sink and stove placement—the *feng shui* of a kosher kitchen.

Most of us do not have that kind of budget, and must make do with preexisting space. Most of us have one sink, stove, refrigerator. You may not be building a new kitchen, but you do need to "design" the space you have. Designate a meat area and a dairy area for work space, and meat and dairy cabinets, for food and for dishes. Do this to avoid accidental incidents of *basar b'chalav*. You want to set your kitchen up to leave the least possible room for mistakes. If one counter is dedicated, for example, solely to meat preparation, you won't ever have dairy products nearby, and vice versa. The larger the kitchen, the easier it is to separate these areas; your design may need to be more creative if you have a tiny kitchen.

Color Coding

Consider drawing a diagram of your kitchen, indicating the cabinets, counters, etc. You are not required to memorize everything. Label! When my family kashered our kitchen when I was a kid, my father, who had taken up calligraphy as a hobby, made beautifully lettered labels indicating which drawers and cupboards were for meat, which for dairy, which for pareve.

One popular method for indicating what's what in the kitchen is color coding, and there are companies that manufacture kitchen supplies such as sponges, flexible cutting boards, and aprons that are labeled and color-coded for meat, dairy, and pareve. Traditionally, red is for meat and blue is for dairy—red like meat, blue like, um, skim milk? (Guess white would be hard to see?) Okay, maybe yellow (like butter or cheese) would make more sense, but red and blue are what have evolved. Yellow or green are often assigned for pareve. You can also get small circular stickers in whatever colors you choose and stick them on cabinets for dishes and cookware.

These red and blue color assignments actually date back to nineteenth-century soap production. Soap is the result of a chemical reaction between fat (an acid) and an alkali, such as lye (also known as sodium hydroxide or caustic soda). Yes, the combination of grease and poison makes a miracle cleaner. Traditionally, many soaps were (and are) made with animal fat, which creates a kashrut issue, especially when cleaning dairy dishes.

In 1870, Israel Rokeach, a Polish Jew, developed a soap made without animal fat, and even obtained certification from Rav Yitzchok Elchonon of Kovno when he devised a unique method to differentiate visibly his kosher soap from treif soap. Not only would the soaps have the word *kosher* embedded on them, they would be available in two colors. According to the Rokeach company lore, Israel Rokeach declared (presumably in Yiddish), "The milchig soap will be blue, and the fleishig red."

Pogroms forced Rokeach to flee Poland twenty years later, and he arrived in New York at the height of American kashrut controversy and development, in 1890. Rokeach was enterprising and built another soap factory, once again producing his trademark red and blue soaps. Red and blue became the standard at-a-glance color codes for kosher kitchens.

While it can be acceptable to use unkosher soap for washing yourself, it is recommended to use kosher soaps and detergents for anything related to food, so no unkosher residue is left behind. There are dishwashing soaps available with a hechsher.

In addition to color coding cabinets and counter areas, you can carry it through to sponges, dishtowels, drying racks—anything to minimize confusion and the opportunity for inadvertent accidents.

Heated Discussion: Kosher Status

If you begin with a brand-new kitchen, untouched by any unkosher foods, and with never-used cookware and dishes, you wouldn't have to think about what items are or are not kosher. But most people going kosher likely already have a stash of kitchenware. So, what exactly makes an item unkosher?

Heat. Heat contained in a medium of transference (a.k.a. a pan or pot). That is, certain substances, when heated, can transfer flavors. Making a cheeseburger in a toaster oven, roasting a pork chop, boiling a lobster—the oven, the roasting pan, the soup pot all become unkosher through the mingling of heat and forbidden foods.

What defines heat? The Talmud, in **Shabbat 40b,** uses the term *yad soledet bo,* which literally means "the hand shrinks back from it [because of the heat]." The rabbis explain that this is the temperature at which you would reactively remove your hand in less than fifteen seconds from something hot for fear of being burned. We have thermometers now, so, more recently, rabbinical scholars looked to determine the precise temperature that constitutes *yad soledet bo,* and even conducted temperature tests with people, to zero in on one exact temperature that would cause someone to remove their hand from a heated surface in less than fifteen seconds. Some people have a higher tolerance for heat than others. One man's *yad soledet bo* is another man's *is the heat on yet?* Naturally, there are many opinions, but basically the temperature of *yad soledet bo* falls between 110° and 120°F.

The areas of your kitchen that are most affected by the concerns of *yad soledet bo* are the oven and stovetop, sink, toaster oven, and dishwasher; also pots and pans that were used for heating, dishes upon which hot food was served, and the flatware used to eat that hot food. All are therefore questionable when kashering your kitchen. How to make these various items kosher? Because heat was involved in making the items unkosher, heat must be involved in making them kosher, again when possible.

Dairy and meat are the two main categories in your kitchen, but there are foods that are neither, that are pareve, such as vegetables and fruit. There are all kinds of exceptions to the rules, but basically you can prepare pareve foods using either meat or dairy utensils. If the food stays cold, you can eat that food with either meat or dairy meals. If it needs to be heated, if you cooked, say, green beans in a pot used to cook meat, the green beans would be considered meat. Therefore, some people keep separate pots for pareve foods, so that foods such as those green beans could be eaten with meat or dairy meals.

K'volo Kach Polto: Rules for Kashering

Kashering your kitchen is at least a two-day process. You will need to clean all the elements discussed later on in this section—and then wait twenty-four hours before kashering them. This goes back to the rule discussed earlier, *eino ben yomo*, "not of the day." A full twenty-four-hour day must pass in order for the various parts of your kitchen to lose any unkosher flavor they might have absorbed. After twenty-four hours, those flavors are considered **ta'am lifgam,** having a bad taste. This minimizes the chance that traces of treif could still contaminate the kitchen while it is being kashered.

The basic rule of kosherizing is **k'volo kach polto,** an expression that means, literally, "as it is absorbed, so is it purged." (Interestingly, the same expression means "easy come, easy go"; not necessarily the case when it comes to kashering.) In other words, the way a potentially kosher item became unkosher determines how you can make it kosher. There are four methods of kashering.

Because a heat source is what caused various items to become unkosher (an oven, a pot, a pan), heat is used to remove unkosher substances from these items. And some items cannot, by nature, be purged.

The methods of koshering include the following:

Libun is used for items heated directly on a fire, such as a grill, baking pans used in an oven, or frying pans used to heat oil. The word *libun* means "purify" and comes from the same Hebrew root word for "white." There are two types of *libun*:

Libun Gamur, "complete purification." When the term *libun* is used by itself, this is the kind of *libun* being referred to. *Libun* means heating a pan or grill until it is red hot. To heat pans until they are red hot usually requires a blowtorch, as your standard oven does not reach temperatures that are hot enough, and this is a procedure most often performed by a rabbi.

Libun Kal, "simple purification." Heating metal hot enough that paper (traditionally, a broom straw) touching it scorches. When an oven goes through a self-cleaning cycle, it gets this hot. This is a method you might use on a frying pan.

Hag'alah, "scouring" or "scalding," is used for items such as pots or flatware that have become treif through contact with hot liquids. *Hag'alah* means kashering the item in a large pot of boiling water.

Irui, "infusion," is kashering by pouring boiling water over something, a method used for countertops and sinks.

Milui v'irui, "filling and infusing," means soaking. It is a procedure reserved only for glassware, and is used most often for Pesach.

The laws of purging don't *exactly* match the laws of absorption. A baking pan, for example, doesn't simply need to be heated in an oven as you would bake it; it needs to be heated until it is *red hot*, which in most cases would damage the pan. The liquid that infused your forks with treif was probably not boiling at the moment the fork pierced the ham, but such higher heat ensures that all treif flavors are removed.

Some materials are undebatably kasherable, namely stone, such as granite and marble; metal; wood; and natural rubber. Other materials are subject to debate, both within the Orthodox movement and between Orthodox and Conservative. Plastics, such as Formica countertops, melamine (Melmac) dishes, and nonstick pans such as Teflon, are debatable, as is glassware used for baking, such as Pyrex. Earthenware, which includes stoneware (contrary to its name, it is not made of stone, but is a category of ceramics), and enameled porcelain are not usually kasherable, but there are some exceptions.

The Four Elements

There are four elements in your kitchen that require kashering attention:

Food: includes nonperishable sundries with a long shelf life, such as dry goods (flour, sugar, grains, legumes, cereals), canned goods, jarred goods; and perishables needing refrigeration, such as meat, cheese, and other dairy products.

Hardware: sink, countertops, cabinets

Appliances: includes large (refrigerator/freezer, stove, oven, dishwasher) and small (microwave, electric mixer, food processor, blender, bread machine, Crock-Pot, coffeemaker, etc.)

Foodware: dishes, utensils, knives, pots, pans

How do we make these various elements kosher? Let's look at each element individually.

Food

Deal with food first, because you will need to purge your kitchen of all unkosher food. Remove *everything* from every cupboard, closet, pantry, the refrigerator, freezer—wherever you keep food.

Ideally, according to both Orthodox and Conservative, you should start with all new food when you begin kashering your kitchen. But there are foods you can keep. Check with a rabbi, especially regarding the status of foods you may have had during Pesach.

What can you keep? Stricter, more *machmir*, Orthodox rules dictate that you get rid of all open food, from spices through pasta, and start with a bare cupboard, waiting to be filled with hechshered items. Lenient, *mekil*, Orthodox rules allow you to keep opened hechshered items, as long as you are certain they did not come into contact with anything unkosher. If you are eating only packaged goods with a hechsher, collect all unopened nonhechshered items to give away.

If you choose to keep "ingredient kosher," check the ingredients of all unopened items carefully, to ensure that nothing contains unkosher ingredients. Sundries such as rice and dried beans may also be kept, as long as you are sure their containers were never exposed to hot unkosher food.

Empty your refrigerator and freezer and examine everything in it. Now might just be the time to get rid of the half-filled jar of gooseberry jam that's been sitting in the back corner of the top shelf for three years, or that bag of unidentifiable ice crystals that falls out whenever you open the freezer.

Obviously, get rid of all unkosher meat. If you are following Orthodox dictates, give away all nonhechshered cheese. If you are being stricter still, any milk that is not *chalav Yisrael* should be discarded.

Refer to "Kosher Foods" to know what should or should not remain in your kitchen.

You should also consider the hechshers you use. Followers of different schools of Orthodoxy honor different hechshers. Consult your rabbi to make sure that all hechshers are acceptable.

Once you've determined which foods to keep and which to discard, and once the cabinets and refrigerator are ready to be refilled with food, you need to organize how you store food.

The two areas where you keep food are the refrigerator and freezer, for perishable items, and room-temperature cupboards for nonperishables.

Contamination through heat is not an issue in the pantry or refrigerator. There are not many nonperishables that are meat (other than, perhaps, canned soups), but you may want to keep dairy items and pareve items on separate shelves, so you don't inadvertently add powdered milk instead of flour to your pareve cake (as if you would! I'm just saying . . .). If you have shelves or cupboards just for pareve items, you can know without reading labels that those items can be used with meat foods.

Hardware

Cabinets and Drawers

Cabinets do not generally hold heated food. Therefore, they can be kashered relatively easily. Kashering basically means cleaning. Remove everything and wash the shelves and the sides. If you use shelf or drawer liners, discard the current ones and replace with new liners. Let them sit, empty, for twenty-four hours, then put away the food.

Countertops

Unlike cabinets, countertops do get exposed to heat. For example, if you have a heat-resistant countertop such as wood or granite, you might put a hot pot directly on it. Or the hot ingredients inside a pot—soup, stew, hot cocoa—might spill onto it.

The material that your counter is made of determines whether or not it is kasherable. Regardless of the material, you need to clean countertops thoroughly and let them sit, unused, for twenty-four hours.

Countertops today are made of a myriad of materials. According to Conservative rules, all countertops are kasherable except for those made of tile, since it is earthenware.

According to some Orthodox ruling, certain types of counters *cannot* be kashered. Materials that are not kasherable include the very common Formica, quartz and resin amalgamations such as Silestone, and mineral and acrylic polymer composites such as Corian. These all fall under the category of plastic, and plastic, according to some Orthodox tenets, cannot be kashered. Some do say that Corian can be sanded down and can be kasherable in that way, but opinions vary.

Opinion is mixed as to what "not kasherable" means in terms of how to use that counter in your kosher kitchen. One Orthodox rabbi I spoke with said such counters should be covered, usually with Contact paper. Another Orthodox rabbi I spoke with said while such counters are not kasherable, it doesn't matter; they do not *need* to be kashered because of how countertops are used. One school of Orthodox thought is that plastic only becomes unkosher if used directly on a fire, which does not apply to a countertop. The countertop may have been splashed with hot unkosher liquid, but in order for that splashed liquid to affect the kashrut status of the countertop, it would have had to be still boiling when it landed on the countertop; invariably this is not the case, as splashes cool quickly as they travel. By the time they reach the countertop, they would not be hot enough for the Formica to have absorbed the secondary heat. According to this stance, the countertop is not really treif, and the cleaned countertop does not need to be covered with Contact paper. However, since there are disagreements about how to treat a Formica-type countertop when kashering your kitchen, check with the rabbi helping you kasher your kitchen.

Wood counters are kasherable but a challenge. According to both Conservative and Orthodox, you need to shave the surface and plane it to even it out, sanding away any cuts and scratches in the wood so they are no longer visible. You need to wash it with both soap and water and bleach, then wait the requisite twenty-four hours.

Metal, stone, and wood countertops, and Formica and other "plastic" countertops, if you are following Conservative tenets, can be kashered through *irui*. Heat a kettle of water to boiling, and pour the boiling water over the entire countertop. Yes, this can get messy, so make sure you have a bunch of clean rags or towels on the floor to absorb all the water.

Regardless of the material your counter is made from, most rabbis recommend that you do not place hot pots or pans directly on the countertop. Rather, place them on dedicated trivets.

The Sink

The kitchen sink is a hotbed of treif. Most likely, before you started thinking about keeping kosher, pots, pans, and dishes with traces of milk and meat products went into that sink, and hot water swirled over them, mixing everything together. The hot water can get quite hot, definitely in the *yad soledet bo* range.

Enameled porcelain sinks are treated as earthenware, a substance that absorbs flavors permanently. These sinks are not kasherable.

Stainless steel sinks can be kashered. The kashrut preference, for both Conservative and Orthodox, is to have two separate sinks, one for meat and one for dairy, because a sink can so easily become treif. A double sink is possible, but difficult to keep kosher, as spills from one to the other can happen too easily. But for many people two separate sinks are not an option.

This does not mean you cannot use your sink. If you have only one sink, even if it is stainless, it will quickly become unkosher through normal use. But you should still kasher it when kashering your kitchen.

Sinks are kashered through *irui*. Scrub the sink thoroughly. Some Orthodox rabbis encourage pouring a bleach solution down the drain, but this is a *machmir* position, as the drain and garbage disposal will never come in contact with food you actually prepare to eat.

Do not use the sink for twenty-four hours. Then boil water and pour it all over the sink, including the faucet and the lip of the sink that overlaps onto the counter (don't forget to put towels or rags on the floor).

Some sinks have a retractable spray attachment, the nozzle of which is usually plastic. According to some Orthodox, this is not kasherable and should be replaced or not used. According to Conservative halacha, it is kasherable—include this nozzle during the *irui* process.

If you have only one sink, how do you use it without causing your dishes to become treif? You cannot soak dishes in a sink filled with water—that could cause any residual unkosher flavors to contaminate your dishes.

If you are dexterous and careful, you might be able to hold the dish or fork or pot in your hand during the entire time you wash it, making sure not to let it touch the treif sink. If it falls—you have to kasher it again. Realistically, get separate plastic tubs that fit in your sink, one for meat and one for dairy. A more lenient approach is to use separate rubber-coated racks, and the dishes can rest on this rack (like hot pots can rest on a trivet on the countertop) as you wash them.

Keep with your color theme here to avoid confusion—for example, red or pink racks and tubs for meat, blue for dairy, yellow for pareve items.

Appliances—Large

Refrigerator/Freezer

A refrigerator is cold, so kashering means basically cleaning. Remove all the shelving, if possible, and wash the shelves, the bins, and the drawers with soap and water. Also wash the walls of the fridge—a task made easier if you can remove the shelves. Only put back food that is kosher.

As with your cabinets, it can be easier if you designate various areas of your refrigerator as meat, dairy, or pareve. When storing cooked food, it is best to let it cool to room temperature before putting it in the fridge. Otherwise, if anything spills, there can be issues of heat transference between dairy and meat items. If your refrigerator shelves are racks, you can cover them with aluminum foil or plastic, so that accidental spills won't spread to the shelf below. If spilled milk gets on the hot chicken soup pot, for example, you may need to rekasher the pot. Anyway, from a simply practical, nonkashrut point of view, it is not a good idea to put hot food in the refrigerator, since it warms up the temperature of the fridge, which can have adverse affects on the food you are trying to keep cold.

Cooktop

There are many kinds of cooktops, from standard gas and electric to futuristic radiant heat with a glass-ceramic surface.

Gas cooktops generally consist of the pilot burner, a hinged cooktop, metal plates around each burner, and grates, or "spiders," that rest on those grates. **Electric cooktops** are similar, but without the grating, as pots and pans rest directly on the heating coil.

Let the cooktop rest, unused, for twenty-four hours. Remove all the burner grates and plates and wash thoroughly. Scour the stovetop. If possible, lift the stovetop and clean underneath. I've been amazed at the amount of food that seems to escape into the seamy underside of my gas stovetop. Make sure to clean temperature-setting dials as well. Once all the separate parts are cleaned, reassemble your stovetop.

Once the cooktop is cleaned thoroughly and reassembled, turn each burner on high. Check with your rabbi as to the amount of time the burner should remain on. One Orthodox rabbi I spoke with said fifteen minutes was sufficient—you want those iron grates or the electric coils to get red hot. According to Conservative tradition, the burners should remain on for forty-five minutes. Some Orthodox say the gas cooktop iron grates may be kashered when you kasher your oven (see page 94). You can put them in the oven during the self-cleaning process, although you may want to check with the manufacturer that this won't cause damage.

In order to ensure that the area immediately surrounding the burners is adequately heated and kashered, one Orthodox rabbi I spoke with recommends placing a *blech* on top of the heating burners. A *blech* is a metal tin, shaped like an inverted cookie pan, which you place on top of the burners to dissipate the heat if you leave the stove on during Shabbat. When you see the *blech* glowing faintly red (most visible with the lights turned off), the burners are kashered (and so is the *blech*). Alternately, cover the burner areas with heavy-duty aluminum foil or a double layer of regular foil.

As with sinks, two cooktops are ideal in a kosher kitchen, but not necessary. The standard cooktop design is to have two columns of two burners, with a space of just under a foot wide between the columns. Food does splatter when being cooked, and the space between burners gets quite warm, past the *yad soledet bo* point, so this area is considered treif, as probably both dairy and meat foods have splattered on it. If you are cooking and some hot meat falls into that space, you would need to discard the meat. (However, if the space was cold and the meat was cold, you could still use the meat.)

If you have a metal cooktop, this space is kasherable with a blowtorch (best done by a rabbi familiar with kashering with blowtorches). Some Orthodox and Conservative rabbis say that *irui* may be used. Enameled cooktops cannot be kashered, according to Orthodox tenets, although the burners are acceptable to use.

If you have a fan above the cooktop, it needs to be cleaned thoroughly, but not kashered in any particular way, as you are not using it for direct food preparation.

The same stovetop can be used for both meat and dairy cooking; however, rabbis recommend not cooking meat and dairy at the same time, or at least not directly next to one another. Steam from one pot can rise and mingle with steam from the second pot, thereby affecting the flavor of the food cooking in each pot.

Smooth glass cooktops can be tricky to kasher, as it is difficult to heat adequately the entire area that a large pan might touch without damaging the surface of the cooktop. According to Orthodox halacha, glassware that is heated needs to be kashered through very high heat, which may damage the cooktop. According to Conservative rules, it does not need such kashering; it is enough to wash the glass cooktop with soap and water.

Oven

To kasher an oven, remove the racks, scrub them clean, and scrub clean the walls, ceiling, and floor of the oven. Let it sit, unused, for twenty-four hours. Some Orthodox rabbis say it is sufficient to clean and heat the oven as high as possible for an hour, or to run the oven through a self-cleaning cycle if that is an option; others feel that the heat of a blowtorch is necessary to kasher an oven effectively. A rabbi will blowtorch the racks and sides of the oven.

From the Conservative stand, cleaning the oven, letting it sit unused for twenty-four hours, and then running it through the self-cleaning cycle, or leaving it on high heat for forty-five minutes, is the acceptable way to kasher an oven.

Actual oven use can be tricky, and the stricter observers strongly recommend separate ovens for meat and dairy. Again, this is not an option for many people, so there is some leniency in this matter.

When you use your oven, you cannot cook meat and dairy dishes at the same time because the flavors of one can permeate the flavors of the other. A more *machmir* Orthodox stand is that an oven has one "gender," say, for example, meat. If you want to cook dairy in that oven, then you need to cover the racks with aluminum foil. Ideally, you should cover the top of the pan with aluminum foil as well, but that may not be an option for items such as cakes or cookies. In such a case, make sure the oven is thoroughly cleaned and kashered.

A more *mekil* stand is that the oven may be used for either meat or dairy, but should be thoroughly cleaned between uses. The Conservative stand is that an oven may be used, but separately, for both meat and dairy cooking.

Dishwasher

Dishwashers weren't an issue for the first few thousand years of kashrut. Now they are, and debated appliances, too. There is some difference of interpretation between Orthodox and Conservative in how you can use the dishwasher. At issue is heat, and the material from which the dishwasher is made. The dishwasher water becomes even hotter than sink water, definitely to the *yad soledet bo* level. So, if you washed a dirty dairy dish and a dirty meat dish together, the flavors from any remnants of food from each would wash over the other and make that dish treif. The walls of most dishwashers are plastic, with some enameled porcelain and some stainless steel, which is becoming more common. The strictest Orthodox ruling is that a treif dishwasher with plastic or enameled walls cannot be made kosher and should therefore be replaced; if finances are a concern, check with your rabbi.

A metal-walled dishwasher can be kasherable. You may need to replace the racks; again, check with your rabbi. To kasher the dishwasher, let it rest, unused, for twenty-four hours. Clean the drain filter and inspect any corners for accumulated debris. Then run the empty dishwasher through an entire cycle, with soap. Some rabbis recommend running it through a cycle three times.

The preferable Orthodox rule is to designate the dishwasher either dairy or meat. You could technically use such a dishwasher for both meat and milk dishes, kashering it in between each use, with separate racks for meat and for dairy, but rabbis recommend against this option. It is too easy for *basar b'chalav* to happen inadvertently because it can become difficult to keep track of whether the dishwasher is in a meat phase or a dairy phase.

According to some Orthodox interpretation, a lenient interpretation at that, you can use the metal dishwasher for meat and dairy under specific conditions:

- You must wait twenty-four hours between running a meat cycle and a dairy cycle. You must run an empty wash in between.
- You must have separate racks for meat and dairy.
- You must use a separate drain filter for meat and dairy.

Remember, according to Orthodox rules, this may not be possible for a dishwasher that is plastic or enamel.

If you have one dishwasher, decide which kinds of dishes you use more often, and designate the dishwasher dairy or meat. One rabbi I spoke with said he considered having "made it" when he could afford two dishwashers.

According to Conservative interpretation, dishwashers *can* be kashered, regardless of the material they are made from. Scrub the interior of the dishwasher, paying attention to the small parts, such as the drain and the part that sprays the water, as particles of food can get caught there. Let it rest, unused, for twenty-four hours, then run it through a complete cycle, empty, using soap. The dishwasher is now ready for use.

According to Conservative rules, you may use the dishwasher for dairy and meat, but not at the same time. Do not wash dairy and meat dishes together. Rinse dishes thoroughly before loading them, getting rid of any obvious particles of food. Even if you have one of those great dishwashers that actually clean hardened crud-covered plates and pots, you still need to rinse all that stuff off because it could get caught in the filter and potentially affect the next load in a *basar b'chalav* way. There are differing opinions, but the standard accepted method is to run an empty cycle between running a dairy cycle and a meat cycle or vice versa; some say this is not necessary. You do not need to wait twenty-four hours. Some advocate using separate racks, but others do not.

Whether Orthodox or Conservative, you should check with your rabbi regarding your dishwasher.

Appliances—Small

The plethora of small appliances that simultaneously provide us with conveniences in food preparation and clutter our kitchens are subject to various methods of kashering. Some small appliances are truly not kasherable, as they have nooks and crannies impossible to clean sufficiently, or they have many plastic parts which, according to Orthodox halacha, cannot be kashered. Fortunately, many small appliances are relatively inexpensive and can be replaced without too high a cost.

A note on doubles: You do not necessarily need two of every electrical appliance you have. One and a half is enough. That is, you will not need doubles of the electrical part of high-ticket items such as food processors or standing electric mixers. You will need two mixing bowls and blades or beaters. You can usually order these from the manufacturer or from kitchenware stores.

With dishes, you can easily have separate sets for dairy and meat that each have distinguishing colors or characteristics. But doubles of such things as beaters for the electric mixer or a bowl for the food processor are virtually identical, so you need to differentiate between the sets. Enter permanent markers or nail polish. In keeping with the red and blue theme, use a red marker or nail polish for the meat utensils and blue for the dairy, and mark the items accordingly.

Microwave Oven

The microwave oven is debated in Orthodox circles. Because the oven itself does not heat up the way a regular oven does, it does not need the same kind of *libun* high-heat kashering treatment required for a regular oven. Some rabbis recommend heating the microwave for a few minutes, then resting your hand on the tray or walls. If you cannot hold your hand there for fifteen seconds, it is considered *yad soledet bo,* and likely cannot be kashered, as the material is either plastic or enamel. Otherwise, it can be kashered. According to Conservative halacha, microwaves can be kashered.

To kasher your microwave, first clean it thoroughly. If there is a glass plate inside, remove and wash it. Let both plate and microwave sit, unused, for twenty-four hours. Return the plate to the microwave. Place a container with a few ounces of water in it and heat until it boils, producing steam. Some Orthodox authorities recommend getting two separate glass inserts because how much a microwave heats containers is debatable, and can vary from oven to oven. If you want to have one tray, you can put a paper towel or piece of Styrofoam underneath any dish you might use.

According to Conservative halacha, do the same treatment with the water, but the glass insert may be used uncovered for dairy or meat. Wash it between uses.

Electric Mixer

There are two kinds of electric mixers: standing and handheld. With both, you need to clean thoroughly the base of the machine. Since that part does not usually come in direct contact with food, you can keep it (but check with your rabbi). The handheld variety usually has two detachable metal beaters. Those beaters can be detached and kashered through *hag'alah,* boiling (see Dishes, page 102). If you plan to use the mixer for both dairy and meat, you need to have separate beaters for each, and you should color-code each set.

Standing mixers, such as a KitchenAid, generally come with a mixing paddle, a dough hook, and a whisk, plus a work bowl, and perhaps a plastic work shield. Since a mixer is not generally used for anything hot (unless you did use it for mixing hot items), you may be able to use the existing items, even if they are rubber-or plastic-coated; check with your rabbi. It is traditional to kasher both the bowl and the attachments with *hag'alah* to be safe. Also, thoroughly clean the mixer stand and all parts; do not use the mixer for twenty-four hours before using *hag'alah*. You will need to have separate bowls for dairy and meat items. Unless you plan to mix up meat mixtures in your mixer bowl, you could have one bowl be dairy and one be pareve so you can use it to prepare pareve desserts to follow meat meals. Just be sure to clean the mixer thoroughly after each use.

Blender

If your blender container is glass, it is kasherable in the same way glassware is kasherable. But many blenders have a plastic container, which may not be kasherable, according to some Orthodox rulings. According to some Conservative halacha, if the plastic can be submerged in boiling water without damage, by *hag'alah,* it is kasherable. The metal blade may also be kasherable; check with your rabbi regarding the plastic lid and rubber gaskets. You can keep the blender base, but it must be cleaned thoroughly. You will need separate blender containers and blades for dairy and meat.

Food Processor

A food processor has restrictions similar to a blender. There is a metal blade, but it is usually attached to plastic. According to some Orthodox ruling, it cannot be kashered. According to Conservative halacha, if the plastic bowl and plastic parts are heat resistant, they can be kashered by *hag'alah*. You will probably need to check with the manufacturer. You may need to replace the parts, but you can keep the most expensive part of the processor, the base. As with other small appliances, you will need separate blades and bowls for dairy and for meat.

Immersion Blender

Creamed soup making became a hundred times easier and neater when these handheld blenders were introduced, and they became our standard hostess gift for several years. However, they are not viably kasherable, and not only because they are made of debatable plastic. *Hag'alah* would be required, as you've most likely used them in hot soup. While you can immerse an immersion blender into liquid up to a point (hence the name), you can't immerse it completely, as would be required to kasher it; this would damage the electrical parts. Fortunately, the price has changed little since we first purchased one fifteen years ago, and they are replaceable. You need separate meat and dairy immersion blenders.

Bread Machine

Bread machines are something of a challenge, as they are in effect a mini-oven. Also, the bread machine pan is coated with a nonstick coating. Nonstick coating, such as Teflon, is not kasherable, according to some Orthodox standards; it falls under the category of plastic. According to Conservative standards, you could put the pan in your regular oven set at the highest setting for one hour, for *libun*, but you should check with the manufacturer to learn if this would damage the pan. You can buy replacement pans, and you should have two, one for dairy and one for pareve. As for dairy breads, remember that the bread must be consumed in one meal, and probably should be mixed up in the bread machine, then baked in a regular oven in a different shape (see Bread, page 65, in the chapter on Kosher Foods).

Bread-machine baking is usually programmed—it is difficult just to turn it on to its highest heat as you would an oven. One possibility is to run it through a bread-baking cycle, empty, but check with your rabbi. It is unlikely that the heating element of a bread machine came into contact with anything treif, as the main ingredient that spills out of the pan during the bread-making cycle is flour. Regular ovens are more susceptible to unkosher spills before being kashered, since unkosher meat has been roasted therein with the possibility of dripping meat juices.

A rabbi I spoke with said steam might be an issue, if you made a dairy bread in the machine; it could embed the sides of the machine with a dairy flavor. You could bake only pareve breads in the machine, but use the dough setting for dairy breads. Since it would not be heated to the point of *yad soledet bo*, there would not be a transference of flavors.

Slow Cooker

A.k.a. Crock-Pot, this consists of a metal base with a heating element, a ceramic pot, and a glass or plastic lid. The ceramic pot is not kasherable. The heating element may be kashered simply by cleaning it, as no food comes in contact with the base. The lid may be kasherable according to Conservative standards; according to Orthodox standards, since the glass was used in cooking, it may not be kasherable and the plastic is debatable. Slow cookers are inexpensive; purchase a new one. You will need separate pots and lids for dairy and for meat. A slow cooker has become practically indispensable for Shabbat afternoon lunch cooking (see the chapters on Shabbat, page 111, and Recipes, page195).

Coffeemaker/Coffee Grinder

Plain, unflavored coffee beans do not have to be certified (although there are those that are). Ground coffee, *as long as it is unflavored* (or instant, which doesn't really apply to a coffeemaker), does not need to be certified either, since it is produced in a dedicated factory. If you have a standard coffeemaker (no special milk-steaming attachments), and you've only ever made plain, unflavored coffee with it, all you need to do is clean it and it can be kosher.

Americans love coffee, and contraptions, so there are coffee machines with fancier and more elaborate attachments, including ones that enable you to steam milk. Since dairy has some issues, you will need to consult with a rabbi concerning the kasherability of such machines. It is possible that such a machine could be used only for dairy meals. If you choose to use only *chalav Yisrael*, there may be other issues.

Flavored coffee, on the other hand, presents problems. Unless you've only used certified kosher flavored coffee, you may need to get a new coffeemaker, as some flavorings can be made from treif ingredients.

As for a coffee grinder, if you used it only for unflavored coffees, nothing special needs to be done to kasher it. However, if you used it for flavored coffees, remnants of those flavors may still leach into the beans, which would then also permeate the coffeemaker, which gets heated. The grinder, however, does not, so you can use it. You should clean the grinder thoroughly and not use it for twenty-four hours.

Toaster Oven

Toaster ovens are difficult to kasher without ruining them. Since a toaster oven is generally used for more than just toast, often to bake both meat and dairy items, it really does need a full kashering. It has to be heated very hot, which can sometimes damage the unit. It should be cleaned and scrubbed thoroughly, and left for twenty-four hours. The rack and the tray have to be kashered through *libun gamur*, and the red-hot heat might melt the thin bands of a toaster-oven rack. Check with your rabbi about the best way to kasher a toaster oven.

Toaster

Toasters are usually dedicated primarily to bread. If you know that you never toasted anything that was expressly unkosher (some pastry items, such as Pop-Tarts, contain gelatin, which may be a kashrut issue for you), clean the toaster by getting rid of crumbs. Let it sit unused for twenty-four hours. Then turn it on and let it heat up. It should be left on for at least five minutes, long enough for the coils to get red hot. You may need to override the mechanism that causes it to shut off automatically. Some rabbis recommend placing aluminum foil over the openings in the toaster top to help retain heat.

Electric Waffle Iron, Griddle, Sandwich Maker, George Foreman Grill

All these appliances are not easily kasherable. Most are Teflon-coated, and they cannot be heated red hot without being irreparably damaged. Some have removable parts that may, according to Conservative ruling, be kashered by placing them in a hot oven until they are *libun kal*; check with your rabbi.

Outdoor Grill

The grill must be cleaned thoroughly. The grates then have to be heated until red hot, *libun gamur*, either through a flame or with a blowtorch.

Foodware

You will need two sets of dishes, flatware, serving platters, pots, and pans for meat and for dairy. There may be certain pots or pans that you won't need to double, as you may have different cooking needs for one or the other. For example, you probably won't need a dairy roasting pan.

According to Orthodox tradition, new or newly kashered glassware, china, and metalware should be *toiveled*, or ritually immersed in a mikvah.

Dishes

Dishes can be made of several substances: china, earthenware, glass, wood, various plastics, metal. Some can be kashered, some cannot, some are debatable.

Leviticus 6:21 says, *"And the earthenware vessel in which it was cooked shall be broken; and if it was cooked in a brazen vessel, it shall be scoured, and rinsed in water."* This verse is the basis for certain rules of kashering dishes, and what may or may not be kasherable.

Whether or not you can keep the dishes you already own depends on the material from which they are made. If the dishes are "earthen," that is, china or stoneware, it is most likely you will *not* be able to keep them, at least not for immediate use. Unglazed earthenware cannot be kashered at all, as the porous ceramic permanently absorbs juices and flavors from foods. Nowadays, glazed chinaware can be relatively inexpensive, especially compared to 50 or 150 years ago. Consequently, Orthodox and Conservative opinions on keeping dishes that were previously used in unkosher kitchens have become stricter. The general opinion is, chinaware cannot be kashered. Thickly glazed china or fine china, family heirloom material, can sometimes be made kosher, but it must sit, unused, for at least twelve months; have a rabbi check your china to determine if this rule is applicable. This is the amount of time deemed necessary for dissipation of all unkosher flavors. If the glaze is thin and could easily flake off, the dish likely cannot be kashered. The alternative is to find a kiln and heat the ceramic items at kiln temperatures (about 2,000°F), but at that heat the china might break.

The rule regarding chinaware applies not only to place settings, but to serving platters, as well as mixing bowls, fruit bowls, and so on. Items that are never used with hot food, such as a ceramic fruit bowl or a sugar bowl, are not treif and don't need kashering.

Teapots, if they were *never* used with flavored tea, may not need to be kashered and can be kept; check with your rabbi.

Glass has been controversial, in both Conservative and Orthodox rulings, in terms of determining what material category it falls under. Glass is made of sand, so is it earthenware? Yet it does not absorb as earthenware does, so is it like metal? In the Shulchan Aruch, Joseph Caro writes that glass dishes "need no kashering since they do not absorb," while Moshe Isserles writes, "And some are more stringent and say that even purging by boiling is of no effect in their case." The ultimate Conservative and more common Orthodox conclusion is that glass is neutral, and can be kashered simply by washing.

However, because glass is neutral, the question has been raised: Could the same dishes be used for dairy and for meat, just washing them in between uses? While technically this is a possibility, both Conservative and Orthodox rules frown upon this as a practice. It is too easy for incidents of *basar b'chalav* to happen. Keeping track of when you used the dish last, if you washed it appropriately, and so on make it problematic to use the same glass dishes for hot dairy and meat foods.

Drinking glasses, however, since they are used only for cold substances, may be used with both dairy and meat meals. A *machmir* Orthodox stand is to have separate drinking glasses for dairy and meat, but using one set of drinking glasses is not only acceptable but common practice.

Glass that is used for baking, such as Pyrex, is a separate issue. The Conservative ruling is that Pyrex and such materials are treated the same as other glassware, and can be kashered simply by washing. The Orthodox stand on Pyrex, on the other hand, is that it and other glassware that has been used for baking *cannot* be kashered, and must be replaced.

There are two ways to kasher glasses: by simply washing them and waiting twenty-four hours, or by ***milui v'irui***. This method, soaking, is primarily used to prepare glassware for Pesach, but it may also be used when going from an unkosher to a kosher kitchen. Place the glassware in a single layer (no stacking) in a large container (this may be done in a cleaned bathtub that hasn't been used for twenty-four hours). Cover with water completely. The glassware needs to soak seventy-two hours, but you must change the water after twenty-four hours and again after forty-eight hours. At the end of the seventy-two hours, drain and wash the glassware.

The kashering method used for most foodware is *hag'alah*. It is used primarily for dishes and flatware made of metal, stone, wood, and rubber. According to Conservative halacha, it can also be used for hard plastic, such as Melmac (the brand name for melamine). Orthodox opinion on this issue varies. Some say plastics are kasherable, some say they are not. Since most plastics are not used in an oven or over a direct flame, there is a certain amount of leniency here.

Hag'alah means "boiling." You need a very large pot for this, ideally one dedicated to the kashering process. When we kashered our kitchen when I was a kid, my mother purchased a huge pot, larger than any we'd ever used. Part of the koshering process calls for a large stone, and my mother asked for the permanent loan of a heavy, smooth stone I had found on the school playing fields some months before. The stone can serve two purposes. One, it helps maintain the heat of the boiling water as objects to be kashered are added. And two, it is used to kasher large pots, by dropping it into the pot in order to cause the water to overflow down the sides.

To do *hag'alah* for dishes, bring the water to a rolling boil. If the plate is platter-sized and is too big to be submerged completely, rotate it. Submerge half, and then rotate it and submerge the other half, holding each part in the water for about thirty seconds. Plates, even smaller ones, should be kashered one at a time. The water has to touch the entire surface of the plate, and if plates are overlapping, there might be part of one that would not be sufficiently kashered. According to Conservative ruling, this method may be used for plastic dishes; according to most Orthodox halacha, it may not.

Cutting Boards

Cutting boards made of wood can be kashered through *hag'alah*, but they must first be sanded down and bleached, similar to the method used to kasher a wooden countertop. This can be tedious for a cutting board, and you may opt to purchase a new one. A plastic cutting board should be replaced.

Metal Flatware

Silverware and stainless steelware can be made kosher through *hag'alah*. The day before kashering, clean all the flatware and let it rest, unused, for twenty-four hours.

Some flatware handles are made of a different material, such as Melmac (a hard plastic) or wood. You can submerge the entire piece, if it can withstand the heat. Otherwise, its kasherability is debatable. Some rabbis I spoke with said you can submerge just the metal part of the flatware; since you don't eat with the handle, it doesn't matter if it is kasherable or not. Others say the entire implement may not be kashered. Check with your rabbi.

It also depends on how smoothly attached the handle is. If it seems loose, if there seem to be cracks or spaces into which food could enter, which would be very difficult to clean, you probably should not use it, and it should be replaced. This is also the case with knives, many of which have handles made of a separate material.

The flatware pieces cannot touch each other, lest those parts touching not be fully exposed to the water, so this is a somewhat tedious procedure, especially if you have a lot of silverware. The Star-K organization recommends tying the individual implements together in a sort of chain, with a few inches between each piece of flatware, so you can easily lower them into the boiling water. Another option is a large net bag, as long as it is large enough for the flatware to spread out on the bottom of the pot in a single layer. The flatware should remain in the water about fifteen to thirty seconds, and then be rinsed in cold water. Make sure you do not rinse it in an unkosher sink!

The rules for koshering flatware are the same for Orthodox and Conservative followers.

As for other kinds of utensils, it again depends on the material. There are some made with newer materials, such as spatulas designed to withstand temperatures above 500°F, 600°F, even 700°F. These could certainly withstand *hag'alah*, but consult with your rabbi, as they are a kind of plastic. Wooden spoons can be kashered by *hag'alah*.

Knives

Sometimes flatware will become unkosher through everyday inadvertent accidents. So will knives. Usually you save up a pile of to-be-kashered items, and then do several at once. Knives can be kashered through *hag'alah*, as with other flatware, but they also can be kashered in another way, by **ne'itzah**, under certain conditions. Literally, *ne'itzah* means "thrusting." You thrust the knife in question into the ground ten times, in ten different spots (next to each other is okay). If you live in an apartment, a plant pot packed with dirt is acceptable too. The thought is that the dirt will effectively clean the knife, and *hag'alah* will not be necessary. *Ne'itzah* is a special procedure used when a smooth-bladed knife becomes unkosher in a few specified circumstances:

- If you use a dairy knife to cut *cold* or *slightly warm* meat
- If you want to use a meat knife to cut pareve bread for a dairy meal
- If you only have an unkosher knife at hand. Use *ne'itzah* so you can use it temporarily.
- If, when cutting vegetables, you inadvertently cut a worm

What the preceding circumstances all have in common is that the foods are cold, or at least below *yad soledet bo*. Knives that you use for cutting hot meat, such as those that are part of a set of flatware, still need to be kashered through boiling, *hag'alah*. A serrated knife, however, because of its nooks and crannies, needs the higher heat of *libun* for kashering. That is, the knife has to be heated with a blowtorch until it is red hot.

You may need to get a new set of knives. Many great cooking knives have bolted plastic or wooden handles; few are one continuous piece, and there is the real possibility that unkosher food might get caught between the various cracks. Check with your rabbi.

Pots and Pans

Pots and pans used on the cooktop to heat liquidy food can be kashered by *hag'alah*. Not frying pans, though. Clean them first, wait twenty-four hours, and then heat a pot of boiling water. If the pots are too big to submerge completely in the *hag'alah* pot of water, use tongs to hold one side of the pot and submerge it partially for about thirty seconds, then turn the pot and continue submerging it, part by part, until the whole pot has been submerged.

If the pot is too big to fit into the kashering pot, you'll make somewhat of a watery mess. Fill the pot to the lip with water and bring to a boil. In the meantime, put a large stone or a brick (cleaned) over another burner so it can heat up. When the water boils, take the hot stone (with tongs!) and drop it into the boiling water. This should cause the water to rise uniformly, spilling over the sides, thereby covering the outside of the pot with boiling water. This is the procedure you can use to create a kashering pot in the first place. You will also need to kasher the kashering pot in this way when you are through doing *hag'alah* on everything else.

Pressure cookers are similarly kashered through *hag'alah*, including the rubber gasket.

Frying pans that used oil, according to Orthodox ruling, should be kashered by *libun kal*. They should be heated on a burner set over high heat until a piece of paper touching the pan gets singed.

Note: Pans that are coated with **Teflon**, according to the Orthodox, *cannot* be kashered; according to Conservative ruling, they can. If the surface is fairly scratched up, which happens with Teflon, the pan should be replaced (as it should be anyway; who knows what's in those flakes of Teflon that might come off into your scrambled eggs?).

Baking Pans

You will likely need to get a new set of metal baking pans. Metal pans used for baking must be kashered by *libun gamur*, that is, heated over an open flame (such as a blowtorch) until they are red hot. This treatment can damage many pans, such as those made from aluminum. If you have heavier pans, they may survive red-hot temperatures, but usually people opt to buy new baking pans. You will also need to scrub off any baked-on residue. As with other items to be kashered, clean the pans and let them rest, unused, for twenty-four hours. According to some more lenient rulings, however, you can kasher metal baking pans by placing them in the oven, set at the highest setting, for one hour or let them stay in the oven during the self-cleaning process.

Glass baking pans just need to be washed, according to Conservative halacha. According to Orthodox rules, they cannot be kashered and must be replaced.

Clothware

Sponges used for washing dishes should be dedicated to meat or dairy washing. Color coding comes in handy here. Dish towels should also be dedicated to one or the other, but can be washed and changed. It is just easier to color-code or design-code the towels so you don't accidentally wipe a meat pot with a milk-stained towel.

Similarly, tablecloths and cloth napkins can be washed and used for meat or dairy.

Tevilat Kelim

You have now kashered everything that can be kashered in your kitchen. You have possibly replaced your previous dishes with a new set and bought a new, second set of dishes. According to Conservative tradition, you are all done now, ready to start cooking in your kosher kitchen. According to Orthodox rules, there is one more mitzvah to perform in the kashering process: *tevilat kelim.*

Literally the "immersion of vessels," the mitzvah is called *toiveling* in Yiddish. *Tevilat kelim* has biblical roots. In **Numbers 31:21-23,** in a chapter recounting how the Israelites are to deal with the spoils of war with the Midianites, the priest Elazar tells the soldiers, "*This is the decree of the Torah, which the Lord commanded Moses: Only the gold, and the silver, the brass, the iron, the tin, and the lead—everything that comes into the fire—you shall pass through the fire, and it shall be purified; nevertheless it must be purified with the water of sprinkling; and everything that does not come into the fire you shall pass through the water.*"

The rabbis interpreted this to mean that any dishes that have been either manufactured or previously owned by non-Jews (such as the Midianites) must be ritually immersed in a mikvah ("purified with the water of sprinkling"). Since most people in the world are not Jewish, the likelihood of non-Jewish manufactured cookware is fairly certain.

A mikvah is a special ritual bath, used for purification. When someone converts to

Judaism, they immerse themselves in a mikvah. Before they are married, the bride and groom, separately, will immerse themselves in a mikvah. *Tevilat kelim* further emphasizes the sanctity of kashrut.

This step is unnecessary according to Conservative traditions; as Rabbi Paul Plotkin says, "There is no official position one way or another on *toiveling*. It has been an orphan issue and is just now coming onto the agenda. We are currently working on it." So *toiveling* may be a Conservative procedure as well in the near future.

Tevilat kelim is a mitzvah subject to much interpretation. Some materials are *toiveled* with a blessing, some without, with various exceptions. If you do decide to *toivel* your dishes, contact your rabbi.

Beyond Your Kitchen:
Keeping Kosher "Out"

In the introduction, I mentioned the concept of eating kosher "out," that is, outside of the home. This is a topic that probably comes up more frequently in Conservative circles. You keep a kosher home, so how should you keep kosher outside of your home, specifically, in a restaurant? Restaurants are an issue because most of them constantly violate lots of laws of kashrut. Meats are cooked in pots used for dairy, treif foods are cooked next to potentially acceptable foods, and so on.

A strictly Orthodox observer of kashrut will eat only in restaurants with kashrut supervision. Some observant modern Orthodox might also eat in vegetarian restaurants, or they could order cold food such as a salad in a nonkosher restaurant, as transference of flavors from heat is not an issue with cold foods.

Strictly observant Conservative Jews also follow this way of eating out. However, many Conservative Jews do eat hot foods in restaurants that do not have kosher supervision, and that do serve unkosher foods. Some simply do not keep kosher "out" at all, and anything goes in restaurant land. Many, however, will observe certain restrictions when they go out, opting to eschew meat, poultry, and shellfish in favor of fish or vegetarian dishes. "It's a common practice for many Conservative Jews to eat in nonkosher restaurants," says Rabbi Plotkin. "But I'm hard-pressed to give a halachic foundation for that practice." Plotkin eats hot food only in kosher restaurants or cold food in a nonkosher restaurant. "My mantra is, if everybody was appropriately strict in the Conservative movement, we would have tons more kosher restaurants."

Other Conservative rabbis I spoke with are more ambivalent about restaurant dining. Rabbi David Starr says, "I fall in a very inconsistent place. Practically, I don't feel comfortable eating hot food in a nonkosher environment. I do it. I do it because I'm inconsistent, but don't really believe it's being kosher to do that. My practice has a geographic quality to it. In New York City, there's no need to eat in a nonkosher restaurant. But in Boston I will eat in nonkosher restaurants. I don't really believe in trying to find a halachic justification for it; I prefer to see it as halachically deviant behavior."

But Conservative Jews, such as Rabbi Starr, who do eat in nonkosher restaurants, do observe some level of personal kashrut, albeit one that might not be halachically correct. They do not order meat or shellfish, they check that no chicken stock was used for soups, and only order fish or vegetarian dishes. Rabbi Mark Robbins says, "Liberal Jews will incorporate kashrut into what they believe, into what they feel like they need to do as a fully participating member of American society. I am supportive of eating out in restaurants. I eat pasta and fish out, and whenever I go into a restaurant, I am cognizant I am Jewish because I have to make decisions about everything I eat. Many may argue that's being hypocritical, but in our society, with kashrut, there's always the next degree you can go to; everyone sets their own level that makes them feel integrity. But if you consider what we do as Conservative Jews as emanating both from the grassroots and from halacha, this is what we do. We do make compromises."

Thank God

Whew! You have just finished the truly hard part, kashering the kitchen. But as Rabbi Plotkin says, "If you want to do something, it's never hard. If you don't, it's overwhelming." Maintaining kashrut is relatively easy, especially in the home. If it happens that you use milk in a meat pot, or vice versa, you can rekasher the item. Sometimes items are not rekasherable—you will need to describe the particular situation to your rabbi to learn about the kashering options.

Once you have kashered everything that can be kashered, replaced what can be replaced, cleaned what needed to be cleaned, *toiveled* what needed to be *toiveled* if you chose to do that, your kitchen is a kosher kitchen. You can drink a *l'chaim*, a toast, to your accomplishment, and to the ongoing fulfillment of keeping kosher. There is no special *bracha*, blessing, to make upon kashering a kitchen. However, it would be appropriate to say the *Shehecheyanu* blessing now, the blessing thanking God for an accomplishment:

> *Baruch ata Adonai, Eloheinu melech ha'olam, shehecheyanu, v'kiyimanu, v'higiyanu lazman ha'zeh.*
> Praised are you, Lord our God, King of the universe, who grants us life, sustaining us, and enabling us to reach this day.

Kashrut is a cornerstone of Jewish cooking for Jewish holidays. From Shabbat to Pesach and throughout the year, all involve culinary traditions and their own dietary laws. These are discussed in the next three chapters.

SHABBAT AND KASHRUT

THE TWENTY-FIRST CENTURY seems to be an era of overscheduling, whether we're single, married, with or without children. All week we rush—to classes or to work, dropping off kids at day care or school along the way, arranging pickups and after-school activities for children and for ourselves, home for a quick dinner, baths, bed. It seems there is barely time to think about and plan for all the things we need to do, let alone to get those things done, yet somehow everything works.

Monday through Thursday, my husband works late, usually arriving home after our children are in bed. I serve the kids one dinner, have my own separately, and then Jeffrey has his, usually after ten o'clock at night. But not on Friday night. Friday night is *Leil Shabbat*, the start of the Sabbath, and Shabbat dinner is the meal we all eat together, at the same time, in the same place, no matter what, often joined by friends.

Shabbat, the weekly Jewish day of rest, joins kashrut as a foundation of Jewish observance. Kashrut sanctifies the act of eating, something we do every day. Shabbat sanctifies time. Setting aside one day of the week that is dedicated to rest and spiritual contemplation sanctifies the week, both by honoring rest for itself and, in contrast, honoring the work we do on the other days of the week. Just as work makes us appreciate rest, Shabbat by itself has no meaning, if not different from the other days of the week.

Shabbat is connected to kashrut in other ways as well. Kashrut affects how we eat. Shabbat is a holiday full of celebratory meals—eating is one of the mitzvot of Shabbat. And there are rituals and restrictions associated with those meals.

As with kashrut, there are different ways to observe Shabbat. Your Jewish community and family will influence your choices in how you celebrate Shabbat. Halacha dictates very specific ways in which Shabbat is to be observed, including the types of activities that may or may not be done. Those who follow certain halachic laws of Shabbat are considered *shomer* or *shomrei Shabbat*, literally "keeper(s) of Shabbat." By using this phrase to describe yourself, you indicate that you don't travel, work, or perform various other prohibited activities on Shabbat. Orthodox and more observant Conservative Jews observe Shabbat in this way.

There are those who are not *shomer Shabbat*, who do cook, turn lights off and on, and so on, but still make the day a holy one, one set off from the week.

For decades the Reform movement eschewed most traditional Shabbat observances, but in the last thirty-five years, the movement has worked to reestablish some lost traditions. In 1972, they published *The Shabbat Manual*, which describes Shabbat as "a discipline and as a source of noble living." The Reform movement does not agree with all the work prohibitions of Shabbat, but recommends following any of the mitzvot of Shabbat you choose to do. In *Jewish Living*, Mark Washofsky writes, "No matter how 'Reform' our Judaism, it would be Jewishly unthinkable without the mitzvoth of Shabbat." He continues, "Shabbat is a day not to be treated as any other. It is not merely a day off; it is rather an expanse of time that is holy, different in quality and essence from all other days, consecrated both to God and to us for the purpose of our fulfillment as Jews. Reform Jews seek that fulfillment in different ways, but they will find it only when they commit themselves with the utmost seriousness to the Jewish responsibility to observe (*shamor*) the Sabbath day."

The Reconstructionist movement also stresses the importance of Shabbat. "Jewish time is lived, first and foremost, from Shabbat to Shabbat," write Rebecca T. Alpert and Jacob J. Staub in *Exploring Judaism: A Reconstructionist Approach*. "There is no greater gift than Shabbat. Shabbat means no work. Budgeted, inviolable time to sit at leisure with family and friends. . . . Communities of individuals who stop together to pray and study and sing and eat." Yet at the same time, the authors acknowledge that, in today's society, this is "easier said than done." To make an effort to observe some kind of Shabbat is important. "There are many points of entry," they write.

The Reform and Reconstructionist movements are relatively open when it comes to certain practices on Shabbat, and what kind of work is and is not permitted. This is not so much the case in Conservative and Orthodox Judaism, although there are many affiliated Conservative Jews who observe Shabbat in a more Reconstructionist manner. Some observant Conservative Jews find this a matter of apprehension. Isaac Klein writes in *A Guide to Jewish Religious Practice*, "Jewish life will not be restored to good health unless the Sabbath regains its sanctity and its central place." He differentiates Shabbat from the weekend, "At best the purpose of a weekend is rest and change. In the case of the Sabbath, however, the . . . day of rest must also become a day of holiness . . . The most important activities for the sanctification of the day are prayer and study."

The laws, rituals, and traditions of Shabbat are extensive, and encompass much more than food-related matters. However, since this is a book about kashrut, Jewish dietary laws, those are the Shabbat-related laws I shall discuss in this chapter.

There can be issues of kashrut regarding how you observe Shabbat. If you observe Shabbat in a halachic manner, you should not light a fire or start cooking food on Shabbat. Food that was cooked on Shabbat, even if accidentally, should not be eaten on Shabbat. Some Orthodox rabbis I spoke with said there could also be an issue as to the kashrut status of your kitchen if you are not *shomer Shabbat* after kashering your kitchen, so that is something to keep in mind when considering how you want to observe Shabbat.

As with kashrut, when determining how you want to celebrate Shabbat, consider who your friends are and the Jewish community you belong to. Just as there are Jews who observe a stricter level of kashrut and eat only in homes that observe a similar level, there are Jews who apply analogous standards regarding Shabbat observance.

The Shabbat Commandment

Shabbat. Shabbos. Shabbes. The Sabbath. Whatever the pronunciation or English spelling, the word comes from the Hebrew word for "rest," and refers to the seventh day of the week, the Jewish day of rest.

Keeping Shabbat is one of the Ten Commandments, but the historical basis for Shabbat comes long before then, at the very beginning of the Torah and of Creation. In **Genesis 2:2–3**, after spending six days creating the world, God rests on the seventh. *"And on the seventh day God finished His work which He had made; and He rested on the seventh day from all His work which He had made."* Not only that, God consecrates that rest, that shabbat—and the seventh day—creating the concept of Shabbat. *"And God blessed the* *seventh day, and hallowed it; because He rested on it from all His work which God in creating had made.*"

Shabbat is not mentioned again in Genesis. Much happens in terms of Jewish history—Noah and the flood, Abraham, Isaac, Jacob, Sarah, Rebecca, Rachel, Leah, Joseph, a move to Egypt, enslavement in Egypt—but there is no mention of Shabbat. It is not until the Jews are freed by God from their enslavement in Egypt and are wandering in the desert, that God introduces the concept of Shabbat to humankind.

In this way, Shabbat is associated with freedom. When we are free, we can work, and we can stop working when we choose, we can take a day off, an option that was not available to the Jews when they were slaves in Egypt. Similarly, when we are free, we have the freedom to keep kosher, to have control over the food we eat.

The first time the Israelites are told to observe Shabbat is directly in connection with food, when God gives them the miracle of the manna. In **Exodus 16,** the wandering Jews complain about being hungry, and God causes food to appear: quail at dusk and, in the morning, covered by dew, a unique bread called *manna.* But God offers it with a stipulation. The Israelites are to gather a prescribed amount of manna each day, and on the sixth day they are to collect twice as much. They are not initially told why. In **Exodus 16:22,** they follow those instructions: "*It happened on the sixth day they gathered twice as much bread, two omers for each one; and all the rulers of the congregation came and told Moses.*" Only after they do what they are told does Moses explain, in **Exodus 16:23,** "*This is what God has spoken. Tomorrow is a rest day, a holy Shabbat to God. Bake what you wish to bake and cook what you wish to cook, and whatever is left over put away for yourselves as safekeeping until the morning.*"

The Israelites of the desert generation did not exactly have a reputation for obedience, and perhaps the instructions about Shabbat had not been explicit enough. Moses said it was a day of rest for *God,* after all. He hadn't said anything about people. There were those who still went out the next day to gather the manna—but found nothing. God, annoyed, says, in **Exodus 16:28–30,** "*How long will you refuse to keep My commandments and My laws? See that the Lord has given you the Sabbath; that is why He gives you on the sixth day the bread of two days. Let every man remain in his place; let no man go out of his place on the seventh day.*" This time, "*The people rested on the seventh day.*"

So the Jewish people were already familiar with the concept of Shabbat when, four chapters later, God gives Moses the Ten Commandments. Again God is explicit in his intentions regarding Shabbat. In Commandment Four, **Exodus 20:8–10,** God says, "*Remember the Sabbath day, to sanctify it. Six days shall you labor, and do all your work; but* *the seventh day is a Sabbath unto the Lord your God; you shall not do any work, you, your son, nor your daughter, nor your slave, nor your maid-servant, nor your animals, nor your stranger that is within your gates; for in six days the Lord made heaven and earth, the sea, and all that is in them, and rested on the seventh day; therefore the Lord blessed the Sabbath day, and hallowed it."*

The Ten Commandments are listed twice in the Torah, first in Exodus and later in Deuteronomy. The commandment regarding Shabbat appears several times, not only in the list of Ten. This time, in Exodus, it carries the unique instruction *Zachor*, "Remember." The word "remember" is not used casually in the Torah, and this is the only time it is used directly in connection with Shabbat. To me, this has a few connotations. It is as if God is reminding the Israelites of the Shabbat they observed a few weeks ago, reminding them of that day on which they were instructed to behave differently from the preceding days. This is when a structured week begins for the Jewish people. It also is a subtle reminder that God freed them from Egypt; the last time the word *zachor* is used is in **Exodus 13:3,** when the Jews have just left Egypt: *"Remember this day, on which you came out from Egypt, out of the house of bondage."*

"Remember" also signifies a covenant, a promise. When God delivers Noah and the Ark onto dry land, he makes a rainbow, and says, in **Genesis 9:15,** *"I will remember My covenant, which is between Me and you and every living creature of all flesh; and the waters shall no more become a flood to destroy all flesh."*

The commandment of Shabbat is repeated in two more chapters in Exodus, but this time the commandment begins with *Shomer,* which means "Keep" or "Guard." Three separate times in **Exodus 31,** God declares, *"You shall keep the Sabbath."*

Again, when the Ten Commandments are repeated in Deuteronomy, "keep" rather than "remember" is the decree. Rashi notes that God had the ability to utter both words, *shamor* and *zachor*, simultaneously. **Deuteronomy 5:12–14** reiterates the Fourth Commandment with a few slight differences: *"Keep the Sabbath day and keep it holy, as the Lord your God commanded you."* In Exodus, God reminds the Jews of his Creation as part of the Fourth Commandment. In **Deuteronomy 5:15,** within the Fourth Commandment, God reminds the Jews of their redemption from Egypt, that in observing Shabbat, they should remember the might of God. *"And you shall remember that you were a slave in the land of Egypt, and the Lord your God brought you out from there with a mighty hand and by an outstretched arm; therefore the Lord your God commanded you to make the Sabbath day."*

There is one additional passage in the Tanach that shapes the way we observe

Shabbat today. **Isaiah 58:13–14** states, *"If you restrain your foot because of the Sabbath, from pursuing your business on My holy day; and call the Sabbath a delight, and the holy of the Lord, honorable; and shall honor it, not doing your wonted ways, nor pursuing your business, nor speaking thereof; then shall you delight yourself in the Lord, and I will make you to ride upon the high places of the earth, and I will feed you with the heritage of Jacob your father; for the mouth of the Lord has spoken it."* The key words here that are part of the mitzvot of Shabbat are *oneg,* "delight" or "be joyful," and *mechubad,* "honorable." We are to delight in and honor the Sabbath day. What better way to do this than with a meal? The Shabbat afternoon meal is sometimes called the *oneg.*

What is the difference between "remember" and "keep"? They refer to different aspects of how we observe Shabbat. *Zachor,* "remember," refers to what we *should* do on this day, the blessings and rituals of Shabbat. *Shamor,* "keep," refers to what we should *not* do on Shabbat, the activities we should refrain from doing, namely, the work.

What Is Work?

What is work? That is the question. Throughout the Torah, there are several different Hebrew words that are translated into English as "work." The Hebrew word for "work" in the Fourth Commandment is *melacha.* It is the only word that is used to describe work in relation to Shabbat. *Melacha* and variations on the word (e.g., plural, *melachot;* possessive, *melachto*) appear sixty-five times in the Torah. It is used both in reference to sublime activities such as creating the world, starting with the establishment of Shabbat, in **Genesis 2:2:** *"And on the seventh day God finished His **work** which He had made,"* and to more mundane situations, such as in **Leviticus 11:32:** *"Whatsoever vessel it be, wherewith any **work** is done."* The rabbis interpreted *melacha* to refer to creative work.

Each time God mentions the commandment of Shabbat, He reiterates the importance of not working, of resting.

In the Torah, God only specifies one type of work one should not perform on Shabbat, in **Exodus 35:3:** *"You shall not kindle fire throughout your dwellings on the Sabbath day."* Yet the Fourth Commandment specifies *"any manner of work."* So the rabbis of the Talmud looked to the text for further elaboration, not unlike the way they searched the text to understand the laws of *shechita* and those determining what types of birds can be kosher.

After God gives Moses the Ten Commandments in **Exodus 20,** He spends the next several chapters describing additional ordinances, including some dietary restrictions, which Moses writes down to tell the Children of Israel. In **Exodus 24,** God summons Moses again, to give him the rest of the Torah, and Moses disappears for forty days and forty nights. During this time, God begins with instructions on how to build the *Mishkan*, a portable sanctuary for the Israelites in the desert, *"That I may dwell among them."* The details of how to construct the *Mishkan* are very precise, from the dimensions and the type of wood to use, to the color of the cloth for priestly clothing. The instructions continue through **Exodus 31,** where, starting with verse 13, God reiterates the Shabbat commandment, twice emphasizing that no work should be done on Shabbat.

Unfortunately, while Moses is gone, the people are concerned that he has not returned, and they decide to make the infamous golden calf. They are in the midst of worshiping this idol when God tells Moses what the Israelites are doing, and Moses descends from Mount Sinai. Moses throws down the tablets he was carrying when he sees the actual idol-worshiping, and punishments ensue (including three thousand idolators killed). God calls Moses back to the mountaintop, and Moses is gone *again* for forty days and nights; this time the Children of Israel sit tight and idolless.

In **Exodus 35,** Moses descends from Mount Sinai once more, and immediately calls out to the Children of Israel, saying, in **Exodus 35:1,** *"These are the words which the Lord has commanded, that you should do them."* And the first thing he tells them is the commandment of Shabbat—where he left off just before the incident of the golden calf. Directly following this, Moses repeats the instructions on how the *Mishkan* should be built.

Now, you may be wondering—what's with all this information about the *Mishkan*? What's that got to do with Shabbat?

Everything.

Because it is the very description of the *Mishkan* that shapes all the laws about what constitutes the work we should not do on Shabbat.

From the double juxtaposition of the Shabbat Commandment with the description of the construction of the *Mishkan*, the rabbis concluded that the work, the *melachot*, forbidden on Shabbat must include all the types of tasks that the construction of the *Mishkan* encompassed, activities such as building or cutting materials to a certain size.

The word *melacha* has the same root as *melach, mem-lamed-aleph-chaf,* Hebrew for "angel" or "messenger from God." Perhaps this is another reason the rabbis determined that all the work that should not be done on Shabbat is that which was associated with building the *Mishkan*, with its altar to God.

The rabbis concluded that there are a total of thirty-nine different *melachot* that cannot be performed on Shabbat. Even though *melacha* means "work," when it is used in reference to Shabbat, it has come to mean "work that is forbidden on Shabbat." Eleven of the thirty-nine *melachot* are directly related to food preparation, including farming activities such as planting and harvesting.

How is food preparation related to the construction of the *Mishkan*? The concept of cooking as one of the thirty-nine *melachot* comes from the descriptions of the colored cloth to use. For example, **Exodus 35:25** states, *"And all the women that were wise-hearted did spin with their hands, and brought that which they had spun, the blue, and the purple, the scarlet, and the fine linen."* The rabbis reasoned, since no cloth is naturally blue, purple, or scarlet, it must be dyed those colors. Dye in those days was made from plants that were cooked in water to extract the colors. Therefore, all activities connected to the use of those plants counts as a *melacha*: plowing (*choresh*), sowing (*zoreah*), reaping (*kotzer*), bundling (*m'amair*), threshing (*dush*), winnowing (*zoreh*), selecting (*borer*), sifting (*miraked*), grinding (*tochen*), kneading (*lush*), and baking (*ofeh*).

There is another thought I had regarding cooking on Shabbat. As mentioned earlier, when the Children of Israel are first given Shabbat, before the Ten Commandments, in **Exodus 16,** they are told to prepare food on the sixth day in anticipation of the seventh day. Specifically, they are told to *"cook and bake,"* and both words are repeated twice. Just as they are told to gather twice as much manna on the sixth day, so too are they supposed to cook and bake twice as much food. They are cooking for two days, so there will be food for Shabbat. The implication, therefore, is that they should not cook or bake on the seventh day, but use the food already prepared. To me, this further supports the *Mishkan*-based *melacha* of cooking.

Each of the eleven food-related *melachot*, along with the injunction against kindling a fire during the Shabbat day, presents challenges in preparing the celebratory meals. And we need to understand exactly what the time constraints are for those activities.

The Sabbath Day

The Jewish theologian Abraham Joshua Heschel writes, "The meaning of the Sabbath is to celebrate time rather than space." Even this celebration of time must have parameters.

"The seventh day is a *palace in time* which we build," Heschel writes. But when is this time, when is Shabbat? The seventh day, yes, but when does that seventh day begin? When does it end?

In our modern secular calendar, the new day begins at midnight. But Jewish "days" start in the evening, based on the description of days in the story of Creation in **Genesis 1.** Each day, God created something (light and dark, sun, firmament, water, heavens, dry land . . .). The Torah concludes each day's work with the phrase *"And there was evening, and there was morning, the first day, . . . the second day, . . . the third day,"* and so on. Therefore, a day starts in the evening and continues through the next morning until the following evening.

Okay—but when exactly does "evening" begin? Specifically, when on Friday evening does Shabbat begin? When can you no longer kindle a fire? Evening begins at sunset, the rabbis determined—but what is sunset? This presents a more complex question than you might think. Because when the sun first disappears past the horizon, it is not really dark yet, a period referred to as *bein hash'mashot* (twilight, literally, "between the suns"). The sages debated the length of this time for centuries—through the Talmud, before and after the Shulchan Aruch, and beyond. Some said sunset is when the sun disappears over the horizon, others said sunset is only when it is totally dark.

Ultimately, sunset is defined as when the sun disappears below the horizon, even though it is not actually dark yet. The start of Shabbat is signified by the lighting of candles, and the practice today, the general conclusion, is that candles should be lit eighteen minutes before sunset. It is better to extend the time of Shabbat a little bit, rather than to shorten it inadvertently. (You could, in fact, light the candles even earlier; Shabbat restrictions begin once the candles are lit.)

Most Jewish calendars list candle-lighting times for several major American cities, and there are useful websites that calculate candle-lighting times based on zip code. The time depends on the latitude and longitude of your location, and modern databases make this "geocoding" calculation easy.

Shabbat is officially over when we can see three stars in the sky on Saturday evening. And, in the case of cloudy skies, there are calendars that indicate the exact time Shabbat is over in different geographical locations. Shabbat is concluded with a ceremony, *Havdalah*.

Shabbat Meals

Celebratory meals are an integral part of Shabbat. "Come over for Shabbat" means come over for a Shabbat meal. Everyone has their traditions, such as gefilte fish, roast chicken, potato kugel. "We always have this on Shabbat," someone will assert. "*This* is our Shabbat specialty," someone else will say. Food as part of Shabbat is more than tradition—it is one of the mitzvot of Shabbat.

The Shulchan Aruch states that we should eat three meals on Shabbat. This is based on the first time the Israelites are introduced to the concept of Shabbat, in Exodus, when they are told to gather enough manna for two days on the sixth day. **Exodus 16:25** explains, *"And Moses said: 'Eat that* **today**; *for* **today** *is a Sabbath unto the Lord;* **today** *you shall not find it in the field."* Because the word *hayom,* "today," is repeated three times in connection with the word "eat," the rabbis concluded that we should have three meals on Shabbat. Since Shabbat begins at sundown, the first meal is the Friday night dinner, the meal that welcomes Shabbat.

The Talmud describes stories of rabbis finding a particularly special morsel during the week and setting it aside, saving it for the Shabbat meal. Nowadays, at least in the affluent United States, all manner of "superior" foods are available all the time. Even so, we need to plan a special menu in advance, and purchase food for it accordingly. Shabbat dinner is not a spontaneous last-minute, let's-see-what's-in-the-fridge kind of meal.

I start thinking about what I am going to make early in the week, shopping in advance, menu planning, determining if guests will be joining us. Sharing a Shabbat meal with friends is a mitzvah, the mitzvah of *hachnasat orechim*, welcoming guests for a meal.

The second Shabbat meal is usually a big luncheon served after services at synagogue on Saturday afternoon, sometimes called the *kiddush*, which comes from the word "sanctify." *Se'udah shlishit*, literally, "third meal," is usually a smaller meal eaten shortly before Havdalah. When I was growing up, we would go to synagogue late Saturday afternoon for *mincha* (afternoon) services. We'd then partake of a simple *se'udah shlishit* replete with joyous *zmirot*, "songs," followed by Havdalah services. It was a meaningful way to mark the end of Shabbat and the beginning of a new week.

What's Cooking?

The mitzvah of festive meals is a great idea in theory; in practice, it requires days of planning, every week. Not only because the Shabbat meal should be a celebratory meal, one that features different foods from the food you have during the rest of the week. But also there is the added challenge of advance preparation, of coordinating cooking and serving hot food with the injunction against kindling a fire and cooking once Shabbat begins. Somehow, a cold Shabbat meal just doesn't seem as festive as one featuring warm food.

The tradition of warm food for Shabbat meals dates to Talmudic times. Having various Jewish affiliations is not a modern convention. During the first century before the Common Era, when the Oral Law was indeed still oral, there were those Jews, the Sadducees, who believed only in the Torah—the Written Law. They would not follow any interpretation made in the Oral Law, the Talmud. They decreed that the commandment against kindling a flame meant that no flame could burn at all during Shabbat. The Pharisees, another sect, were determined to put the joy in Shabbat, as recounted by Isaiah, and concluded that a flame lit *before* Shabbat began could continue to burn and could be used to keep food warm for Shabbat. Ultimately, the followers of the Talmud prevailed, and having warm food on Shabbat serves as a reminder of the importance of the Talmud.

The most significant *melachot* related to Shabbat meal preparations are cooking and kindling or extinguishing a flame, and they present the kashrut challenge of Shabbat.

Once the Shabbat candles are lit, no more cooking can be done, although meal preparations invariably continue, such as putting out salads, setting the table, and so on. And food that began cooking before Shabbat started can continue to cook.

So, how do you have a hot meal Friday night, not to mention Saturday afternoon? How can you have your steaming cuppa in the morning before shul, without cooking, without lighting a fire? There are ways. Elaborate, well-conceived ways.

Cooking, by halachic definition, means food plus heat, heat as in *yad soledet bo*—so hot your hand would recoil from the temperature in less than fifteen seconds. Preparing a cold salad is not cooking. Roasting, frying, boiling, grilling, and baking are cooking.

As I mentioned earlier, cooking is not the only food-related *melacha*. Other *melachot* directly affect food preparation:

Sifting (*miraked*) means passing ingredients through a screen, which includes flour, as well as straining liquids, such as pouring broth through a sieve.

Threshing (*dush*) means separating an item from its natural container, such as wheat from the chaff. This includes cracking open nuts and squeezing fresh juice from fruit.

Grinding (*tochen*) includes coffee and pepper (no fresh-ground pepper on your salad). The meaning has been extended to include grating, such as with cheese and vegetables, although cutting and chopping are permitted.

Kneading (*lush*) includes combining liquid and dry ingredients to make a paste. This precludes making something such as instant pudding, even if no heat is involved. It also includes kneading bread.

Selecting (*borer*) means separating the inedible parts of food from the edible—such as removing the bones from fish, which led to the creation of boneless gefilte fish as a traditional Shabbat dish. If you have a bowl of fruit, such as berries, you can't pick out and remove the bad berries. However, you can pick out and eat only the good berries.

The foregoing restrictions are relatively easy to deal with before Shabbat. You can grind pepper in advance, pick out the bones and make gefilte fish the day before, and sift the flour and knead the challah long before Shabbat begins. The real challenge is cooking. Having food be warm for the meal—that cannot be done in advance. While you cannot kindle a flame (i.e., turn on the stove) once Shabbat begins, and you cannot *begin* cooking after Shabbat starts, a stove turned on *before* Shabbat can stay on, and food that started cooking before Shabbat can continue to cook after Shabbat begins. There are specifics about Shabbat food preparation that make warm meals possible.

Over the millennia, the rabbis both in ancient times and today developed halachically acceptable methods to have warm food without violating the commandments not to cook on Shabbat. Nowadays it is much easier to prepare warm food for Shabbat, with timers and electrical appliances that can be set to start or turn off after Shabbat begins. A coffeemaker with a timer enables you to have hot coffee on Shabbat morning. Slow cookers enable you to have hot soup Friday night, or a warm *cholent* for Shabbat afternoon. Also, having your own appliance-filled kitchen (as opposed to communal ovens and such) makes food preparation *much* easier!

The Vocabulary of Shabbat Cooking

Shabbat cooking has its own vocabulary.

In brief, key terms are **bishul,** cooking; **shehiya,** leaving food on a heat source where it is cooking; and **chazara,** returning food to a heat source where it had been cooking. **Hagasa** refers to stirring. A **blech** is a metal covering that goes over your cooktop burners.

Kli rishon, literally, "first vessel," is the pot in which food is cooked. **Kli sheni,** "second vessel," is a container into which you might pour the contents of a *kli rishon*. And **kli shlishi,** "third vessel," is the container into which you might pour the contents of a *kli sheni*. These terms are relevant to Shabbat and kashrut in that food in the *kli rishon* is considered cooked, but food in the *kli sheni* has less heat, since the sides of the container were cool to begin with, so it might not be considered a cooking vessel.

There can be great complexities and variations and special cases involving all these terms. If you have any specific questions, check with your rabbi.

Bishul

Bishul literally means cooking, and is used as a catch-all word to include baking, frying, boiling, grilling, and roasting. In other words, *bishul* means changing the properties of food by applying heat. It is forbidden to start cooking *after* Shabbat begins. However, you can start food cooking *before* Shabbat, and the food can continue cooking on Shabbat. You can also attach a cooking appliance, such as a coffeemaker, to a timer that will turn it on at a set time as long as you yourself are not starting the actions of cooking after Shabbat begins. You can leave burners and the oven on, but they need to be covered. You can also use a hot plate and a slow cooker, such as a Crock-Pot.

Issues of *bishul* also involve the vessel in which the food is cooked, as in the various *kli* situations previously described. This can involve brewing coffee or tea. If you pour heated water onto a teabag from a *kli rishon* into a *kli sheni*, some say *bishul* does not occur; others feel a *kli shlishi* is necessary. The jury is out on this one, and it depends on your level of observance. Check with your rabbi on the matter of coffee and tea preparation.

Shehiya

Alert readers may notice this resembles the term used in reference to *shechita. Shehiya* literally means "delay" or "interruption." In *shechita, shehiya* refers to the act of pausing midslaughter. Delaying, dragging out the slaughtering process, is forbidden.

In the case of Shabbat food preparation, *shehiya* refers to a pause in that preparation, pause meaning extension, extending the time it may take to cook a dish so that the food can be ready and warm for Shabbat.

This permitted extension starts from a prohibition. The rabbinic rule is that you cannot leave a pot of food that is not done cooking on the flame where it was cooking once Shabbat begins. In times of hearths, the concern was that you may be tempted to stir the coals under the fire, effectively kindling more flames while speeding up the cooking process.

The halachic rule of *shehiya*, made when people had hearths rather than gas and electric cooktops, stated that leaving a pot directly on the flames was a no-no. But because of that temptation to stir the embers, if you covered those flames with ashes, thereby preventing the stoking of the fire, you could leave the pot over the diminished heat.

However, we no longer cook with wood and fuel (I'm not talking about outdoor grills here). We have cooktops with individual burners, whose flames or heat is controlled with a knob. There are two actions that are modern-day equivalents to hiding the flame with ashes that must be implemented in order not to violate the rabbinical prohibition of *shehiya*.

The first is to cover your lit burners with a *blech*. No, it doesn't mean yucky. *Blech* is Yiddish for "tin," and it is a rectangular piece of metal shaped like an inverted cookie pan that fits over two or four cooktop burners. (They are available by mail or at Judaica stores.) You could also use a Flame Tamer or heat diffuser, a round metal plate that fits over a single burner. (Note: Glass cooktops may crack if covered by a *blech* or heat diffuser; check with your rabbi on how to use a glass cooktop on Shabbat.) The *blech* fulfills the tradition of covering the flames with ashes.

However, since you don't really adjust the gas flame or electrical coil directly by stirring the embers, as in days of yore, what you really need to cover are the cooktop control knobs, the modern-day equivalent of stirrable embers, the fuel source, as it were. Use visible tape to cover the knobs so that there will be no inadvertent flame-adjusting.

Not all food left on the stove requires a *blech*, only food that is not fully cooked. Food that is almost raw before Shabbat begins needs a *blech*, because this is food that you would be most tempted to attend to by adjusting the flame. Food that is partially cooked does not need a *blech*.

What is "partially cooked" food? Not surprisingly, there is more than one definition of "partially cooked." In defining such food, the rabbis of the Talmud immortalized a famous contemporary robber, known as Ben Drosai. One of the stories that circulated regarding Ben Drosai was that he only had enough time to cook his food until it was just barely edible, since he was always on the run. Ever since, food partially prepared before Shabbat begins is called *maachal Ben Drosai*, literally, Ben Drosai's food. How cooked is "barely edible"? Rashi determined that, in order for food to be considered partially cooked for Shabbat, one-third cooked is enough; Rambam declared that one-half cooked is required.

Although you technically *can* leave food that meets the Ben Drosai cooking requirement on an uncovered burner, this falls under the category of "permissible but not recommended." It is a good idea to cover the burner with a *blech,* especially if you have a gas stove, purely for safety's sake. (I get nervous at the thought of an uncovered, untended flame burning overnight, as you cannot extinguish a lit flame either.) There is also the issue of **michaze k'mevashel,** literally, "appearance of cooking." Someone passing by might see the food cooking on an uncovered stove and get the impression you were cooking on Shabbat in the traditional manner of cooking, thereby violating Shabbat.

If you have food on the cooktop that is not *maachal Ben Drosai,* but rather is barely cooked before Shabbat begins, you also cannot stir the food. Stirring is called **hagasa,** and it is forbidden because stirring affects the speed at which the food cooks, so you would effectively be actively cooking the food if you stirred the pot.

The point of a *blech* is to allow you to start cooking raw or inedible food right before Shabbat begins. This is more likely to happen in the winter, when Shabbat starts early. You may not be ready to eat immediately when the sun sets at four in the afternoon. If you make a slow-simmering stew, you can put it on the *blech* just before lighting the candles in order for it to be ready to eat a couple hours later. Note: Once the candles are lit, it is traditional not to eat anything until the Shabbat meal begins.

Chazara

Literally, *chazara* means "returning," and this refers to the prohibition of returning a pot of food to the cooktop (or oven) once it has been removed. Again, the issue is *michaze k'mevashel,* that someone may think you are starting to cook food after Shabbat begins. There are ways around this prohibition. You can remove a pot from the cooktop and return it to the heat source under the following conditions:

- The food must have started out being on top of a *blech.*
- The flame must still be covered with a *blech.*
- The food is completely cooked and retains its heat.
- You intended to return the pot when you removed it.
- You did not put the pot down on any surface and held it the entire time (indicative of your intention to return the pot to the *blech*-covered flame).

A more lenient, *mekil,* ruling states that the pot may be returned directly to the *blech;* a stricter, *machmir,* ruling indicates that you can put the removed pot on top of another pot that is resting on the *blech,* clearly demonstrating that you are not cooking food in the normal manner.

Another kind of *chazara* is heating up cold food, such as food that has been refrigerated overnight. Solid foods—for example, potato kugel—can be reheated because there is no such thing as *bishul acharei bishul,* "cooking after cooking."

Since something that has already been cooked cannot technically be recooked, you can reheat the kugel on a hot plate or *blech* (as long as the heating element of it was in place before Shabbat began). However, you can't apply a different *type* of cooking to an already cooked food because then you might be creating something new. You can't boil something that has been roasted, or fry something that has been baked. For example, you can't add heated water to a powdered vegetable soup with dehydrated vegetables. Those vegetables were baked; now you would be boiling them and creating something new.

Different rules apply to liquids; you can't, for example, heat water that has been boiled and then cooled down. Liquid food, on the other hand, such as soup, cannot be reheated, because heating up the cold liquid is like a cooking anew. In-between foods, such as a liquidy stew, are generally regarded as solids, but can be controversial. If you want to be certain of the practice in your community, check with your rabbi.

Oven Rules

The rules regarding cooking on a cooktop and in an oven are ostensibly the same, but there are more challenges when it comes to an oven.

The first challenge may be easy to sidestep, depending on the oven you have. Turning a light off and on, according to Orthodox dictates, is forbidden on Shabbat, as it is akin to lighting a flame. Some ovens have a light that goes on automatically when you open the door; simply disable that light. Some, on the other hand, have an electric temperature-indicator light that goes on when you open the door, and this can be more difficult to disable. If this is an issue for you, and you can purchase a new oven, kosher certifying organizations such as Star-K have data indicating the best types of ovens to purchase for easiest use on Shabbat.

Further, most ovens have a thermostat that regulates the temperature. When you open the oven door, the loss of heat may cause the oven thermostat to fuel the oven, effectively kindling a flame. Check with your rabbi if this is an issue. Stricter observance prohibits removing something from an oven and returning it; more lenient observance allows the same exceptions that are permitted for a cooktop.

Shabbat Meal Preparation

The fact is, Shabbat preparation can be anything *but* relaxing, even if you don't observe the prohibitions against cooking once Shabbat begins. Any special meal requires advance planning, and a special meal on a work night is that much more challenging. Yet, no matter how much time I've spent in preparing the meal, ultimately it always feels worthwhile because the Friday night meal is the meal I most enjoy. I try to make extra food, so that we can benefit from the leftovers on Shabbat afternoon the next day.

Preparing for Shabbat requires scheduling forethought. Traditionally, this has been the domain of women, as women were in charge of all cooking in a traditional Jewish household, and tended not to work outside the home. Today, many kosher households have two people working full time outside the home; a shared responsibility in preparing for Shabbat makes for a more relaxing time for all involved. But regardless of how or if you divvy up the work, advance preparation is necessary.

Part of the Shabbat meal challenge can be preparing two meals at once, since traditionally the second of the three required meals is also supposed to be a feast. (By the time you get to the third meal, you'll have been eating so much, you won't need anything elaborate; the third meal usually is simple and often served cold.)

Getting the kitchen ready for Shabbat is like a miniature kashering, with various steps needed to set up for the *melachot* that can't be done once Shabbat starts. If you choose not to use electricity, according to Orthodoxy, this includes unscrewing the light inside your refrigerator, which comes on automatically every time you open the door. You need to set timers for lights and food that will be timed, to set up the *blech* on your stovetop, start the food in the slow cooker if you're using it, and so on.

And then—Shabbat arrives, and all the prep work comes to a head. We greet the meal with songs, we light and bless the candles, and the meal begins.

Erev Shabbat Meal

I have been planning and cooking Shabbat meals since I was twelve or thirteen. When I was growing up, my parents both worked, so my younger brother, Avi, and I cooked dinner four nights a week, alternating turns to prepare the Shabbat meal for Friday night. Friday morning before we left for school, we would take an uncooked frozen challah from the freezer and set it on a pan to rise. When we got home, the soft, swollen challah would go in the oven, and we'd start the dinner preparations.

Today, I haven't relinquished the entire responsibility of Shabbat-dinner making to my children, but the whole family is involved in the preparation of the table and setting up for the meal.

Every family has their Shabbat dinner traditions, but even so, there seem to be universal foods everyone enjoys and even expects for Shabbat dinner. There is also a Shabbat *seder*, which means "order," similar to the Pesach seder. We light candles to indicate symbolically the beginning of the holiday. We sing songs, bless children, make a kiddush, a prayer that begins by quoting the description of the first Shabbat in Genesis. We wash our hands. We bless the challah and eat it, indicating the beginning of our celebratory meal.

Traditional Shabbat foods may vary from community to community, and from family to family. When I was growing up, my family had a tradition of serving apple butter to spread on the challah, a treat we enjoyed much more than pareve margarine. We rarely had it the rest of the week. We would pick up a lemon-meringue pie from Danny's kosher bakery. Our Friday night meals now begin with a snack of pistachio nuts or olives, or a special cheese.

Regardless of your personal Shabbat traditions, there are two food elements that are universal: wine and bread, specifically, challah.

WINE

Wine is used ceremonially for many Jewish celebrations, even when not part of a meal. It represents the joyousness of the holiday. Kosher wine should be used for the Shabbat kiddush. The word *kiddush* comes from the same root as "holy" or "sanctification."

We use special kiddush cups for our wine, and a tradition in our family has developed around those cups. We have the family kiddush cup, a silver cup given to us on our wedding that we also use at the conclusion of Shabbat, as part of the Havdalah ceremony. Each of our three children has his or her own small personalized kiddush cup, which was given to them by their Great-Aunt Eve. Eve was the oldest sister of my husband's Bubbe, and her custom was to give kiddush cups as a birth gift to all in the generation of her great-grandchildren. She lived until a week before her 104th birthday. This way we are reminded of this transgenerational family connection each Shabbat.

Sweet wine is the kiddush wine of choice. Not exactly wine for the connoisseur, but the sweetness seems appropriate for welcoming in the holiday.

CHALLAH

Challah actually has two meanings, when it comes to the Jewish dietary laws. One refers to its ceremonial use, described in the chapter on Kosher Foods, in the section on bread; it is a reminder of a priestly ceremony. The most well-known meaning, of course, is the challah bread we eat on Friday night.

Bread is symbolic of a meal, and no Jewish meal is considered a *meal* (as opposed to a snack) without bread. Since the Shabbat meal is an exceptional one, the bread served should be special. Basic bread can be made simply with flour, yeast, and water; the Shabbat challah is enriched with eggs, oil, and a sweetener.

The first meal of Shabbat starts with two *challot*. Two loaves represent the double portion of manna offered in the desert on Shabbat. Sometimes this isn't so practical, as your family may not actually eat the two challot and you don't want to waste food. Some people have one large and one small loaf. Some kosher bakeries make so-called kiddush loaves that are medium-sized.

The word *challah* is used in the Torah only twelve times, each time in reference to a special bread (or "cake," as it is also translated) used as part of a ceremonial offering. Calling the bread we bless at the beginning of Shabbat *challah* recalls the sanctity of that biblical bread.

Like many traditions, challah as part of the Shabbat ceremony feels ancient, but the bread we know as challah dates back probably to the fifteenth century, according to culinary historian John Cooper in *Eat and Be Satisfied: A Social History of Jewish Food.* Cooper found references to challah from that period, and references that called the bread consumed on Friday night *berches.* The etymology of this word, which appeared in Germany, is vague, though a likely source is the Hebrew word *bracha* or *birkat,* "blessing."

Cholent

Another part of the Shabbat meal challenge is preparing two meals at once, since traditionally the second of the three required meals is also supposed to be a feast. *Cholent* is a slow-cooking stew that has been made for centuries (Cooper cites a reference dating to the 1200s), usually for Shabbat afternoon lunch. Cholent is a rib-sticking one-pot meal, usually a combination of barley, beans, potatoes, other root vegetables, and pieces of meat.

The name *cholent* may be related to an Old French word (Modern French *chaud*) meaning "hot," perhaps combined with *lent,* slow. Cholent is cooked slowly, over low heat, so you can have warm food on Shabbat, and in past years it was made in a pot left overnight on the ash-covered embers of the hearth. Today, slow cookers such as Rival's Crock-Pot are indispensable for Shabbat preparations. You can set them up in the morning so as to have hot, steaming soup for the *Shabbat* evening meal, and you can get them started just before Shabbat begins for a Saturday afternoon hot meal. If your slow cooker has an adjustable knob (and most do with High and Low settings), you need to put tape over this knob too, as with the stovetop knobs, to avoid the prohibition of *shehiya*.

A slow cooker is an effective modern-day Shabbat cooking tool, since it can take six to fourteen hours to cook a particular dish. Food can be put in it before sundown on Friday night and left to finish cooking overnight, so that a hot meal can be enjoyed after synagogue on Saturday afternoon.

Similarly, you can plug in a coffeepot or hot-water heater and have hot drinks on Shabbat. However some *machmir* interpretations find that transferring the water from a coffeepot is akin to the pouring from a *kli rishon* into a *kli sheni*, and, with coffee and tea, this may count as cooking. The *machmir* practice is to then pour the water into a *kli shlishi*, which would effectively avoid *bishul*, cooking, but you should check with your rabbi.

Havdalah

Havdalah is the ceremonial conclusion of Shabbat. The word *Havdalah* comes from the root "differentiate." This is when we differentiate between Shabbat and the rest of the week. We begin Shabbat by lighting candles; so, too, we end Shabbat by once more lighting a candle, the first since we lit the Shabbat candles welcoming the day of rest more than twenty-four hours before.

The Havdalah candle is a special braided candle that should have at least two wicks, as the blessing for this candle is different from the blessing for Shabbat candles. The Shabbat blessing concludes, *vitzivanu lihadlik ner shel Shabbat*, "who has commanded us to light the candle of Shabbat." In contrast, the Havdalah candle blessing concludes, *borei m'orei ha'esh*, "who has created the lights of the fire." Because the plural "lights" is used, the Havdalah candle should have more than one wick. Standard Havdalah candles are braided wax ropes of blue and white, usually with four wicks; some have as many as twelve. This can be beautifully symbolic, the coming together of many flames into one, the individual as part of a family or community, the connection to the light of Creation, the integration of Shabbat with the rest of the week.

The only light comes from the multiwicked Havdalah candle. We bless and sip wine, smell sweet spices that remind us of the sweetness of Shabbat. We note the contrast between the candlelight and the surrounding darkness, between Shabbat and the rest of the week. And then we extinguish the flame in the wine, turn on the lights, and are ready to start the next week, renewed and refreshed.

KASHRUT THROUGH THE YEAR: THE JEWISH HOLIDAYS

SHABBAT IS OUR WEEKLY HOLIDAY, but there are also holidays throughout the year. These fall under a few categories. Several holidays are described in the Torah. Others are described elsewhere in the Tanach. And some are modern additions to the calendar. Most holidays have dietary laws or culinary traditions.

The Jewish calendar is not the same as the secular January-through-December calendar, called the Gregorian calendar. The names of the months are different, and the basis and the structure of the calendar itself are different.

The Jewish Year

The Jewish calendar can be confusing. According to the Gregorian calendar, dates of various holidays are the same every year. New Year's Day is always January 1. Independence Day is always July 4. In the Jewish calendar, the Jewish New Year is sometimes in early September, sometimes at the end of that month, sometimes in early October. The Jewish holidays *do* fall on the same date every year—the date in the Jewish calendar, which does not directly correspond with the Gregorian calendar. Since most people in this country follow the Gregorian calendar, we need a Jewish calendar to know when to celebrate our holidays.

The Jewish calendar is *lunisolar*—that is, based both on the cycle of the moon and on the tropical year—the time that passes between spring equinoxes, which is the cycle of the earth around the sun and the basis for the Gregorian calendar. The cycle of the earth around the sun is roughly 365 days. The cycle of the moon around the earth is roughly 29.5 days; twelve lunar months are roughly 354 days. To make up for that roughness in the Gregorian calendar, we add an extra day to February every four years. To make up for that roughness in the Jewish calendar, we add an extra month every few years.

In the Jewish calendar, the months are based on the cycle of the moon. The moon waxes and wanes, becoming full midway through the lunar month. If you see a full moon, you know invariably that it is the fifteenth of the Hebrew month. There are twelve Hebrew months, which run alternately twenty-nine or thirty days (to compensate for the half day in the lunar month). Certain months gain or lose a day some years, depending on when certain holidays fall, yielding a year that varies in length from 353 to 355 days. Leap years, however, are longer.

If the calendar were solely lunar, the seasons in which the Jewish months occurred would change over time, falling ten to twelve days earlier each year. After a decade, Pesach would be a winter holiday, and Rosh Hashanah would be celebrated at the beginning of the summer. But the Jewish holidays are tied in with the seasons—Pesach being a spring holiday, Sukkot celebrating the last harvest in the fall. To stay coordinated with the seasons, the Jewish calendar adds an extra month every few years, based on a nineteen-year cycle; these are leap years and range in length from 383 to 385 days. Nineteen years is the time it takes for the lunar year and the solar year to coincide. Over a nineteen-year cycle, the leap years occur seven times, on the third, sixth, eighth, eleventh, fourteenth, seventeenth, and nineteenth years. Those years, the intercalary month is a second Adar. Adar Aleph (Adar I) is considered the extra month, even though it comes first. Adar Bet (Adar II) is the month during which all full-scale Adar holidays fall—notably Purim.

Because of the periodic leap year, the corresponding Gregorian calendar dates of Jewish holidays (the dates we look at because the Gregorian calendar is the one most commonly used) can vary by as much as a month, while still staying in the same season. This is why sometimes Rosh Hashanah falls in September, sometimes in October.

It actually gets a little more complicated. The year length varies based on when the first of Tishri (Rosh Hashanah) is to be celebrated. Rosh Hashanah cannot fall on a Sunday, Wednesday, or Friday because this would affect the day when two other holidays occur, Yom Kippur and Hoshanah Rabbah. The fast day of Yom Kippur must not fall on a Friday or a Sunday because we shouldn't have two days in a row with restrictions. Hoshanah Rabbah, which is celebrated at the end of Sukkot, cannot fall on Shabbat because the *melachot* of Shabbat preclude properly observing this holiday.

The Jewish months (and their length), in the order they are used today, are Tishri (thirty days), Heshvan (twenty-nine or thirty days), Kislev (twenty-nine or thirty days), Tevet (twenty-nine days), Shvat (thirty days), Adar [Aleph] (thirty days), Adar [Bet] (twenty-nine days), Nisan (thirty days), Iyar (twenty-nine days), Sivan (thirty days), Tammuz (twenty-nine days), Av (thirty days), and Elul (twenty-nine days). These names come from the time of the Babylonian exile; in the Torah, the months are usually called "the first month," "the seventh month," and so on. In books of the Tanach, however, certain months are named.

Ah, but what is the first month? How do the months correspond to the Babylonian-named months? In the Talmud, there was a showdown between Tishri and Nisan, when Pesach is observed. One conclusion was that Tishri was considered the first month until the Exodus; after the Exodus, Nisan was considered the first month. Some say the first of Nisan is the new year for festivals, while the first of Tishri is the new year for counting years, akin to the fiscal year, which starts on a different date from the calendar year. The current Jewish calendar, the one used today, was established around the fourth century C.E. This calendar starts with Tishri as the first month of the year.

Sources of the Chagim

The Hebrew word for holiday is *chag*. The same root means "go round," indicative of the cyclical nature of the holiday year. I mentioned earlier there are a few different types of holidays, and the different types have certain dietary rules.

The Torah describes the following holidays: Shabbat, Pesach, Sfirat Ha'Omer, Shavuot, Rosh Hashanah, Yom Kippur, Sukkot, and Shemini Atzeret. Later, the Tanach mentions Purim and five fast days, including Tzom Gedalia, the Tenth of Tevet, Ta'anit Ester, the Seventeenth of Tammuz, and Tisha B'Av. Then there are postbiblical holidays, including Simchat Torah, Chanukah, Tu B'Shvat, and modern holidays such as Yom Ha'Aztmaut, Israel Independence Day.

Some holidays are mere celebrations, some are days of fasting, some are *"Yom Tov"* festivals, and some include a mix. The holidays described in the Torah are the ones that have the most significant dietary rules.

Fast Days and Fasting

Fasting is indirectly an element of kashrut; the requirement to abstain from food is effectively a dietary law. On Jewish fast days, we neither eat nor drink, for a set amount of time.

There are a total of six public fast days during the Jewish year. There are others, according to some traditions, but these six are the public fasts that have been observed at least since Talmudic times. The six fasts fall into three categories: *teshuvah* (repentance), as on Yom Kippur; *avelut* (mourning), mourning a tragic event in Jewish history, such as Tisha B'Av, which recalls the destruction of the Temple in Jerusalem; and *bakasha*, fasting as a way of making a request, as was done by Queen Esther in the story of Purim. These categories are not set in stone and can overlap.

Yom Kippur and Tisha B'Av are full-day fasts, starting before sunset and continuing through the next sunset. The other four fasts last from sunrise to sunset. There are a few more minor fasts that do not apply to everyone, such a the Fast of the Firstborn, undertaken just before Pesach. Traditionally, a bride and a groom fast on their wedding day, breaking the fast together after the ceremony.

Four fasts are referred to in **Zachariah 8:19,** *"Thus said the Lord of Hosts: The fast of the fourth [month], and the fast of the fifth, and the fast of the seventh, and the fast of the tenth, shall be to the house of Judah joy and gladness, and cheerful seasons; therefore love truth and peace."* These fasts were determined to be the Seventeenth of Tammuz (Fast of the Fourth Month), Tisha B'Av (Fast of the Fifth, in Av), Tzom Gedaliah (Fast of the Seventh, in Tishri), and the Tenth of Tevet (Fast of the Tenth), all of them involving the destruction of the Temple and Jerusalem. This passage in Zechariah expresses hope for a time when fasts will be transformed into feasts, into "cheerful seasons."

Why fast at all? The tragic events are over, we've already been rescued from the fate Haman wished upon us, Jews are living independently in Israel, why should we fast on days other than Yom Kippur?

The fasting that we do now can help lead to that time of redemption, according to *Sichos in English* (an online publication produced by the Lubavitch movement), which elaborates: "The transformation of these communal fasts depends on *teshuvah* [repentance], which transforms evil into good. *Teshuvah* is not bounded by time. Therefore on the communal fasts, our people are able to atone for misdeeds committed in previous generations, even those, like the assassination of Gedaliah, which were carried out in the distant past."

In *How to Run a Traditional Jewish Household,* Blu Greenberg writes, "Fasting, then, and the feelings of grief it crystallizes are a testimony to the power of memory. Through the process of remembering, we can never let ourselves become reconciled to defeat and destruction. . . . Memory is protest, memory is activism, memory is the incredible power to turn grief and destruction into hope."

Yom Tov Chagim

All the Jewish holidays, both biblical and modern, have associated traditions, some involving ordinances, some involving prayers, some involving food and food preparation. When the Torah describes holidays such as Rosh Hashanah, the word *Shabbaton* is used, implying that the holidays should be observed in a manner similar to Shabbat. These days are now referred to as *Yom Tov*—literally, "Good Day"—or *yontif* in Yiddish. As with Shabbat, the beginning of a *Yom Tov* is marked by lighting candles.

The number of *Yom Tov* days differs in Israel and the Diaspora, the rest of the world. Most *Yom Tov* holidays are celebrated an extra day outside of Israel. This dates back to the monthly biblical observance of Rosh Chodesh. Literally "head of the month," Rosh Chodesh was an important day, because keeping track of each month was essential to celebrating the holidays at the proper time. The months were lunar based, and the Jews counted on reliable witnesses in Jerusalem who had seen the new moon to know when each month ended and began.

That information was then disseminated by messengers to the rest of the country. This took time. To avoid any uncertainty that they might have missed the first day of a holiday, it was decreed that everyone outside of Jerusalem should celebrate the holidays for two days. Today that custom continues, with all of Israel standing in for Jerusalem. The exception is Rosh Hashanah, which is celebrated for two days everywhere. In the days when the new moon was determined by witnesses, no one could be sure in advance what day would be the first of Tishri. On the other hand, because a month is about 29.5 days, they would know in advance from the date of the previous Rosh Chodesh the only two days that were possibilities for Rosh Hashanah. The tradition of celebrating Rosh Hashanah for two days in Israel continued even after the calender was established in advance through calculations rather than through monthly sightings. Because of the fasting required on Yom Kippur, it is celebrated for only one day everywhere, as are the other fast days.

Yom Tov holidays and restrictions include the two days of Rosh Hashanah, the first two days of Sukkot (just the first day in Israel), Shemini Atzeret and Simchat Torah (observed together on one day in Israel), the first two and last two days of Pesach (just the first day and the last day in Israel), and the two days of Shavuot (just one day in Israel). The Reform movement traditionally has celebrated all *Yom Tov* holidays for one day, including Rosh Hashanah, although this is now changing in many congregations.

Yom Tov holidays have similar restrictions to Shabbat, with some exceptions, regarding food preparation. Cooking is permitted. According to Orthodox tenets, you cannot *ignite* a fire, but you can light something from an existing flame, and you can adjust a flame, although you cannot extinguish it on *Yom Tov*. There are mixed opinions concerning electric appliances, although the majority rule is against their use, including electric ovens; check with your rabbi.

If you have a gas stove with an automatic pilot light, this counts as remaining lit; on the other hand, if you have one that is lit electronically, check with your rabbi. Although a *blech* is not required, since you are allowed to cook, you may want to put it on the stovetop for safety's sake.

According to Conservative rules, you may turn your stove off and on, regardless of whether it is electric or gas, and you may use electric appliances on *Yom Tov*.

For both Orthodox and Conservative followers, cooking is allowed on *Yom Tov*, within certain parameters. This is based on **Exodus 12:16,** *"And on the first day there shall be to you a holy convocation, and on the seventh day a holy convocation; no manner of work shall be done on them, save that which every person must eat, that only may be done by you."* This passage refers to Pesach, but it also applies to other *Yom Tov* holidays.

Eruv Tavshilin

The restrictions for cooking on *Yom Tov* are that you can cook on that day—but only for that day. Since most holidays are two days, you can't cook food for the second day on the first day.

There is a special challenge when there are two days of *Yom Tov* followed by Shabbat, with no break in between. (This happened one year at Pesach, when my parents had their ten children plus grandchildren at their house for the holiday—lots of meals to prepare, plus all the restrictions of Pesach adding to the challenge.) In order to prepare food for Shabbat on a *Yom Tov* day, you need to perform a ceremonial procedure called **eruv tavshilin,** literally, "mixing of dishes." Before the first day of *Yom Tov,* you need to prepare a symbolic amount of food, the size of an olive or an egg. *K'zayit* (like an olive) and *k'beitzah* (like an egg) are standard food amounts referred to in the Talmud. (For example, in order to fulfill a mitzvah of eating something, such as bread, after saying a blessing, you have to eat at least a *k'zayit,* an olive's worth.) Often a hard-boiled egg is used. You must bless this food, along with a piece of bread or matzo, then set the two pieces of food aside and save them.

The *eruv tavshilin* blessing is

Baruch ata Adonai, Eloheinu melech ha'olam, asher kidshanu b'mitzvotav vitzivanu al mitzvat eruv.
Praised are you, Lord our God, King of the universe, who has sanctified us with His commandments and commanded us with the mitzvah of *eruv.*

You also say, "With this *eruv,* let it be permitted for us to bake, cook, insulate, light the Shabbat candles, prepare for and perform all our Shabbat needs on *Yom Tov.*"

The *eruv tavshilin* symbolically indicates that you already started Shabbat food preparation before the *Yom Tov* began, so anything you might make on Friday is actually a continuation of that process.

The Jewish year has a full cycle of holidays, with various spiritual and culinary traditions. Dates are indicated according to how the holidays are observed in the Diaspora. As with the basic laws of kashrut, there are some differences in holiday observances in various communities. Check with your rabbi to understand your community's traditions.

Tishri

1–2 Tishri—Rosh Hashanah
3 Tishri—Tzom Gedaliah
10 Tishri—Yom Kippur
15–21 Tishri—Sukkot

21 Tishri—Hoshanah Rabbah

22 Tishri—Shemini Atzeret

23 Tishri—Simchat Torah

As you can see, almost half the month of Tishri is occupied by holidays. It seems appropriate that Tishri is sandwiched in between two months with no holidays. The month before Tishri is Elul, the last month of the year, when we have time to contemplate and get ready for the month of *chagim*. Heshvan, the month that follows Tishri, gives us time to recover from the festivities.

Tishri falls in September or early October, which feels like a time of new beginnings, as it coincides with the school year. Many of us take vacations in the summer, and the fall holidays have a "back to" element to them.

Tishri is also a month loaded with a tradition of historical events, according to one view expressed in the Talmud, **Rosh HaShana 10b–11a:** *"R. Eliezer says: In Tishri the world was created; in Tishri the Patriarchs were born; in Tishri the Patriarchs died."*

The first ten days of Tishri, from Rosh Hashanah through Yom Kippur, are called the *Yamim Noraim*, the Days of Awe, or the Days of Repentance. It is a time of self-reflection, a time to consider our behavior of the past year, a time for *teshuvah*, "repentance," when we ask forgiveness from God and from people whom we may have hurt. Judging begins on Rosh Hashanah, and we have until the end of Yom Kippur to repent fully. This period starts as a time of joy and feasting, but grows more somber and concludes with a fast.

1–2 Tishri—Rosh Hashanah

The commandment to observe Rosh Hashanah is given by God twice in the Torah. In **Leviticus 23:24,** God says, *"In the seventh month, on the first of the month, there shall be a solemn rest unto you, a remembrance proclaimed with the blast of horns, a holy convocation."* And in **Numbers 29:1,** God says, *"And in the seventh month, on the first day of the month, you shall have a holy convocation: you shall do no manner of servile work; it is a day of blowing the horn unto you."*

When the holiday was established in the Torah, Nisan, the month of the Exodus, was regarded as the first month of the year; this is why Tishri is referred to as the seventh month. Rosh Hashanah has three other names: *Yom Teruah* (Day of Blowing the Horn, because we blow the shofar), *Yom HaZikaron* (Day of Remembrance), and *Yom HaDin*

(Day of Judgment). This is the time of judgment, when we remember how we have behaved the past year—toward others, toward God, toward ourselves. We repent for poor behavior, and plan to behave better in the coming year.

There are a total of four celebratory meals eaten on Rosh Hashanah; *Yom Tov* cooking restrictions apply. The holiday begins with candle-lighting on the evening of the first day, as with Shabbat, eighteen minutes before sunset, followed by services and a festive meal. The next morning is spent in synagogue, with a kiddush after services. Usually we're so full from this meal, a celebration with friends and family, that the meal on the second evening is much smaller than that of the first evening. We light candles again on the second evening (from a flame that was left burning, according to Orthodox tenets), but this time they are lit after sunset, so as to avoid the appearance of lighting the candles twice on the same day. The second day we also celebrate with a kiddush after services.

The Torah does not require us to eat any particular foods on Rosh Hashanah, but it has become customary to eat certain foods. One of the basics is challah. As on Shabbat, we have two challot, but these challot are shaped differently. The most common shape (the only one I have ever seen, and the easiest to make) is a spiral round. The round shape has various symbolic attributes: the cycle of the year; it resembles a crown; also, it is not merely a round loaf, but a spiral round, symbolic of our prayers spiraling toward heaven. Other shapes include a ladder and a bird, again with the thought of prayers heading upward.

Apples and honey are perhaps the most well-known food custom of Rosh Hashanah. The apples-and-honey ritual is accompanied first by a *bracha* (blessing) and then a prayer. With the *bracha*, we thank God for what He has provided; the prayer is a request. Whenever we eat something, we should make the appropriate blessing; with the blessing, we thank God for the mitzvah of eating whatever we are about to eat. We then eat the item, such as apples and honey, followed by a prayer that begins,

> *Yehi ratzon milfanecha, Adonai Eloheinu vi'Elohei avotainu . . .*
> May it be your will, Lord our God and the God of our forefathers . . .

After we dip apples or challah into honey, we conclude the prayer with the words *shetichadesh aleinu shana tova umituka,* "that you will renew for us a good and sweet year."

Apples and honey are the most famous of the Rosh Hashanah foods. Why honey?

Why apples? Sweetness is the theme for Rosh Hashanah, and honey is the biblical sweetener mentioned in the Torah to describe the bounty of the Land of Israel when the Jews were ending their Exodus in the desert: *"a land flowing with milk and honey."*

As for apples, I always associate apples with fall, when they are in season both in the United States and in Israel, and that probably has something to do with the tradition. They are also sweet themselves, and round; there are several foods we eat on Rosh Hashanah because their round shape represents fullness and the cycle of the year.

Rabbi Jacob Moellin, known as the Maharil, a fourteenth-century rabbinic authority in Austria, gives a rather complex reason for apples involving the incident where Jacob disguises himself as Esau in order to receive the blessing intended for his minutes-older twin. The elderly, blind Isaac thinks he recognizes his favored son by his smell, as he says in **Genesis 27:27,** *"The smell of my son is as the smell of a field which the Lord hath blessed."* Isaac proceeds to bless Jacob. While the type of field referred to was debated, the general consensus was that it was a field of apple trees.

Apples and round challah are not the only symbolic foods traditionally consumed on Rosh Hashanah. Eating symbolic foods dates back to the Talmud. In **Kritot 5b–6a,** there is a debate regarding the validity and permissibility of looking for "signs" that a coming year might be good. The conclusion is that you shouldn't rely on signs for making decisions, but symbolism is acceptable. The Talmud states, *"Said Abaye: Since you hold that symbols are meaningful, every man should make it a habit to eat on New Year pumpkin, fenugreek, leek, beet and dates."*

Post-Talmudic commentators give instructions on how to use foods symbolically. Notes in the ArtScroll Talmud, **Horayot 12a,** say, *"Magen Avraham ad. loc. writes that one may use any food whose name carries the implication of a blessing, even if it is not the Hebrew name of the food."* Another commentator indicates that *Yehi Ratzon* prayers should accompany partaking of the symbolic foods. The commentary continues, *"Meiri writes that these utterances have the effect of inspiring one to repentance and good deeds . . . and thereby serve the purpose of preventing the omen from becoming a form of divination."*

Now, we don't *need* to eat symbolic foods in order to make anything happen, and eating them will not guarantee a sweet year, a full year, a prosperous year. The point of these foods is to make us think about the year, and our hopes personally and as a people. Just as kashrut makes us think about what we eat, eating certain foods on Rosh Hashanah serves as a reminder also. Rabbi Yehudah Prero, on the *torah.org* website, writes, "As soon as the person realizes that now is the time that he is being judged, he will realize that omens alone will not be enough for his salvation, and that repentance is needed."

The foods mentioned in the Talmud, as well as other symbolic food traditions, have been largely incorporated by Sephardic communities, although there are Ashkenazic culinary customs as well.

The foods mentioned by Abaye in the Talmud are symbolic either because of the sound of their names in Hebrew or because of certain physical attributes. You can tell that these foods were used during difficult times for the Jews, as many of the prayers have to do with the destruction of our enemies, perhaps a less than lofty wish, but reflecting the reality of the times.

The first food mentioned is **karah, pumpkin** or **squash. *Karah*** has the same root as the term "call out" or "proclaim"; it is also a play on words, as it is a homonym for the Hebrew word for "tear" or "abolish." The accompanying prayer is *she'tikra g'zar de'nainu v'yikaru l'fanecha zechu'yotainu*; in English, "that the decree of our sentence be *torn up* and may our merits be *proclaimed* before you." It is easy to think of other ways in which squash or pumpkins can be symbolic. The seeds can represent fertility or a multitude of good deeds, and pumpkins in particular are very sweet. Some say the pumpkin is used because it is a fast-growing plant.

The second word, ***rubia,*** is **fenugreek,** a seed that is used as a spice. It sounds like the Hebrew word for "increase," *yirbu*. The accompanying *Yehi Ratzon* prayer concludes, *she'yirbu zechu'yotainu*, "may our merits increase."

Karti means **leek,** and it sounds like *keret*, "to cut off." The accompanying prayer concludes, *sheyikartu sonainu*, "that our enemies be decimated."

Beets, *selek,* have a similar theme. *Salek* mean "get rid of," so the prayer concludes, *she'yistalku oyvainu*, "that our adversaries be removed."

Finally, **dates, *tamar*** in Hebrew, sound like *yitamu*, "be removed," and the prayer concludes, *she'yitamu oyvecha v'sonecha v'chol ra'atenu. Yitamu chata'im min ha'aretz,* "who removes your enemies and your hated ones and all who do evil upon us. May the wicked of the earth be removed."

However, the symbolism of these foods is subject to interpretation, and some have different *Yehi Ratzon* prayers. For example, dates. In *The Sephardic Kitchen*, Rabbi Robert Sternberg writes that the word *tamar* is similar to *tamah*, "causing wonder." The conclusion for his *Yehi Ratzon* is "to create a sense of wonder and amazement in the eyes of our enemies, make them acknowledge Your Greatness, and respect You as Sovereign of the World."

According to Sternberg, *rubia* is Aramaic for black-eyed peas, so they may be an alternative to fenugreek.

In *Sephardic Holiday Cooking*, Gilda Angel offers *Yehi Ratzon* prayers in both Hebrew and English, making puns with the English word for the food, rather than being a direct translation of the Hebrew. For example, for leeks, Angel offers this prayer, *"Like* as we eat this *leek* may our *luck* never *lack* in the year to come."

The concept of symbolic foods is fairly open, with some whimsical plays on words in languages other than Hebrew. For example, carrots can be cut into coin shapes to represent prosperity, and the Yiddish word for "carrots" is *mehren*, which means "to multiply"; the prayer is for blessings to multiply. A play on English words I've seen repeated is to eat a raisin and a stalk of celery, symbolizing the hope for a *raise in salary*.

Other customs have developed as well. It is traditional on the second night of Rosh Hashanah to eat a new fruit—a fruit that is new for the season. A pomegranate is popular, in part because of its many seeds. One claim is that pomegranates have 613 seeds, which corresponds to the number of mitzvot. Even if they don't have that number, they have a lot; the thought is to fill the year with mitzvot. The accompanying *Yehi Ratzon* concludes, *she'nihyeh mal'ey mitzvot k'rimon,* "that we will be filled with mitzvot like a pomegranate."

The reason for eating a new fruit is because of the odd nature of this two-day holiday—the only two-day holiday in the Jewish year both here and in Israel. Although it is two days, it is celebrated as an entire unit. On the first day, we say the *Shehecheyanu* blessing, the prayer celebrating the beginning of holidays and new experiences. Normally, we wouldn't say the *Shehecheyanu* on the second night because we already said it on the first, and the second day is a continuation of the same holiday. But if we eat a new fruit—or wear new clothing—we have a new reason to say the *Shehecheyanu*.

In researching these culinary traditions, I came across all kinds of reasoning—puns in Hebrew, English, Yiddish plays on words. They all come down to the purpose of this holiday: reflection. The symbolic significance of the food—whether it be the sweetness of the honey or the multitude of pomegranate seeds—inspires us to reflect, on ourselves as individuals and as part of a community.

3 Tishri—Tzom Gedaliah

The famous fast of Tishri is Yom Kippur. However, one of the five other fasts of the year also takes place this month. The day after the festivities of Rosh Hashanah are over, we commemorate a terrible event that occurred during the Babylonian exile. According to the Tanach, in the Book of Jeremiah, a few Jews remained in Israel, governed by Gedaliah ben Ahikam. Under the guise of friendship, another Jew, Ishmael, came to assassinate him. Though Gedaliah had been warned, he fatally refused to hear any negative talk of this visitor.

The passage of betrayal is poignant, in **Jeremiah 41:1–3:** *"Now it came to pass in the seventh month, that Ishmael the son of Nethaniah . . . came unto Gedaliah the son of Ahikam Mizpah; and there they did eat bread together in Mizpah. Then arose Ishmael . . . and the ten men that were with him, and smote Gedaliah . . . with the sword, and slew him, whom the king of Babylon had made governor over the land. Ishmael also slew all the Jews that were with him, even with Gedaliah, at Mizpah, and the Chaldeans that were found there, even the men of war."* Ishmael went on to slay several other Jews; and the last Jews in Israel fled.

If the third of Tishri falls on Shabbat, this fast is delayed one day. It is a sunrise-to-sunset fast. Work is permitted.

10 Tishri—Yom Kippur

Yom Kippur, or *Yom HaKippurim*, means "Day of Atonement." The commandment for Yom Kippur is given in four different places in the Torah, as in **Leviticus 16:29–30.** *"And it shall be a statute forever unto you: in the seventh month, on the tenth day of the month, you shall afflict your souls, and shall do no manner of work, the home-born, or the stranger that sojourns among you. For on this day shall atonement be made for you, to cleanse you; from all your sins shall you be clean before the Lord."*

"Afflict your souls" is interpreted to mean, among other things, "refrain from eating and drinking," that is, to fast, based on other biblical passages, such as **Isaiah 58:5,** *"Is it such the fast that I have chosen, the day for a man to afflict his soul?"* Yom Kippur is the longest of the fast days, lasting from before sunset to after sunset, some twenty-five hours. *Yom Tov* restrictions regarding food preparation apply.

On Yom Kippur we fast to contemplate ourselves and our behavior, to refrain from thinking about the needs of the body. This used to strike me as slightly ironic, especially on the invariably sweltering Indian summer days that always seem to characterize Yom Kippur. Because *not* eating and drinking would make me think about eating and drinking. Except that, in reality when you fast, there are no concerns about treif and kosher, meat and dairy, cooking, feeding, cleaning up after food. Because I know, on this particular day, I'm not going to eat, therefore I am not going to think about meal preparation or what food I'm going to have at the next meal. It is a time of self-reflection and atonement, not self-fulfillment and satiation.

Yom Kippur is the only fast day that supersedes Shabbat. The other five fast days are moved a day earlier or later if they fall on Shabbat, but not Yom Kippur. Yom Kippur is the culmination of the Days of Awe, of this period of our self-examination. The most significant dietary aspect of this holiday is the fast. Just as on Rosh Hashanah the foods we eat remind us of this period of repentance, on Yom Kippur, our hunger pangs remind us that the period of asking for forgiveness, of examining our behavior and knowing how to change, of asking for a positive judgment before the book of judgment is sealed is almost over.

Leviticus 23:32 has a slightly confusing passage: *"It shall be unto you a Sabbath of solemn rest, and you shall afflict your souls; in the ninth day of the month in the evening, from evening to evening, shall you rest on your Sabbath."* But everywhere else Yom Kippur is mentioned, the Torah says "the tenth day."

The Talmud, in **Brachot 8b,** addresses this: *"Khiya ben Rav of Difti recited* [the following]: *It is written* [Lev. 23:32]: *And you shall afflict your souls, in the ninth day of the month in the evening. Now, do we fast on the ninth? Why, we fast on the tenth! But this teaches you that if one eats and drinks on the ninth, Scripture accounts it to him as if he fasted on the ninth and tenth."*

Thus, on the day before Yom Kippur, 9 Tishri, not only is it recommended that you eat a full meal in anticipation of the fast, it is an obligation, a mitzvah. Several explanations are given as to why. Rashi says that by eating on the ninth you are preparing yourself for the fast, thereby making the eating part of the fasting. In other words, you need to eat, to fill your stomach, in order to feel the effects of fasting, in contrast. If you actually fasted the day before Yom Kippur, you might not experience the fast as fully. Another reason to eat a full meal on the ninth is that *chagim* traditionally should be celebrated with a festive meal. Since you can't eat on Yom Kippur itself, you should have a festive meal beforehand.

However, it is also traditional to minimize obvious discomfort. Highly spiced and salty foods should be avoided, as they will cause extra thirst on Yom Kippur.

One indirectly food-related Yom Kippur custom is that of *Kapparot*, which literally means "forgivenesses" or "pardons," but refers to a controversial practice. At the time of the Temple, the high priest would perform a sin offering, using a goat to take symbolically the sins of the people into the wilderness, and perhaps the *Kapparot* custom has roots there.

Kapparot involves taking a live chicken (rooster for a man, hen for a woman), grasping its feet, and rotating it around your head three times, while declaring, "This is my substitute, this is my exchange, this is my atonement. This fowl will go to death, and I will enter upon a good and long life." The bird is then slaughtered by a *shochet* and either donated to charity or eaten by the person who purchased it, and its cash value is given to charity.

I have to admit, this was not a custom I grew up with, and when I first read about it, I imagined it was obsolete. On the contrary, there are many observant Jews, including Chassidim, who continue this practice today. Some participate in an altered *Kapparot* ceremony; rather than a one-to-one ratio of person to chicken, there may be a group *Kapparot* session, in which one chicken represents the sins and fate of a community, not unlike the biblical goat.

Kapporot seems to have roots in Talmudic times, but it has been controversial throughout history. There were rabbis who found the custom barbaric and paganlike, and did not sanction it, yet there were other rabbis who approved of it, and the practice continues despite periodic condemnation.

The idea is that the chicken, as the prayer states, is a substitute for us. The bird demonstrates that none of us can be free from sin, and that the fate of the chicken is what we deserve. Actually seeing the live chicken killed drives home the point of the fragility of life (especially to the chicken). It does seem unnecessarily cruel to the chicken. While there are those who hold the bird gently and slowly move it in a circle, there still are some who really swing that chicken around.

So that *shochetim* do not get inundated with last-minute chickens needing to be slaughtered, and thereby inadvertently becoming unable to be as careful as they should be due to volume demand, *Kapparot* can be done anytime between Rosh Hashanah and Yom Kippur.

For Jews who choose not to follow this custom—and it is a custom, *not* a mitzvah, *not* a commandment—but like the idea in theory, there is a symbolic *Kapparot* ritual. *Tzedakah*, giving money to charity, is encouraged on Yom Kippur, and some use a package of money to symbolize the practice of *Kapparot*. Rather than holding a chicken and circling it, they hold some money, saying instead, "This is my substitute, this is my exchange, this is my atonement. This money will go to charity, and I will enter upon a good and long life."

In some communities, as a nod to the ritual of *Kapparot* perhaps, chicken is served as part of the meal before Yom Kippur.

Yom Kippur is spent primarily in synagogue, concluding with the *Neilah* service. After the final shofar blowing of the High Holy Days, we return home to break the fast with a simple meal. Traditionally, construction of your sukkah should begin as soon as Yom Kippur is over.

15–21 Tishri—Sukkot

Chag HaSukkot, literally, "Festival of the Booths," is the third of the *Shloshet HaRegalim*, the Pilgrimage Festivals, so called because these were festivals on which the Jews of ancient Israel would travel to the *Beit HaMikdash*, the Holy Temple in Jerusalem, to celebrate. (The other two Pilgrimage Festivals are Pesach and Shavuot.) It is usually referred to simply as Sukkot, which means "booths" or "tabernacles," and is also called *Chag Ha'Asif*, "Festival of Ingathering" because it celebrates the final harvest of the year.

The way to observe Sukkot is described in great detail in **Leviticus 23:34–43**: *"On the fifteenth day of this seventh month is the Festival of Sukkot for seven days unto the Lord. . . . You shall dwell in booths seven days; all that are home-born in Israel shall dwell in booths; that your generations may know that I made the children of Israel to dwell in booths, when I brought them out of the land of Egypt; I am the Lord your God."*

Sukkot is a weeklong festival, immediately followed by two more holidays, *Shemini Atzeret* and *Simchat Torah*. The first two days of Sukkot are *Yom Tov* days (only the first day in Israel), and the same cooking parameters for Rosh Hashanah apply.

The significant food-related aspect of Sukkot is where we eat all our meals for the week: in a *sukkah*, a "booth." A sukkah is a temporary structure, reminiscent, as God says in the preceding passage in Leviticus, of the temporary structures the Israelites lived in as they wandered the desert after the Exodus.

Traditionally, you should begin construction of your sukkah as soon as Yom Kippur is over. Realistically, this is nighttime; not only can it be difficult to see properly, but neighbors might object to the hammering and drilling. You can begin construction symbolically, perhaps hammering a couple of planks together, and then complete the sukkah in the next few days.

Building a sukkah is a special experience. My husband and I are not exactly "handy" people when it comes to carpentry and such, but for several years we've managed to construct a sukkah that stays standing throughout the holiday.

As a child, I loved the experience of eating in a sukkah—we began doing this a few years before we started keeping kosher. I remember the first sukkah my father built, more than thirty-five years ago. "It seemed like a very nice thing to do," my father says. "It's a great holiday." He had not grown up building sukkot, but had become increasingly interested in various Jewish practices and traditions. Perhaps this step toward being more observant eventually led to our keeping kosher a few years later. Once my father built that first sukkah, we always built a sukkah.

We lived in a row house on Capitol Hill then, in Washington, D.C., and our sukkah was wedged into a small space between the porch and the back of the house. My father, an amateur engineer, designed the sukkah in such a way, with hook-and-eye connections, that it could easily be assembled and disassembled from year to year. My parents still use the same base for their sukkah today, although they did expand it when we moved to a house with a slightly larger yard, so a picnic table rather than a card table could fit inside.

The sukkah has to be a temporary structure. Even though my parents' sukkah has survived for nearly four decades, it is still a temporary structure. If it were left outside all year, it could never remain standing. The transitory nature of the structure reflects the booths our foreparents lived in in the desert.

A sukkah can be made from almost any material, as long as it meets certain dimensional criteria outlined in the Shulchan Aruch. (Check with your rabbi for more precise details.) It has to be at least big enough for one person to stand in, which is about a twenty-seven-inch square. It should have at least three complete walls. It is acceptable to use the walls of your house for this; the roof is what really makes a sukkah temporary. It also should be at least three feet high and not more than thirty or thirty-five feet high (based on converting the handbreadth system of measurement).

The roof of the sukkah must be made of something that grows in the soil that has been cut. The roofing material is called *schach*, which means "thatch." The Jewish day school I attended as a child used to have a *schach* sale as a fund-raiser every Sukkot, and we'd line up to fill our car trunk with cut evergreen branches. Evergreen branches make the best *schach*, I now know. It smells nice and stays green through the whole holiday. Other types of leaves dry out and shrivel in a few days.

While the sukkah is a temporary structure, it should still be strong enough to stand up to normal winds and weather. The *schach* should be placed on the roof so that you can see the stars at night, yet the branches should be close enough together that there is more shade than sun inside. We always use new freshly cut *schach* for our sukkah, but I have seen bamboo roofing mats sold as certified kosher *schach*.

The size of the sukkah and the *schach* to use have halachic requirements. Although not required halachically, it is customary to decorate the sukkah, usually with produce. When I was growing up, my father made carefully designed harnesses out of twine that securely held apples, oranges, carrots, gourds, and other sturdy produce, adding color to the sukkah and reminding us of the harvest nature of the holiday. Depending on the weather, they'd stay preserved or gradually ripen and soften as the holiday progressed.

What produce holds up the best in a sukkah? For our sukkah, the answer is none. We have another issue altogether when it comes to décor, because our very aggressive city squirrels have come to regard our sukkah as a giant feeder. Initially, the sukkah was in our yard; we subsequently moved it onto our back porch, but the proximity to the house did not discourage the squirrels.

When we first built a sukkah, we considered which fruit was sturdier and would last the holiday. We started out with apples and oranges. The fruit disappeared from the sukkah in a day. Another year we tried pomegranates and coconut. Somehow, the squirrels figured out how to open the coconut, smashing it onto the asphalt lot next door.

The following year we went with gourds and mini-pumpkins. I saw a squirrel in action one morning as I was washing dishes in the kitchen. I had been impressed that most of the produce had survived more than a day. But maybe that was only because rain had kept the squirrels under cover. Out of the corner of my eye, I saw movement.

I turned and watched, mesmerized, as a squirrel leaped onto the roof of our sukkah. Thin pieces of pine wood were stretched across the top to support the *schach*. Tied to these with twine were the colorful gourds and pumpkins I had chosen for that year. The squirrel walked across one of the lengths of pine. And began to shake. He shook the wood with determination and watched as, one by one, each gourd and pumpkin tied to that plank fell to the ground. The squirrel then jumped down, picked up a mini-pumpkin and carried it off over the fence.

I gathered the fallen ones and doused them with Tabasco sauce, thinking that might deter the scoundrels, and retied them. No such luck. By the next day, all the gourds were gone.

Another year I tried Indian corn. The squirrels didn't bother removing it; they just hung upside down and munched, dropping dried corn bits all over the table. Even spraying the corn with cleaning fluid did not deter them.

Not having learned from the Tabasco fiasco, I tried habanero chile peppers the next year. Bright yellow and orange, they added autumnal color to our sukkah. For one day. Another year I tried mountain ash, a bright orange berry that is poisonous. It stays on trees for several weeks, untouched. In our sukkah it lasted three days.

Finally, I went with colorful orange Japanese lanterns, puffs of papery dried flowers, again hoping for festive color. Unbeknownst to me, nestled inside the papery flower is . . . a berry. The squirrels pointed that out within two days.

My determination to stick with natural produce representing the harvest came to a defeated end. Now we go with construction-paper chains and decorations made by our children.

The mitzvah of eating in the sukkah is described as the only mitzvah that physically surrounds us. There is something peaceful and refreshing about sitting in the sukkah for breakfast, lunch, and dinner, a different feel from merely sitting in the backyard at a picnic table. The parameters of the sukkah sanctify the space surrounding the picnic table—make it more than just eating outside. Even though it is far from a permanent dwelling, the sukkah gives you a feeling of shelter. As kashrut is a connection to generations of Jews eating the same way, the sukkah evokes the same sense of connection to history, to Jews throughout the world, over the centuries, sitting, eating their meals, sharing this mitzvah together.

It is also a mitzvah to invite guests for a meal in the sukkah, especially those who do not have a sukkah of their own. We hold an Open Sukkah party, inviting dozens of friends for a buffet meal.

Another mitzvah on Sukkot is that of the *Arba Minim*, the "Four Species," also known as the *lulav* and *etrog*. **Leviticus 23:40** outlines this commandment, *"And you shall take for yourselves on the first day the fruit of hadar trees, branches of palm-trees, and boughs of thick trees, and willows of the brook, and you shall rejoice before the Lord your God seven days."* Those Four Species were interpreted to include the *etrog* (citron) as the fruit of the *hadar* tree (also called the "goodly fruit"), which resembles an oversized lemon and has a special pistil, called a *pitom* or *pitma*, which makes it whole and considered kosher for use on Sukkot, plus date-palm leaves (*lulav* in Hebrew), myrtle leaves, and willow leaves. Traditionally, the three sets of leaves are bound together with a sort of three-branched holder made out of dried, woven palm fronds. The three sets of leaves together are named for the palm and are called the *lulav*. The mitzvah is to hold the *lulav* and *etrog* together and to shake them methodically in all directions, after saying appropriate blessings. You should perform the mitzvah of the *lulav* and *etrog* every day of Sukkot, except for Shabbat.

Each species represents something, in part based on their characteristics. The *etrog* has both scent and taste, palm trees have taste in the date fruit, but no smell; myrtle leaves have a fragrant scent but can't be eaten, and willow leaves have neither scent nor taste. These various characteristics represent the diversity of the Jewish community. Rabbi Bradley Shavit Artson, from the Ziegler School of Rabbinic Studies at the University of Judaism, writes on the Jewish Community Federation of Greater East Bay website, "According to Pesikta De-Rav Kahana, each of the plants symbolizes a different type of Jew:

one who is learned in Torah and rich in good deeds, one who is learned but has performed no good deeds, one who is uneducated but active in demonstrating loving kindness, and one who is uneducated and has not performed loving deeds. By binding all four plants together, we pray that God will also consider the entire Jewish people as a single unit, each responsible for the other, each Jew compensating for the shortcomings of the others. Thus, *lulav* and *etrog* demonstrate our unity as a people and celebrate our diversity as individuals and as religious movements within the umbrella of Judaism."

Another interpretation is that the Four Species represent the four-letter name of God, *yud-heh-vav-heh*. A third looks at the three branches as representative of the patriarchs and the *etrog* as representative of God. When you perform the mitzvah of the Four Species, you hold them all together, unifying the four. I like to think of the Four Species as representing the fours matriarchs. Holding them together represents the unifying power of God.

The culinary traditions of Sukkot are more customary than historical. Since it is a harvest festival, fruit-based dishes are popular. The first two nights are festive *Yom Tov* meals. The night of the seventh day, *erev* Shemini Atzeret is also a *Yom Tov*, and time for a festive meal, complete with challah. The challah for Sukkot is usually round.

21 Tishri—Hoshanah Rabbah

The seventh day of Sukkot is not a *Yom Tov*, but it is time for the *Hoshanah Rabbah*, literally, "many praises," a special synagogue service that includes the final shaking of the *lulav* and *etrog*.

22 Tishri—Shemini Atzeret
23 Tishri—Simchat Torah

Shemini Atzeret and Simchat Torah are celebrated on the same day in Israel and as two separate *Yom Tov* holidays everywhere else. The word *atzeret* comes from the root word "stop" or "hold back." Shemini Atzeret literally means "Eighth Day of Assembly." It is like an extra, eighth day of Sukkot. It is a separate holiday described in **Leviticus 23:36,** *"Seven days you shall bring an offering made by fire unto the Lord; on the eighth day shall be a holy convocation unto you . . . it is a day of solemn assembly."* It is observed as an eighth day of Sukkot, and traditionally we have our last meals in the sukkah that day, although we no longer do the mitzvah of the *lulav* and *etrog*.

Shemini Atzeret is the day when we begin to pray for rain, signaling the start of the rainy season, which in Israel does begin around this time.

Simchat Torah, "Rejoicing of the Torah," is a celebration of the Torah, of reading the Torah, and a celebration of the knowledge we gain from reading the Torah. Over the course of the year, every Shabbat we read a portion of the Torah aloud at synagogue. During the morning service of Simchat Torah, the last verses of the Torah are read, immediately followed by the beginning verses, symbolizing the ongoing cycle of reading the Torah, and that there is always new knowledge to be gleaned from that reading.

Simchat Torah, while celebrated with a festive meal complete with candle-lighting, is very much a synagogue-oriented holiday. Simchat Torah is also a holiday of great merriment and dancing, a fitting celebratory conclusion to the month of holidays known as the High Holy Days. Our synagogue in Cambridge, Massachusetts, Temple Beth Shalom, is renowned for its Simchat Torah celebration. The Tremont Street Shul, as it is referred to for this holiday, is *the* place to go for Simchat Torah in the Greater Boston area. The street is closed off, and the place is packed and spilling out onto the street. All the Torahs are taken out and carried for each of many *Hakafot*—the traditional circlings around the shul carrying the Torahs—and the *Hakafot* extend beyond the confines of the synagogue, into the closed-off street, accompanied by clapping and dancing.

The daytime celebration is much more low-key; for that reason, I like it. This is when the Torah is actually read, and everyone in the congregation has an *aliyah*, is called up to the Torah. So that we don't stay in synagogue all day, there are several group *aliyot*. In Conservative, Reform, and Reconstructionist synagogues, men and women are honored with *aliyot*; in Orthodox shuls, only men have *aliyot*.

There is something joyous about seeing hundreds upon hundreds of Jews celebrating this holiday together. And then there is something cozy about celebrating with those who take time off from work to come to shul in the morning, to have small *Hakafot* just in the courtyard in front of the shul.

Kislev

25 Kislev–2 or 3 Tevet—Chanukah

(The end date of Chanukah varies because sometimes Kislev is twenty-nine days, and sometimes it is thirty days long.)

Chanukah as it is celebrated today is a favorite among children because of the presents thing. And the latkes thing. However, Chanukah did not start out as a gift-exchanging day, and it is a relatively minor holiday religiously, compared with Rosh Hashanah or Pesach or Shavuot. (And Chanukah probably has more transliterated spellings than any other Jewish holiday.) However, it is a holiday of fun, and one that celebrates a few miracles. It is a home-centered holiday, as the primary mitzvah, lighting candles, is done at home.

The story of Chanukah is not part of the Tanach. It is told in one of the extra books, the Book of Maccabees, which was written in Greek. The popular opinion is that the original story was written in Hebrew, but the only extant copies are in Greek.

During the second century B.C.E., Greeks had taken over Palestine and issued edicts against Shabbat and Torah study. There were those Jews who assimilated, called Hellenists, but there were also those Jews who resisted, protested, and revolted.

A small band of rebel fighters, led by Judah Maccabee of the Hasmonean family, fought the Greeks for three years and ultimately succeeded in overpowering the much larger army, a miraculous victory. They took over as rulers of Palestine once again, and set about rededicating the Holy Temple, the *Beit HaMikdash*, which had been inaccessible to Jews for several years, and had been defiled by the Greeks. As the Book of Maccabees recounts the story, Judah and company returned to the Temple, cleaned it up, and rededicated it, declaring an eight-day festival. *Chanukah* means "dedication."

1 Maccabees 4:52–56 describes the rededication ceremony: *"Early in the morning on the twenty-fifth day of the ninth month, which is the month of Kislev, in the one hundred and forty-eighth year, they rose and offered sacrifice, as the law directs, on the new altar of burnt offering which they had built. . . . So they celebrated the dedication of the altar for eight days, and offered burnt offerings with gladness; they offered a sacrifice of deliverance and praise."*

Why eight days? One theory is that the Maccabees were celebrating a delayed Sukkot. Since they had still been fighting and had not reclaimed the Holy Temple during the actual Sukkot of that year, they decided to celebrate it when the Temple was restored to them, since Sukkot is a holiday of celebration traditionally observed at the Holy Temple. The eighth day was similar to the inclusion of Shemini Atzeret at the end of Sukkot.

No mention of the famous miracle of the oil is in the Book of Maccabees. That comes a few hundred years later, in the Talmud. The Talmud adds a spiritual element to the story of Chanukah. A seven-armed menorah was part of the Temple, and it was always kept lit. No candles in those days, but wicks floating in oil. The menorah had not been kept lit during the Greek occupation. The oil used for the lamps had to be kosher, as oil (fat) can come from animal sources as well as plants. Only oil sanctified and sealed in a container to ensure that it would not be mixed with tainted oil could be used for the menorah in the Temple. According to the Talmud, **Shabbat 21b,** the Greeks defiled all the oil, save for one small flask. There was only enough oil for one day, but miraculously the oil burned for the eight days needed to obtain more oil. For this reason, Chanukah is also called *Chag Ha'Orot*, "Festival of Lights," and we celebrate the holiday by lighting candles for the eight days in a special menorah called a *chanukiah*, which has nine branches rather than seven. There is a branch for each day of Chanukah, plus an extra for the *shamash* (which means "servant"), the candle used to light the other flames.

Candles are a relatively recent convention, those blue boxes of forty-four-plus available now in supermarkets. Wicks in oil, preferably olive oil, had been more widely used, though some used a candle for the *shamash*. (Much easier to light oil lamps with a candle than with another oil lamp.)

How the candles are lit was yet another topic of debate between the schools of Hillel and Shamai (Talmud, **Shabbat 21b**), two Talmudic scholars who often had contrasting views on how to follow certain laws. Shamai said we should begin with eight candles lit, decreasing the number each day, down to one. Which makes sense, if you think about it. But Hillel's ruling prevailed, which seems to make sense visually, building up another light each day, culminating in a glorious eight candles lit.

As for how the candles (or wicks in oil) are placed in the *chanukiah* and lit, there are two orders. First is how you *insert* the candles into the *chanukiah* (or pour oil and add wicks), the second is the order in which you light the candles. The candles should all be at the same height, with the *shamash* slightly higher. The Chanukah candles themselves should not be used for any purpose other than for viewing pleasure. The first candle should be inserted in the far right, the second next to that, and so on, working toward the left. However, you light the candles in the opposite direction, starting with the most recently inserted candle, working toward the right.

On the Shabbat that falls during Chanukah, light the Chanukah candles just before you light the Shabbat candles, since candles can't be lit after Shabbat starts. But Chanukah candles should burn during each day of Chanukah. So, use longer Chanukah candles on Shabbat, candles that will still be ignited when the sun actually goes down half an hour later.

There are no dietary rules regarding Chanukah, just culinary traditions. It is a festival, not a *Yom Tov* holiday, so there are no restrictions on working or cooking—except, since it is a joyous occasion, you should not mourn or fast during this time. Also, some Orthodox women have a tradition of stopping any household work while the candles burn.

Because of the miracle of the oil, it is customary to eat fried foods. The word for oil, *shemen*, and the word for eight, *shmona*, also sound similar, which is another connection. Either way, it's a valid excuse, I mean reason, for latkes and *sufganiot*, jelly doughnuts.

Another tradition is to eat cheese-based foods, which comes from the story of Judith, who was thought to be of the Hasmonean family. Judith encountered the Greek general Holofernes. She offered him salty cheese to eat, which made him thirsty, so he drank great quantities of the wine she then offered, and fell asleep. While he was sleeping, Judith beheaded him, causing his troops to retreat.

Other Chanukah traditions are not food-oriented. Dreidel, a spinning-top game, is usually played with gold foil–wrapped chocolate coins. For centuries, card playing was popular among adults, a sort of lighthearted gambling, although this practice seems to have faded. Then there is the practice of exchanging gifts. This is somewhat controversial within each affiliation.

The sources of the gift giving are vague. Older writings refer to the practice of giving children money, Chanukah *gelt*, as an inducement to study Torah. This was traditionally done on the fifth day of Chanukah, which never falls on Shabbat (money cannot be handled on Shabbat). Gifts seem to be a later twentieth-century development (the practice certainly was common when I was a kid in the 1960s and 70s).

Some stricter Jews eschew the practice of exchanging gifts. The Conservative Rabbi Isaac Klein writes in *A Guide to Jewish Religious Practice*, "In America, the proximity of a Christian holiday, and its prominence on the secular calendar, has influenced the celebration of Hanukkah both positively and negatively. The positive influence expresses itself in the greater and more widespread observance of Hanukkah. Negatively, Hanukkah has become more important to many American Jews than some of the major festivals in the Jewish calendar and is celebrated more and more lavishly in order to compete with the celebration of the non-Jewish holiday." That would be Christmas, which has elevated the stature of Chanukah in the eyes of non-Jews, and probably has also contributed to the gift-giving aspect of the holiday.

Blu Greenberg has a more positive view of presents. In *How to Run a Traditional Jewish Household*, she writes, "I'm not sure of the origin of this gift giving, but I'm pretty certain one won't find it in rabbinic literature. Nevertheless, Jews are human too, and not highly ascetic at that, and since gifts never hurt anyone, especially children ages two to ninety, it is rather sweet that gift giving came to be associated with Chanukah. . . . Contrary to the naysayers, gifts do not distort one's perspective on the holiday nor confuse it with Christmas in the mind of a firmly anchored Jew."

In his detailed book *The Jewish Festivals*, published in 1938, Hayyim Schauss mentions several Chanukah traditions, including that of giving children coins, but makes no mention of the exchange of presents. However, he writes, "With the spread of the Zionist sentiment the importance of Chanukkoh increased in Jewish life. The close of the last century and the beginning of this century saw a new epoch in the history of Chanukkoh. The festival emerged from the mistiness in which it had been obscured for two thousand years, during which it existed as a semi-holiday. . . . Chanukkoh is rapidly becoming one of the greatest of Jewish festivals."

A Jewish victory and a miracle of light are certainly worth celebrating.

Tevet

10 Tevet—The Fast of the Tenth of Tevet

This is a fast day that mourns the beginning of Nebuchadnezzar's siege against Jerusalem, as described in **Kings II 25:1**: *"And it came to pass in the ninth year of his reign, in the tenth month, in the tenth day of the month, that Nebuchadnezzar king of Babylon came, he and all his army, against Jerusalem, and encamped against it; and they built forts against it round about."* The fast is a sunrise-to-sunset fast.

The Israeli rabbinate also declared this day to be a day of mourning for those whose date of death or place of death is unknown (*Hakaddish HaKlali*).

Shvat

15 Shvat—Tu B' Shvat

The Mishnah, in **Rosh Hashanah 1:1**, describes four different New Year days in the Jewish calendar:

1 Nisan, the New Year for kings and the festivals;
1 Elul, the New Year for the tithing of animals;
1 Tishri, the New Year for the counting of years;
15 Shvat, the New Year for the Tree.

This last date was actually debated: The school of Shamai advocated for 1 Shvat and the school of Hillel, which prevailed, advocated for 15 Shvat. The word *Tu* comes from pronouncing the two Hebrew letters that make the numerical value of 15 (*tet* and *vav*).

It is significant that the Mishnah says *Rosh Hashanah La'Ilan*—the "New Year for the Tree," singular. Why singular and not plural? Some have commented that by using the singular, the term can have multiple meanings. *The* Tree can refer to the *etz hadar*, the *etrog* tree, the "goodly tree." On Tu B'Shvat, we pray for a beautiful *etrog* on the coming Sukkot. *The* Tree can also be a reference to the Tree of Life, symbolic of the Torah.

In more recent times, Tu B'Shvat has been referred to as *Hag Ha'Ilanot*, "Festival of the Trees," and is also called "the birthday for trees." This date is more than just a tree-appreciation day. I mentioned earlier that produce grown in Israel has certain kashrut concerns. One is *orlah*, that a tree must be over three years old before we can eat its fruits. The age of a tree is measured relative to Tu B'Shvat. Certain tithes are required as well, based on the age of the tree.

Although this holiday happens in midwinter (usually mid-January to early February), this is the time when winter starts to abate in Israel, when the rainy season is more than half over, and sap starts to run in the trees. It is not a religious holiday, but one that celebrates trees and what they offer. As with Chanukah, fasting is forbidden, and there are no dietary or cooking restrictions.

In the sixteenth century, Safed was a center for Jewish mysticism, which was based on the teachings of Rabbi Isaac (Yitzchak) Luria. These teachings were central to the later development of Chassidism. Luria is credited with establishing the custom of a Tu B'Shvat seder. The order of the seder was later documented in an eighteenth-century publication called *Pri Etz Hadar* (from **Leviticus 23:40**), which means "fruit of a beautiful or majestic tree"; this has been interpreted to mean the *etrog*.

Ashkenazic communities developed traditions of eating fruit, nuts, and dried fruit (since little fresh fruit is available at this time of year in Eastern European countries). Sephardic communities also celebrate the holiday with fruit, but developed it into a more ceremonial celebration, along the lines of Luria's seder, called *Las Frutas* or *Fruticas*. Different communities have slightly different rituals, but have several practices in common. The Tu B'Shvat seder is highly symbolic.

The common elements of the Tu B'Shvat seder include four cups of wine of changing color, the Seven Species of fruit mentioned in the Torah, and fruits that fall under at least three categories, with a debatable fourth category. Appropriate blessings are made before eating each element of the seder, followed by commentary from the Tanach, Talmud, Zohar, and other sources, explaining the symbolic significance of each fruit.

The fruits include those of plants and vines as well as tree fruits; what they have in common is that they have seeds or pits—no roots, stalks, or leaves. The number of fruits to be eaten varies. Some say at least twelve; fifteen is common, as it parallels the date of the holiday. Ascent of Safed, a learning center-cum-youth-hostel in Safed, Israel, tries to include at least thirty kinds of fruit in their elaborate annual Tu B'Shvat seders.

Bear in mind that the seder I describe is not set in stone, and the order varies. That said, most Tu B'Shvat seders begin with the Seven Species. Actually, the seder begins with a lengthy introduction, not unlike the Pesach seder, before the food is consumed. Then the Seven Species are introduced. These are the fruits listed in **Deuteronomy 8:8**, in which Moses describes the land of Israel that God will soon be giving to the Israelites: *"A land of wheat and barley, and vines and fig-trees and pomegranates; a land of olive-trees and honey."* Vines means grapes as well as wine; the honey referred to is interpreted as date honey.

The food of the seder begins with **bread** or **cakes** made with **wheat. Barley** is not always included in the seder, but is referred to, as the counting of the *omer* (see *Sfirat Ha'Omer,* pages 165–167) is based on the barley harvest. If the wheat is in the form of bread, you say the blessing for bread:

> *Baruch ata Adonai, Eloheinu melech ha'olam, hamotzi lechem min ha'aretz.*
> Praised are you, Lord our God, King of the universe, who brings forth bread
> from the earth.

If it is in cakes, you say the blessing for snacks:

> *Baruch ata Adonai, Eloheinu melech ha'olam, borei minei mizonot.*
> Praised are you, Lord our God, King of the universe, Creator of all kinds of
> foods.

Wheat represents the sustenance bread provides—but it is sustenance that comes through the work of farming.

Before the first fruits are eaten, the appropriate blessings are made. Most of these are tree fruits, so the blessing is for the fruit of the tree.

> *Baruch ata Adonai, Eloheinu melech ha'olam, borei pri ha'etz.*
> Praised are you, Lord our God, King of the universe, Creator of the fruit of
> the trees.

Fruits from vines or bushes are blessed with the fruit of the earth blessing:

Baruch ata Adonai, Eloheinu melech ha'olam, borei pri ha'adamah.

Praised are you, Lord our God, King of the universe, Creator of the fruit of the ground.

The order of the species can be your choice, but usually **olives** are consumed next. There is a Midrash that says, "Just as olive oil brings light into the world, so do the people of Israel bring light into the world." The olive tree is an evergreen, representing endurance.

Dates are the fruit of the palm tree. The sturdiness of the palm tree is used metaphorically, as is its utility. One Midrash describes how the entire tree is used—its leaves for thatch, its trunk for building houses, its fruit for eating. **Grapes** represent versatility. They can be dried into raisins and eaten year-round; they can be made into wine, the ceremonial basis for rituals and joyous occasions.

Figs can have multiple interpretations for what they represent. Ascent's website states, "Figs must be picked as soon as they ripen, for they quickly go bad. Similarly, we must be quick to do mitzvot at hand before the opportunity 'spoils.'" The Talmud, in **Eruvin 54a,** likens a fig tree to the study of Torah. The fruit is not all ripe at once, so you have to keep looking for more. We don't gain all the knowledge the Torah offers at once; the more we study, the more we learn.

Pomegranates, mentioned under Rosh Hashanah, are said to have 613 seeds, representing the 613 mitzvot.

At least one of the fruits included should be new to the season, so you can say the *Shehecheyanu* blessing (see page 110).

Four glasses of wine are then drunk, interspersed with the eating of several other fruits. Any fruit can be used, but fruit that grows in Israel is encouraged. The three main categories of fruit each represent an aspect of the spiritual world, as described by Kabbalists. Those aspects are *Asiah*, "Action"; *Yetzirah*, "Formation"; and *Briah*, "Creation." The fourth, highest, realm is *Atzilut*, "Emanation of Godliness." Some include a fourth category of fruit representing this level; others do not.

The glasses of wine are also compared with those four Kabbalistic aspects by some authorities; others say they represent the seasons, and the characteristics of trees in each season. Say the blessing over wine before drinking each glass:

Baruch ata Adonai, Eloheinu melech ha'olam, borei pri hagafen.

Praised are you, Lord our God, King of the universe, Creator of the fruit of the vine.

The first cup of wine should be pale white, representing winter, when trees are dormant.

Follow the first cup with **fruit with inedible skins**, such as avocado, banana, nuts, and carob. (Some include oranges and lemons in this category; others say that, since the skins are edible when cooked or preserved, they do not qualify for this category. So stick with fruit whose skins you would never eat.) When I was growing up, we used to get carob pods in school for Tu B'Shvat, representing a mysterious sort of fruit from Israel. Yitzhak Buxbaum in *A Tu BeShvat Seder* describes this kind of fruit as representing *Asiah*, "the lowest of the spiritual worlds—a world which is enveloped by materialism, just as the fruit is enveloped in its peel/shell."

The second cup of wine should either be a more golden white or a white wine slightly colored with a drop of red wine. This represents the early spring, when the sap in the trees begins to build and move. The accompanying fruit should be **fruit with an edible skin but an inedible pit**, such as peaches, mangoes, or cherries. Buxbaum writes, "This stage is comparable to the realm of formation (**yetzirah**). The edible parts of the fruit represent holiness. Pits represent impurities which have penetrated the holiness." This fruit also represents potential—we can't eat or use the seed now, but if we plant it, it will grow into a tree, which will bear more fruit, something useful.

The third cup of wine should be a rosé, a darker pink, or white wine mixed with more red. This symbolizes early summer, with trees in bloom. It should be accompanied by **fruit that is entirely edible**, such as strawberries, blueberries, apples (considered wholly edible, even if the cores are less than desirable). "This is the realm of creation (*briah*), the highest level in the created world," Buxbaum writes. "Things are coming close to their full potential. Even the seeds are now edible. They not only have future potential, but are also delicious and ready to eat right now."

The fourth glass of wine should be red, representing the late summer and fall harvests, when trees bear fruit. Some do not accompany this glass with any fruit. Rabbi Chaim Vital, a student of Isaac Luria's who wrote down much of what Luria taught, writes, "*Atzilut*—the World of Emanation—is too purely divine to have physical representation." Buxbaum, however, includes the *etrog*, the *pri etz hadar*, in this category, not for its physical attributes, not for its taste, but for its fragrance. He explains this choice: "The sense of smell is the purest and most elevated. It is through the nose that God invested Adam with a soul, as it says, 'God breathed into man's nostrils a breath of life' [**Genesis 2:7**]. Since there is no perceptible physical matter to smell, it is the most spiritual and Godly of the five senses."

When Tu B'Shvat falls on Shabbat, incorporate the seder into one of the Shabbat meals.

Adar

13 Adar—Fast of Esther
14 Adar—Purim
15 Adar—Shushan Purim

Purim is a holiday of great fun and celebration—a celebration of the deliverance from a near genocide of the Jewish people. It is a very food-oriented holiday, and certain mitzvot of this *chag* are directly connected to food.

Each holiday has special associated biblical readings, both from the Torah and from the Tanach. Five of the additional books that are part of the Tanach are known as *Megillot*, "Scrolls," and are read on five different *chagim*. They include the *Song of Songs* (read on Pesach), *Ruth* (Shavuot), *Lamentations* (Tisha B'Av), and *Ecclesiastes* (Sukkot). The *Book of Esther* is read on Purim. It is probably the most famous *Megillah*; when the word is used alone, as in the phrase "read the *Megillah*," invariably it is referring to the *Book of Esther*. Perhaps this is because, of the five *Megillot*, only the reading of the Book of Esther is so central to the celebration of the holiday itself. *Megillat Esther* explains exactly how Purim came to be and how we should celebrate it.

In the ancient Persian city of Shushan, Esther, also known as Hadassah, is the new wife of King Achashverosh. Unbeknownst to him, she's Jewish. Achashverosh's adviser, Haman, has it in for the Jews and convinces the king to sign an edict to destroy all Jews in Persia. Mordechai, Esther's cousin and adopted father (she was orphaned), works with Esther to foil these dastardly plans. Esther reveals her heritage to the king, along with the truth about Haman and his plans to murder her people. In the end, it is Haman himself who is hung from the prepared gallows, along with his ten sons. Jews throughout the land consequently celebrate their near miss with death.

The name of the holiday comes from the method Haman used to choose the date of death for the Jews. He cast lots, *purim*, and 14 Adar was the designated date. It seems particularly apt that we appropriated the randomness of this death sentence and turned it into the name for this holiday of celebration.

In discussing the Jewish calendar, I mentioned that during a leap year there are two months of Adar, known as Adar Aleph (Adar I) and Adar Bet (Adar II). So do we get two full-scale Purims? Not exactly. The first Adar is treated as the extra Adar. On 14 and 15 Adar Aleph, there is a celebration called *Purim Katan,* "Little Purim." The *Megillah* is not read and none of the mitzvot of Purim are required, but the day is supposed to be festive, and fasting and mourning are not allowed. The full-scale Adar holidays are observed during Adar Bet.

13 Adar—Ta'anit Ester

While Purim is a time of fun, the day before Purim is *Ta'anit Ester*, the Fast of Esther. Unlike the four other public fast days, this one does not mourn a tragic event. Rather, it commemorates the *bakasha* fast that Esther undertook, and asked the Jewish people to undertake with her, as a way of praying for spiritual guidance when she learned of Haman's plans for the Jews. In **Esther 4:16**, she tells Hatach, a trusted chamberlain, to tell Mordechai, "*Go, gather together all the Jews that are present in Shushan, and fast you for me, and neither eat nor drink three days, night or day; I also and my maidens will fast in like manner; and so will I go in unto the king, which is not according to the law; and if I perish, I perish.*"

The fast is now observed on 13 Adar, unless 13 Adar falls on Shabbat. In that case, the fast is moved to the preceding Thursday, so as not to interfere with Shabbat preparations. It is a sunrise-to-sunset fast, although there are those who continue the fast until after the *Megillah* reading. Esther's fast was actually round the clock for three days, but she was fasting to make a request specific to the situation of the Jewish people in her time, one we no longer need to make.

14 Adar—Purim

Purim has become one of the most joyous of Jewish holidays. There are four mitzvot associated with Purim. The first is to listen to the reading of the *Megillah*, in a public place, at synagogue. The *Megillah* is read both in the evening and in the morning. People wear costumes and everyone carries a noisemaker (*grogger*)—whenever Haman's name is read, we attempt to block it out with these groggers and by stamping our feet.

The *Megillah* itself contains the remaining three mitzvot to be performed on Purim. In **Esther 9:22**, Mordechai writes a letter to Jews throughout Achashverosh's kingdom, saying, "*The days wherein the Jews had rest from their enemies, and the month which was turned unto them from sorrow to gladness, and from mourning into a good day; that they should make them days of feasting and gladness, and of sending portions one to another, and gifts to the poor.*" Naturally, as befits most Jewish celebrations, food and drink are very much a part of the festivities.

"Days of feasting and gladness" is the requirement to partake in a festive meal, during the day, called *Seudat Purim*. This can be a challenge for those who work; Purim is not a *Yom Tov* day, so all work is permitted, though more observant Jews recommend taking the day off work. The Purim feast has no particular dietary customs, except for the tradition of excessive drinking.

Wine is part of all Jewish rituals, but drunkenness is normally frowned upon—except on Purim. The Talmud says, in **Megillah 7b,** "*Rava said: A person is obligated to drink on Purim until he does not know the difference between 'cursed be Haman' and 'blessed be Mordechai.'*" In Israel we celebrate with an *Ad-lo-yada*, an outdoor festival and parade. The name *Ad-lo-yada* comes from the above Talmudic quote, and means "until he does not know." In the United States, synagogues hold Purim carnivals—I remember always trying to win a goldfish.

The most famous food for Purim is hamantashen, triangular-shaped pastries made with a bread or cookie dough and filled, traditionally, with poppy seeds or prune. Those aren't exactly American kid–oriented fillings; we usually use raspberry jam, chocolate chips, and other things my children like. According to Rabbi Robert Sternberg, executive director of the Hatikvah Holocaust Education and Resource Center in Springfield, Massachusetts, and author of *Yiddish Cuisine* and *The Sephardic Kitchen*, yeast-raised hamantashen came first. "The first hamantashen probably originated during eighteenth-century Austro-Hungary," Sternberg says. "There's a tradition—which has not been documented—that 'hamantashen' is a corruption of 'mohn tashen,' pastries stuffed with a poppy seed filling. 'Mohn' means poppy seed and 'tashen' is pocket."

Many Jewish cookbooks assert that hamantashen represent the shape of Haman's hat, but Sternberg disagrees. "The triangle shape was more a part of the Napoleonic tradition, rather than the shape of a Persian hat," he says. Some say that the three corners of the pastry represent the three patriarchs, and the hidden filling represents the hidden attributes of God. In Israel the same pastries are called *oznei haman*, which means "Haman's ears." In her book *The New Jewish Holiday Cookbook*, Gloria Kaufer Greene observes, ". . . the man had pretty strange ears. Actually, the appellation probably came about because it was an old custom to cut off a condemned criminal's ears before execution."

Greene describes Sephardic deep-fried cookies, *Orejas de Haman*, that do more closely resemble ears.

I prefer to make dairy hamantashen because I like the flavor of butter, but many will only make pareve hamantashen, so that people can eat the pastries with any meal. While it is likely that poppy seeds were used because they were popular in Austro-Hungarian pastries, some say that poppy seeds are representative of Esther's diet while she was hiding her Jewishness from Achashverosh. In order to maintain kashrut, she ate a vegetarian diet of beans and seeds. For this reason, too, some cookbooks, especially those highlighting Sephardic traditions, feature bean recipes for Purim.

Another unusual dairy Sephardic pastry, described by Gilda Angel in *Sephardic Holiday Cooking*, is *foulares*, sometimes translated as "Haman's feet." A dough enriched with grated cheese is rolled and cut into a foot shape. A hard-boiled egg, in the shell, is secured to the foot with additional strips of dough. The significance of the foot shape or of the egg is not clear, but it makes for an intriguing element to the Purim feast.

The next mitzvah Mordechai describes is *mishloach manot*, also referred to as *shalach manot*; the Yiddish pronunciation is *shalach manos*, and means "sending of portions." It refers to the practice of sending small plates of food to friends and acquaintances. The package should contain two different types of food. A baked good is invariably one of these types of food, usually hamantashen, the traditional Purim delicacy. It is also a chance to use up flour in anticipation of Pesach, which begins a few weeks later. The second food might be some kind of fresh or dried fruit. I always enjoy preparing these packages—I like an excuse to bake. Hamantashen making is a ritual my kids value and start talking about in midwinter ("Can we make hamantashen now?" they'll ask beseechingly on dreary January days). In our *shalach manot* packages we usually include hamantashen, clementines, which are in season then, nuts, and pieces of chocolate.

The final mitzvah is to give money or goods to at least two people or charities. Our synagogue, as do many, collects food and clothing for several weeks before Purim and then donates the packages to a food kitchen or homeless shelter on Purim—the mitzvah is supposed to be performed on that day. In the evening, before the *Megillah* reading, a basket is passed around the synagogue for donations to the selected charity.

One commentary states that if money is tight, you should spend less on the Purim feast so you can give more to charity.

15 Adar—Shushan Purim

When Esther told Achashverosh about Haman's plan, he didn't exactly reverse it; apparently, that couldn't be done. What he did do was give Jews permission to defend themselves, and on 14 Adar that is what Jews in most of the kingdom did, victoriously. But in the capital city of Shushan, fighting lasted an additional day, and so the Jews there celebrated the holiday on 15 Adar. The rabbis determined that cities that had been walled cities at the time of Joshua should celebrate Purim a day later. Only Jerusalem definitively qualifies. A few other towns are questionable (including Jaffa, Safed, Acco, and Tiberias); in those towns the main celebration is on 14 Adar, but the *Megillah* is read on both days.

We spent our honeymoon in Israel in 1986, and happened that year to celebrate two Purims. We were in Tiberias on 14 Adar, and heard the *Megillah* read on national television in a restaurant. The next night we were in Jerusalem, and heard the *Megillah* read at a yeshiva. There is something special about being in Israel for Purim, where you walk by a bar and the program being broadcast from the elevated TV set is a *Megillah* reading.

Purim proper, 14 Adar, never falls on a Shabbat. However, Shushan Purim can fall on a Shabbat, and there are consequently a few exceptions in terms of observance. Shushan Purim ends up being a three-day holiday. The *Megillah* is read the day before, on Friday. Giving to the poor is also moved to Friday, with the thought that they should have provisions for Shabbat. On Shabbat a special prayer, *Al HaNisim* (About the Miracles), is read. And on Sunday, *mishloach manot* are sent and the *seudat Purim*—festive meal of Purim—is observed.

Nisan

15–22 Nisan

Pesach is the major Nisan holiday. And because there are so many dietary laws concerning Pesach, I have devoted a whole chapter to the subject.

16 Nisan–6 Sevan—Sfirat Ha'Omer

Sfirat Ha'Omer means "Counting of the *Omer*," and refers to the period that begins on the second night of Pesach and continues until Shavuot, seven weeks later. During this entire time, we count the *omer*, a symbolic countdown of the days until Shavuot. The *omer* is a unit of measurement in the Torah, and here it refers to a sheath of the first barley harvest (the same word is used to describe how much manna each person ate in the desert).

During the time of the Temple, Jews would bring an *omer* of the new barley harvest as an offering in the Temple. The counting period is named for that offering. The commandment to do so comes from **Leviticus 23:15–16,** "*And you shall count unto you from* *the morrow after the day of rest, from the day that you brought the sheaf of the waving; seven weeks shall there be complete; even unto the morrow after the seventh week shall you number fifty days; and you shall present a new meal-offering unto the Lord."* The "morrow after the day of rest" refers to the second day of Pesach.

In the Diaspora, where we have two seders for Pesach, we start counting the *omer* during the second seder. Every day, for forty-nine days, we recite the blessing for counting the *omer*, followed by announcing the number day of the *omer*. The "sheaf of the waving," *Omer HaTnufah*, refers to a biblical ceremony. Pesach was the first of the Three Pilgrimage Festivals. The Jews would go to Jerusalem to make sacrifices for the festival. Barley was the first plant to be harvested, so Jews would bring their first sheaves of barley as a sacrifice. The offering had to be made to God before they could use any barley for themselves. The high priest would go out into a field and declare, "Is this an *omer*?" Sfirat Ha'Omer is named for this ceremony.

Over the centuries, however, the Sfirat Ha'Omer period has become one of recurring tragedies, and is now regarded as a period of mourning. No weddings should take place during this time, or events scheduled that include music and dancing. No haircuts—some men don't shave as well.

The most significant tragic event occurred around the time of the Bar Kochba revolt (132–135 C.E.). Twenty-four thousand students of Rabbi Akiva died. The story is recounted in the Talmud, in **Yevamot 62b:** *"It was said that R. Akiba had twelve thousand pairs of disciples, from Gabbatha to Antipatris and all of them died at the same time because they did not treat each other with respect. . . . A Tanna taught: All of them died between Pesach and Shavuot. R. Hama b. Abba or, it might be said, R. Hiyya b. Abin said: All of them died a cruel death. What was it?—R. Nahman replied: Croup."*

In just over a month, a plague, "croup," killed 24,000 students; some believe they were actually wiped out during the revolt of Bar Kochba against the Romans.

Naturally, the sages had to determine a reason for such devastation, whether it was by plague or by Romans; the claim was that the students did not respect one another sufficiently, they did not honor one another. The plague was believed to have abated on the thirty-third day of the Sfirat Ha'Omer, called *Lag Ba'Omer*, pronouncing the Hebrew letters *lamed* and *gimmel* that represent the number 33. Consequently, Lag Ba'Omer is a time of celebration, during which all mourning practices are suspended.

Other tragedies in Jewish history are also thought to have occurred during Sfirat Ha'Omer, including a massacre on German Jews during the Crusades.

As for dietary laws, the first seven days of the Sfirat Ha'Omer (six in Israel) are Pesach, so those dietary restrictions apply. After that, there are no particular dietary or cooking restrictions.

Sivan

6–7 Sivan—Shavuot

Shavuot, literally "Weeks," is celebrated on the fiftieth day after the second day of Pesach, after counting the *omer* for seven weeks. One English translation is Pentecost, which means "fiftieth [day]." It is the second of the Three Pilgrimage Festivals, at which time the Jews of ancient Israel would travel to the *Beit HaMikdash,* the Holy Temple, in Jerusalem. The holiday is described in **Deuteronomy 16:9–11:** "*Seven weeks shall you count for yourselves; from when the sickle is first put to the standing crop shall you begin counting seven weeks. And you shall observe the Festival of Shavuot unto the Lord your God after the measure of the freewill-offering of your hand, which you shall give, according as the Lord your God will have blessed you. And you shall rejoice before the Lord your God.*"

Traditionally, Shavuot is regarded as the time when God gave the Jews the Ten Commandments and the Torah at Mount Sinai. For this reason, Shavuot is also called *Zman Matan Torateinu,* "Time of the Giving of Our Torah." Shavuot is a *Yom Tov* holiday, celebrated one day in Israel, two days in the Diaspora. *Yom Tov* restrictions apply regarding cooking. Often one day of Shavuot falls on Shabbat, so advance planning is necessary for the obligatory festive meals.

Like Sukkot, Shavuot is a harvest holiday—this time honoring the first harvest of the season. Another name for the holiday is *Chag HaBikurim*, "Festival of the First Fruit." It is also called *Chag HaKatzir*, which means "Holiday of the Cutting of the Crop." This refers to the wheat harvest.

On the first day of Shavuot, the Ten Commandments are read. On the second, *Megillat Ruth* (Book of Ruth) is read, the story of a Jew by choice, perhaps the most famous convert, Ruth, great-grandmother to King David. A significant part of the story takes place during the wheat harvest.

There are certain Shavuot customs—some recent, some hundreds of years old, that are enjoying a renaissance. One is *Tikkun Leil Shavuot,* "Study on the Evening of Shavuot," another practice initiated by the followers of Rabbi Isaac Luria in Safed. The custom is to study Torah all night long on the first night of Shavuot, in anticipation of the holiday that celebrates the giving of the Torah.

One of the culinary Shavuot customs is to eat dairy foods. There are a few reasons given. One is that until they received the Torah, Jews were unsure if they could drink milk or not, based on the dietary law given after the story of Noah, *ever min hachai,* the injunction against eating "flesh torn from a living body." The dietary laws that are given when God gives the Israelites the Torah indicate that dairy is acceptable to eat, so we celebrate this by eating cheesecake, cheese blintzes, and other tasty forms of dairy.

Another reason is that when they received the Torah, the Jews were not yet familiar with all the laws of *shechita,* so they played it safe by eating dairy. Also, according to Talmudic tradition as expressed in **Shabbat 86b,** *"Everyone agrees that the Torah was given on Shabbat."* Slaughter is forbidden on Shabbat; therefore the Jews ate dairy, and now we eat dairy. Another reason comes from *gematria,* Jewish numerology. The numerical value for *chalav,* the Hebrew word for milk, is 40. Moses was gone for forty days, receiving the Torah from God. All these reasons are acceptable. When else could eating cheesecake be construed as a mitzvah?

Some people also celebrate by following the dairy meal with a meat meal, as there is a tradition that a meat meal is symbolic of rejoicing.

Tammuz

17 Tammuz—Fast of the Seventeenth of Tammuz

This is a mourning fast, recalling the breaking down of the walls of Jerusalem by the Romans, which led three weeks later to the destruction of the Second Temple around 70 C.E. Traditionally, it is also considered to be the day Moses broke the Tablets of the Ten Commandments, when he came down from Mount Sinai and discovered the Israelites worshipping the golden calf. This fast is a sunrise-to-sunset fast.

Shivah-Asar B'Tammuz also marks the beginning of a three-week period of mourning, called *Bein HaMetzarim,* "Between the Straits," or sieges. Restrictions similar to those observed during Sfirat Ha'Omer are followed: weddings do not occur, the *Shehecheyanu* blessing is not said, and people don't cut their hair or listen to music. During the first nine days of the following month, Av, there are those who also refrain from eating meat or drinking wine, except on Shabbat.

Av

9 Av—Tisha B'Av

Tisha B'Av, the Ninth of Av, is a day of great mourning. Tradition says that many tragedies befell our people on Tisha B'Av. The first was the relegation of the Israelites whom God had freed from Egypt to a life of wandering in the desert.

When the Israelites were near Canaan, they sent twelve spies into the land of Canaan. The land was wonderful, the spies reported, but ten of the twelve insisted the current residents were too powerful; there was no way we could take them on. Joshua and Caleb disagreed, but the ten prevailed and succeeded in convincing all the Israelites in the desert of the hopelessness of such an endeavor.

Naturally, God was not pleased with yet another example of the Israelites' lack of faith, and declared, in **Numbers 14: 29-30,** *"You that have murmured against Me; surely you shall not come into the land, concerning which I lifted up My hand that I would make you dwell therein."*

Both the First and Second Temples were destroyed on this date. In more recent history, tradition dictates that the Jews were expelled from Spain on the Ninth of Av, though that is debatable. They certainly were expelled during Bein HaMetzarim.

Tisha B'Av is a fast day. Like Yom Kippur, this fast lasts from sunset to sunset. However, if Tisha B'Av falls on Shabbat, the fast is postponed until Sunday. Work is permitted. The last meal before the fast should be eaten before sunset. It is called *Seudah HaMafseket*, "the Separating Meal." A larger meal can be eaten at lunchtime; this meal should be simple and shouldn't contain more than one type of cooked food. No meat or fish; traditionally, the cooked food is a hard-boiled egg, which can represent the cyclical nature of mourning. Some also dip bread into ashes. However, if the day before the Tisha B'Av observance is Shabbat, these restrictions do not apply, as the mitzvah of celebrating Shabbat supercedes them.

Cooking after noon on Tisha B'Av is permitted, although the fast shouldn't be broken until nightfall. Traditionally, people refrain from eating meat at this break fast until after noon the next day, because the Temple continued burning through the night.

KOSHER FOR PESACH

✦

I DID THE MATH. I have been a participant in at least seventy-one Pesach seders (the number is odd because I spent one Pesach in Israel, where only one seder is observed). And every year I look forward to the retelling of the Exodus, and to the various symbolic elements of the seder. Because at every single seder I learn something, catch a new reference that's always been there, waiting to be noticed, and I get a different perspective on a passage I've read dozens of times.

Seder means "order," and this meal follows a set order, as outlined in the *Haggadah*, which means "story." Parts of the *Haggadah* date at least to Talmudic times. The last chapter of the tractate **Pesachim** is like an expanded version of the *Haggadah*.

Pesach, observed on 15–22 Nissan (21 in Israel), is among the most significant of the Jewish holidays. It is the holiday that recounts the birth of practical Judaism. It is the holiday with the most stringent and explicit dietary laws. And it is the holiday that requires more preparations than all the other holidays put together—including Sukkot, with its sukkah-building requirement.

Pesach celebrates the fundamental core of Judaism as it came to be observed through the millennia, because it is the celebration of the Exodus from Egypt, which led to our receiving the Torah and the Ten Commandments.

The Book of Genesis is, in effect, the *pre*history of the Jewish people, setting the stage for us to understand just who we were at the time of our enslavement in Egypt. Understanding the early evolution of nomads such as Abraham and Isaac, Sarah, Rebecca, and Leah, gives us a sense of who we were before we arrived in Egypt. The story of our enslavement and redemption from that slavery is first recounted in the Book of Exodus.

This enslavement was perhaps necessary, in order for the redemption to be appreciated and understood. And to ensure that we are never enslaved again, it is essential for us to remember the story of our enslavement in Egypt.

Pesach Roots

The commandment to observe Pesach is spelled out explicitly by God. It is not merely a case of this memorable thing happened, so we celebrate it with this holiday. No. The redemption from Egypt was a Big Deal. We are told to observe Pesach before we are given Shabbat, before we are given the Ten Commandments. In fact, God gives the commandment for observing Pesach—the commemorative holiday that marks what is about to happen—*before* it has happened.

In seven verses, **Exodus 12:14–20,** God repeats the instructions for Pesach twice: "*. . . Seven days shall you eat matzos; but on the first day you shall put away leaven out of your houses; for whosoever eats leavened bread from the first day until the seventh day, that soul shall be cut off from Israel. . . . And you shall observe the [holiday of] matzos; for on this very day have I brought your hosts out of the land of Egypt; you shall observe this day throughout your generations by an eternal decree. . . .*" It is as if God is telling the Israelites: What is about to happen is Important. Remember it.

The story of Pesach in brief: Jacob and his family (seventy people in all) move from Canaan to Egypt, when there is a famine in Canaan. Egypt, under the direction of Joseph, has storehouses of food to spare. Initially, things are fine for the Israelites, who *"were fruitful, and increased abundantly, and multiplied,"* (**Exodus 1:7**). Life is good until after the death of Joseph, as it says in **Exodus 1: 8–9,** *"Now there arose a new king over Egypt, who knew not Joseph. And he said unto his people: 'Behold, the people of the children of Israel are too many and too mighty for us.'"* To deal with this, Pharaoh enslaves the Israelites and orders all newborn male offspring killed. But Moses is saved, and is brought up by Pharaoh's daughter. Eventually, this pharaoh dies, and the new pharaoh continues the enslavement of the Israelites.

God chooses Moses to represent Him, and to lead the Israelites out of Egypt. Before the Jews are actually led out of Egypt, God causes a series of miracles to happen, specifically the Ten Plagues. Why didn't God just take the Israelites out of Egypt right away? Why was it necessary to go through the Ten Plagues, to have Pharaoh agree to let them go, ostensibly to pray in the desert, only to change his mind repeatedly? It was necessary, in part, to demonstrate God's strength, both to the Israelites and to Pharaoh. The Israelites, as much as they complained of being slaves, needed time to prepare for their own freedom. The miracles of the Ten Plagues would encourage them to believe in God, to believe that they really would be redeemed, and to perform the tasks they were assigned when the time to leave came.

Performing those tasks is a sign of commitment to God. In **Exodus 12,** God gives Moses and Aaron the instructions they are to convey to the Israelites, the steps they will need to take to save their firstborn children and to prepare for the actual redemption from slavery and from Egypt. They are told to mark their door frames with the blood of a sacrificial lamb, as God says in **Exodus 12:13,** *"And the blood shall be to you a sign upon the houses where you are; and when I see the blood, I will pass over you, and there shall no plague be upon you to destroy you, when I smite the land of Egypt."*

The commandment to keep Pesach is repeated three times before the slaying of the firstborn, before the Israelites leave Egypt. And then the Israelites are led out of Egypt and redeemed from slavery. The commandment is repeated again after God gives the Israelites the Ten Commandments, and it is repeated again in Leviticus, Numbers, and Deuteronomy.

In the Torah, the holiday is called both *Chag HaMatzot,* "Feast of the Unleavened Bread," and *Pesach.* The word *pesach* literally means "skip" or "pass over." God commanded the Israelites to mark their doorposts with the blood of a lamb that they were then to roast and eat; this lamb is also called the *pesach.* God would pass over all houses so marked during the tenth plague, the killing of the firstborn. This is why this holiday is translated as *Passover* in English. The commandment to keep Pesach is obviously very important. It essentially recalls the beginnings of Judaism. The Jewish people began with Abraham, but Judaism as a practicing religion began with the redemption from Egypt, when we could truly understand and appreciate freedom.

Freedom does not mean chaos, does not mean we can do whatever we want, who cares about the rest of the world, and God makes sure we understand this immediately upon embarking on that journey away from enslavement. Freedom means the ability to be moral, to control our actions toward our fellow human beings, without another person stopping us. Freedom gives us the ability to follow God's word, to follow the mitzvot God commanded us. Freedom means the ability to shoulder responsibility.

Shabbat is a sign of freedom. When we were slaves, we could not choose our own day of rest. When we were slaves, we couldn't choose how to observe our holidays. And we couldn't choose our foods, either—the dietary laws are not given to us until we are a free people.

Pesach Yom Tov

The Torah indicates that the first and last days of Pesach should be *Yom Tov* days. In keeping with the custom of adding an extra day, in the Diaspora the first *two* days of Pesach are *Yom Tov*, and an extra day is added at the end, making Pesach an eight-day holiday. The last two days are also *Yom Tov* days.

Yom Tov cooking restrictions apply to these days. That is, most *melachot*, working restrictions, apply except those regarding food preparation—namely, lighting a fire and cooking. However, especially on the second day, the rules about how the fire may be lit apply. Consult your rabbi concerning the special challenge of having Shabbat directly follow the two seders.

Chametz

God gives us two specific commandments regarding food on Pesach. We are told to eat matzo, not just don't eat *chametz*, if you want to eat bread it should be matzo, but we are actually *commanded* to eat matzo. The flip side is, we are not to eat chametz, "leavened foods." As **Exodus 12:18-20** states, *"In the first [month], on the fourteenth day of the month in the evening, you shall eat matzos, until the twenty-first day of the month in the evening. Seven days shall there be no leaven found in your houses; . . . You shall eat nothing leavened; in all your dwellings shall you eat matzos."*

Now, just what is chametz? There are two words the Torah uses that are translated as "leaven" in English. "Leaven" by itself is *s'or*, which is also the Hebrew word for "evil inclination." This in itself is symbolic—for one week, we are consciously to avoid any evil inclinations, which we should do all the time, anyway, but it is a focus, something to remind us each time we eat matzo during the holiday, each time we avoid eating regular bread. Chametz refers to leavened bread. *Spice and Spirit*, a cookbook produced by the Lubavitch movement, describes the difference between chametz and matzo: "The only difference between them is that *chametz* rises, while matzah remains flat. *Chametz* is thus indicative of inflated egotism, arrogance, and self-love. Matzah . . . symbolizes the qualities of selflessness and humility."

The rabbis determined that there are five grains that when combined with water can yield chametz, that is, the chemical reaction we call the leavening process: wheat, barley, rye, oats, and spelt. If the water is cold, it takes a little bit of time for the leavening process to occur. The exact time is debatable; the Talmud, in **Pesachim 46a,** states that dough becomes chametz in the amount of time it takes to walk a certain distance called a *mil*. (The debate over the amount of time this is was also used regarding when to light the candles for Shabbat.) Rashi said this time is 22.5 minutes, Rambam, 24 minutes. But the Shulchan Aruch, which is what more people follow for this particular ruling, says that dough starts to leaven after eighteen minutes. Therefore, in order for matzo to be *unleavened* bread, it has to be made, from start (when water is added) to finish (baking), in under eighteen minutes.

Any food that is made with those five grains, except for matzo and matzo products, is considered chametz. Because the commandment against eating chametz on Pesach is so strict, there are several fences around the Law to ensure that we don't inadvertently eat it.

Unlike unkosher foods such as pork or *basar b'chalav*, the mixture of meat and milk, no amount of chametz can be nullified—during Pesach. Chametz can be nullified *before* Pesach, but *during* Pesach it cannot. That is, even if a speck of bread got mixed with chicken soup, for example, the entire pot of chicken soup would be considered chametz, and could not be eaten on Pesach.

As with regular year-round kashrut, there are different levels of Pesach observance, but many people who are more casually kosher during the year are stricter during Pesach, because of the stringency of the commandment not to eat chametz. For example, Conservative Jews who might eat out at a nonkosher restaurant—even a vegetarian restaurant—will not eat out during Pesach, and will only eat in homes that have been kashered for Pesach. Similarly, Jews who keep "ingredient kosher" throughout the year might eat only products marketed with a "Kosher for Passover" hechsher.

Any company that manufactures food that is supervised as kosher for Pesach must go through stringent cleaning protocols and strict supervision, to ensure that not a single grain of wheat, for example, be mixed in with the kosher-for-Pesach products. This includes derivatives made from chametz, such as grain-based alcohol and vinegar. Some additives and flavorings also might originate from chametz products. Hechshers that indicate a product is kosher for Pesach will say so, or they might simply include the letter *P* next to their regular hechsher.

Incidentally, there are some foods that logic tells us are chametz, such as baking soda—we use it to leaven cakes and cookies, right? True, but still baking soda is not chametz because it does not contain one of the five grains. You will therefore find kosher-for-Pesach—hechshered boxes of Arm & Hammer. And if you read the ingredients labels of Pesach cake mixes, you will notice that the mixes contain bicarbonate of soda—baking soda.

Any product that contains one of the five grains, technically called an "admixture," is considered chametz. This means any cookies, crackers, bread, cereal, and so on. In addition, cookware and foodware that you use during the year is considered *chametzdig*. For Pesach, you need either to kasher the dishes you have or, preferably, have separate dishes, pots, and pans for Pesach use. Since it is not practical to purge your house of all *chametzdig* cookware and so on, it is included in a special procedure known as **Mechirat Chametz,** "Selling of the Chametz," described later in this chapter.

There are other foods, while not technically chametz according to Talmudic dictates, that are loosely called chametz to indicate they are not kosher for Pesach. This is a separate category of foods called *kitniyot*.

Kitniyot

Literally, *kitniyot* means "legumes." For Pesach, the term *kitniyot* includes legumes as well as some grains, such as rice and corn. The list includes spices like mustard, anise, and cumin. None of these are considered true chametz, but, according to Ashkenazic tradition, they are considered forbidden for consumption on Pesach. Sephardim, on the other hand, eat them on Pesach. The rules are not as strict as those for chametz—you are allowed to keep kitniyot in your possession, unlike true chametz products. The list is quite expansive for those who are truly *machmir* about kitniyot, and this perhaps has sparked a pro-kitniyot movement in some circles.

The kitniyot I was familiar with growing up were rice, corn, and all legumes—lentil soup became my mother's signature Pesach-is-almost-here dish. Much to my childhood dismay (not), peas were out, and green beans too (though this prohibition is debatable in some kitniyot circles, as green beans don't have the same issues as dried beans).

Another kitniyot issue is kitniyot derivatives, namely corn syrup and starch and soy products, such as lecithin. Whether or not kitniyot derivatives should be included was also a subject of debate. Peanut oil for some reason was okay, while peanuts and peanut butter were not, as determined by Rabbi Moshe Feinstein, author of many Orthodox Responsa.

For certain products, the ban on kitniyot is a taste plus. When Coca-Cola decided to become kosher, an issue was the corn sweetener used. They adapted their recipe to use cane sugar for all their kosher-for-Pesach sodas, as do other brands that are kosher for Pesach. I am not a soda drinker, but my husband insists that sugar-based soda tastes far superior to soda made with corn syrup. Similarly, my Aunt Raya likes the chocolate that Manischewitz manufactures for Pesach—it doesn't have lecithin as an emulsifier, and she claims it makes for smoother, better-tasting chocolate.

The Talmud discusses grains such as rice and millet in **Tractate Pesachim**, and concludes that they are permissible to eat during Pesach, and that they are not permissible for making matzo. At some time during the ensuing six hundred years, eschewing certain kitniyot for Pesach became a practice in some Ashkenazic communities. This was first documented in the thirteenth century by Rabbi Isaac ben Rabbi Joseph of Corbeil, who is called by the acronym of the work he is most famous for, the *SeMaK*, which stands for *Sefer Mitzvot ha-Katan* or *ha-Kitzur*, "The Small Book of Commandments." While acknowledging that kitniyot are not technically chametz, the Semak cites several reasons given by the sages for not eating kitniyot—even though the Talmud says it is acceptable. Because they look similar to some chametz grains, legumes and grains such as rice and millet might have chametz grains mixed in with them. Since chametz can't be nullified from a mixture, the kitniyot would become a chametz mixture.

Also, kitniyot products can be ground into a flour and made into bread- and cereal-like products. People might think a forbidden grain dish was a kitniyot dish and eat the chametz product. This reasoning is similar to the reason that fowl are considered meat—because they look like meat. Also, some kitniyot grow next to fields where chametz grows, and the two might accidentally be mixed together.

By the time Joseph Caro wrote the Shulchan Aruch, with Moses Isserles's Ashkenazic addendum, three hundred years later in 1569, the Sephardic and Ashkenazic traditions on kitniyot were firm, and opposite. Today still, the custom is for Ashkenazic Jews not to eat kitniyot and for Sephardic Jews to eat kitniyot, although some Sephardic communities avoid rice.

Since more Jews in the United States are of Ashkenazic origin, and the Conservative, Reform, and Reconstructionist movements have Ashkenazic roots as well, the custom here has been not to have kitniyot. In Israel, however, which is much more of a melting pot of Jewish roots, people are more aware of the Sephardic customs. When we lived in Israel, markets sold products such as rice cakes, with the label declaring "Kosher for Pesach for Those Who Eat Kitniyot." These products are more difficult to find here.

There are other reasons given over the years for why particular products are considered kitniyot. Various seeds and spices, such as anise and *kimmel* (which has various translations, including caraway, cumin, and fennel), were said to grow near wheat fields, and therefore might be mixed with chametz. Mustard also belongs to this group because it grows in pods similar to those of beans. Canola oil is made from rapeseed, which is in the mustard family, so some avoid canola oil on Pesach.

Further, there are so-called *kitniyot shenishtanu*, literally, "altered" kitniyot. Products including citric acid, ascorbic acid, dextrose, and glucose are often made from corn. Some rabbis say that this is acceptable; others that it is not. I read a ruling by a Sephardic rabbi that indicated those products can now be made from wheat, so Sephardim, too, need to be careful of such products on Pesach.

In all, the following have been included in lists of kitniyot; as always, check with your rabbi for your local custom.

Spices and seeds: anise, caraway seeds, coriander, cumin, fennel, fenugreek, flax seeds, mustard, poppy seeds, sesame seeds, sunflower seeds

Legumes: beans such as lentils, chickpeas, green beans, peas, peanuts (although peanut oil was determined to be acceptable by Rabbi Moshe Feinstein, which is why you may remember buying peanut oil years ago; nowadays it is more difficult to find kosher-for-Pesach peanut oil)

Soy products, including soy beans, tofu, lecithin

Corn and corn products, including popcorn, corn syrup, cornstarch (found in confectioners' sugar), corn oil, glucose, dextrose, citric acid

Buckwheat (kasha), rice (although Sephardim are wary of enriched rice, as some added vitamins are chametz derivatives), millet, canola oil

There are some strongly worded statements indicating that eating kitniyot is not a choice—if it is your *minhag*, custom, it is acceptable; if not, you should not switch.

That said, there is activity in the Conservative movement in Israel to end the ban on kitniyot for Ashkenazim. Rabbi David Golinkin, chair of the Va'ad Halakhah of the Rabbinical Assembly of Israel, which gives halachic guidance to the Masorti/Conservative movement in Israel, wrote a Responsum in 1989 advocating the relinquishing of the custom of not eating kitniyot on Pesach, for several reasons. "In our opinion it is permitted (and perhaps even obligatory) to eliminate this custom. It is in direct contradiction to an explicit decision in the Babylonian Talmud **(Pesachim 114b),**" Golinkin writes. ". . . Nevertheless, the reason for the custom was unknown and as a result many sages invented at least eleven different explanations for the custom. As a result, R. Samuel of Falaise, one of the first to mention it, referred to it as a 'mistaken custom' and R. Yerucham called it a 'foolish custom.'" Golinkin then cites several reasons *why* kitniyot should be permitted. He notes that restricting the foods permitted on Pesach can detract from the holiday while at the same time giving kitniyot more importance than chametz. Further, it can be divisive in setting up different customs among different ethnic Jewish groups in Israel. He concludes, "Therefore, both Ashkenazim and Sephardim are permitted to eat legumes and rice on Pesah without fear of transgressing any prohibition."

This Responsum was approved unanimously and is the official stand of the Va'ad Halakhah for Conservative Jews living in Israel. However, Golinkin notes, "It was not intended for the U.S., where you cannot buy, for example, peanut butter that says 'Kosher for Pesach.'"

Matzo

Matzo is almost synonymous with Pesach—we are commanded to eat it for the seder, and it helps us recall those final moments in Egypt. For much of the few thousand years that it was being eaten, matzo was made by hand. This changed during the Industrial Age in America, with the development of the matzo factory. This was during the period of kashrut controversy that was dogging *shechita*, during the development of the hechshering system that began slowly at the end of the nineteenth century. Bakeries such as Manischewitz, Horowitz, and Goodman all began in the late nineteenth century, and as the supervising controversies settled down, commercially made matzo—that is, matzo made by machines—was considered acceptable for kosher-for-Pesach use.

For years, all matzo was made only with wheat. But as wheat allergies seem to grow, kosher-for-Pesach matzo made from other grains has gained acceptance.

Not all matzo is acceptable for Pesach use. There are matzo products, such as small, bite-sized matzo crackers, that are not supervised as kosher for Pesach. Just because a package says "Matzo" on the label does not mean it is kosher for Pesach. Check the labels carefully.

Today, there are a few different kinds of matzo: *shmura*, regular, egg, and matzo made from other flour.

Shmura means "guarded." *Shmura* matzo is matzo made from grains that were supervised from the time the wheat was harvested until the finished product was completed. Guarded from what? From moisture. The necessity to guard the flour comes from the passage in **Exodus 12:17**, *"And you shall guard the matzos."* The word *shamor* is used, which can also mean "keep" or "observe," and this line also gets translated as "You shall observe the holiday of the matzos." But the rabbis went with the first translation, and interpreted it to mean the matzo must be guarded to ensure that it not become leavened. Regular matzo is guarded from moisture as well, but only from the time the grain is ground into flour.

Matzo is also called *lechem oni*, "bread of affliction" or "poverty." In contrast, egg matzo is called *matzo ashira*, "rich matzo." Egg matzo, while kosher for Pesach, is not considered true matzo. Egg matzo is made with flour, eggs, and juice. True matzo has to be made with water only. More stringently observant Jews will not eat egg matzo, deeming it to be acceptable only for small children, the elderly, and the "infirm."

Today, in consideration of the rising number of people with wheat and gluten allergies, matzo made from other flours can be found, such as gluten-free oat matzo, made from special oats (regular oats contain gluten). There is also kosher-for-Pesach matzo made with grape juice. Again, because it is not made with water, it is not considered true matzo. True matzo has the potential to become chametz. According to some rabbinic authorities, chemicals in fruit juices inhibit the reaction necessary to produce leavening, so matzo made with juice would not fulfill the commandment to eat matzo. It is not, however, chametz.

Gebrochts

Gebrochts is Yiddish for "broken." It refers to broken matzo, such as matzo farfel and matzo meal. A very *machmir* observance during Pesach, primarily among Chassidim, is to eat nothing made with *gebrochts*. The concern (unproven, but this certainly is a fence around the Law) is that there might be bits of uncooked flour contained within the matzo. If the matzo is then moistened, as it is with dishes such as matzo brie, or matzo balls, or any of the myriad kosher-for-Pesach cake mixes, there is a chance that chametz could happen. To play it safe, they avoid anything made with *gebrochts*. However, the eighth day of Pesach is in a way an extra day. Those who do not eat *gebrochts* or kitniyot during the first seven days of Pesach may eat them on this day.

Preparing for Pesach

I see Pesach as comprising two parts: the seders and the rest of the holiday. The seders are the focal point of the holiday, in that they include the rituals and practices we associate with Pesach. The rest of the holiday basically concerns going about daily life following the Pesach dietary restrictions. However, the preparations we need to make are for the holiday in its entirety.

Pesach itself requires elaborate preparations. This sometimes strikes me as ironic because one thing that characterized the Israelites' departure from Egypt was haste—they had to leave with barely any possessions, and they had to leave so quickly, they did not have time to make leavened bread. Yet preparing for Pesach takes weeks (certainly several days if you are a less organized person).

Well before Pesach begins, cleanup must happen. Cleaning the house for Pesach is like preparing your house for kashering all over again. It truly is a spring cleaning. You use up food you have, make room for new food. And clean, clean, clean.

I remember that first Pesach after my family began keeping kosher when I was a kid. We had just renovated the kitchen that particular year and we were able to use our Formica countertops not covered with aluminum foil. My parents stayed up late into the night, packing up all our year-round dishes, hauling up boxes from the basement containing our *Pesachdig* dishes, one set for dairy, one set for meat. There were not two extra sets of flatware, however. The *hag'alah* pot was brought out and water set to boiling, to kasher all our silverware for Pesach. Fortunately, we had two bathrooms as well, because one bathtub was occupied by all our glasses for three days.

Pesach Food

When purchasing food for Pesach, there are certain Before and During rules that apply: You cannot purchase food on Yom Tov days, namely the first two and last two days of Pesach, and on the Shabbat that falls during Pesach. At most, you'll have the four days of *chol hamo'ed* to purchase foods.

Most people who are observing Pesach kashrut will buy only prepared foods with a kosher-for-Pesach label. Check with your rabbi which hechshers are reliable for Pesach; usually the "Big Four" are acceptable—that is, OU, Star-K, Kof-K, and Circle K (OK). There are a number of products imported from Israel, which certain communities do *not* find acceptable for Pesach. Every year, the different organizations publish lists of acceptable kosher-for-Pesach items, by brand name.

The most reliable sources for lists of kosher-for-Pesach items are available online, as those are updated regularly. There is also an annual publication, *The Laws of Pesach: A Digest*, by Rabbi Avrohom Blumenkrantz, available at most Jewish bookstores. Each year, it gives a thorough explanation of Pesach, from an Orthodox point of view, along with a list of kosher-approved products for the year.

According to the "Rabbinical Assembly Pesah Guide," published by the Conservative movement, certain foods may be purchased *before* Pesach and do not require a kosher-for-Pesach hechsher. These include the following: "Unopened packages or containers of natural coffee without cereal additives (however, be aware that coffees produced by General Foods are not kosher for Passover unless marked KP); sugar; pure tea (not herbal tea); salt (not iodized); pepper; natural spices; frozen fruit juices with no additives; frozen (uncooked) vegetables; milk; butter; cottage cheese; cream cheese; ripened cheeses such as cheddar (hard), muenster (semi-soft) and Camembert (soft); frozen (uncooked) fruit (with no additives); baking soda."

Orthodoxy allows items to be purchased before Pesach, but would not advocate cheeses without a hechsher. You also need to be careful about cottage cheese and cream cheese, as these can sometimes have *chametzdig* stabilizers added.

Some Orthodox have a tradition of not purchasing milk during Pesach. According to the OK certification website, ". . . cows eat grain, and grain becomes chametz upon prolonged contact with liquid. The custom to purchase dairy products before Pesach is rooted in the fear that a chametz particle may be present in the milk." If the milk is purchased before Pesach, the chametz *can* be nullified. Chametz *cannot* be nullified during Pesach. Milk that is certified kosher for Pesach is acceptable to purchase during *chol hamo'ed* Pesach.

If you are keeping a more *machmir* kashrut during Pesach, all prepared products, including items such as ketchup, vinegar, and gefilte fish, should have a kosher-for-Pesach hechsher.

Kashering Your House for Pesach

Much of kashering your house for Pesach is similar to kashering your house for the first time. The main exception is, you need to clean thoroughly any room that may have had food in it over the course of the year. If you eat snacks in your bedroom, your office, the kids' playroom, the living room, dining room—sweep, dust, clean everywhere. Check the pockets of your clothes for crumbs. And clean the car, too. I know people whose cars are spotless, with nary a crumb (or Cheerio) to be seen (usually they don't have children). Ours is not one of those cars. Especially when my children were younger and we had a car seat. All kinds of *chametz* gets caught under a car seat. It says in **Exodus 13:7**, "*. . . There shall no leavened bread be seen with you, neither shall there be leaven seen with you in all your borders.*" This includes all your property, including the car.

Still, the food center, the kitchen, is where most of the Pesach preparations will take place. Much of the instructions here refer you to those in the chapter on Kashering Your Kitchen; much is similar, with a few exceptions. Kashering for Pesach is much stricter. Certain items, which may have been kasherable when converting your kitchen, must be put away or hidden from view.

Hardware

CABINETS AND DRAWERS

Cabinets and drawers that are not going to be used on Pesach and are going to contain chametz do not require special cleaning—they just need to be marked and sealed, at least symbolically. Cabinets you will use during Pesach, including those that will hold dishes, need to be cleaned thoroughly. Although it is technically not a requirement, shelves and drawers should be lined with shelving paper, making a symbolic separation from the shelves used throughout the year.

COUNTERTOPS AND TABLES

Thoroughly clean all countertops, then cover with aluminum foil or a non-absorbent paper such as wax, parchment, or contact paper. Technically, if you have a countertop that is kasherable, you do not need to cover it. The tradition, nonetheless, for both Orthodox and Conservative, is to cover the counter, indicating a higher level of strictness than during the rest of the year, and separation from what is used for chametz. Cover the countertops with tinfoil or paper of choice and secure with masking tape, making sure that all seams are sealed with the tape.

Your kitchen and dining room tables should also be cleaned and covered. A freshly washed tablecloth is sufficient to cover the tables; use separate cloths for dairy and meat meals.

THE SINK

As as with kashering your kitchen, stainless steel and stone sinks are kasherable for Pesach, porcelain sinks are not. If you have two sinks, use one for dairy and one for meat, as you do the rest of the year.

Kasher the sink as outlined in the chapter on kashering your kitchen. Make sure to give yourself enough time before Pesach begins so the sink can sit, unused, for twenty-four hours. If you have one sink, use plastic racks and tubs. These should be separate from the racks and tubs you use the rest of the year, as those are *chametzdig*.

Appliances—Large

REFRIGERATOR/FREEZER

Thoroughly clean the refrigerator, just as you did in kashering your kitchen. If you are keeping some refrigerated chametz (albeit sold to a non-Jew, see page 187), keep it in a separate, sealed-off section of the refrigerator. Sometimes there are items kept on the shelves on the door. Seal the shelves off so you won't accidentally use them, using wax paper or aluminum foil adhered with masking tape.

The shelves of the refrigerator do not need to be covered during Pesach, but many people do so anyway, using aluminum foil, wax paper, or special lightweight plastic trays sold just for that purpose.

COOKTOP

Cooktops should be thoroughly cleaned and not used for twenty-four hours, then kashered the same way you would when kashering your kitchen.

OVEN

Ovens are also to be cleaned throughly and kashered. Some cover the racks during Pesach; a more *machmir* Orthodox observance is to have separate racks for Pesach use.

DISHWASHER

The same Orthodox versus Conservative rulings regarding kashering dishwashers for general use apply to kashering them for Pesach use. According to Conservative rules, dishwashers may be kashered for Pesach as they are when kashering your kitchen. According to Orthodox halacha, dishwashers cannot be kashered for Pesach unless they are made from metal. Although they can be kashered when made from metal, most Orthodox do not recommend using such dishwashers during Pesach.

Appliances—Small

MICROWAVE OVEN

May be kashered for Pesach as outlined in the chapter on kashering your kitchen. Those with a browning element cannot usually be kashered for Pesach; check with your rabbi.

ELECTRIC MIXER, BLENDER, FOOD PROCESSOR

Although electric mixers can be kashered when you are kashering your kitchen, both Orthodox and Conservative do not advocate using them for Pesach. Even if you have separate bowls or beaters for Pesach, since mixers are used primarily for baking, there is a possibility that bits of chametz may be lodged on the base or near the motor, in places impossible to clean thoroughly. Purchase an inexpensive handheld mixer to reserve for Pesach use, and put away the mixer you use the rest of the year.

Similarly, most rabbis recommend not using the blender or food processor you use during the year. We grate our apples for haroset by hand for Pesach.

IMMERSION BLENDER

Do without, or get a new one for Pesach.

SLOW COOKER

Not kasherable for Pesach.

COFFEEMAKER/COFFEE GRINDER

You may use your coffeemaker, but you need to have separate, kosher-for-Pesach parts, even if you clean it thoroughly. For standard coffeemakers with a glass pitcher and removable plastic filter insert, this may be possible. Some coffeemakers now have a metal thermos pitcher, which can be a more expensive option.

TOASTER OVEN AND TOASTER

Not kasherable for Pesach.

ELECTRIC WAFFLE IRON, GRIDDLE, SANDWICH MAKER, GEORGE FOREMAN GRILL

Not kasherable for Pesach.

OUTDOOR GRILL

Kasher as outlined in the chapter on kashering your kitchen.

Foodware

The rules for kashering dishes for a kosher kitchen apply to Pesach as well; again, they are a bit more stringent. Rabbis recommend that you have separate dishes for Pesach, different from those you use the rest of the year. This is a practice made easier by the mass production of chinaware; I wonder if four sets of dishes were *de rigeur* in kosher households a thousand years ago. Or even more recently. Mimi Mazor, a librarian at the Hebrew College Library in Newton, Massachusetts, is married to a Syrian Jew who grew up in Israel. She remembers when they were living in Israel, that his family had a custom of *hag'alah*, "boiling"—but they would do it for the china dishes they used year round, to kasher them for Pesach. "Who had four sets of dishes?" Mazor asks rhetorically. This is not an accepted form of kashering for Pesach in the United States today. Both Conservative and Orthodox rulings indicate that earthenware cannot be kashered for Pesach.

Many people do kasher their flatware for Pesach using *hag'alah*. Both Conservative and Orthodox rule that pans used for baking, both glass and metal, cannot be used for Pesach.

The Shabbat *blech* can be kashered through *libun gamur*, being heated until it is red hot, but most recommend that you have a separate *blech* for Pesach. Similarly, pots and pans can be kashered through *hag'alah*, but most people have separate pots and pans for Pesach to avoid confusion.

According to Conservative ruling, glassware not used for baking can be kashered, by *milui v'irui*, or simply by scrubbing. Check with your rabbi. The Orthodox ruling is the same, although a stricter ruling is to have separate glassware for Pesach.

Getting Rid of Chametz

During the month before Pesach, you should be gradually getting rid of all chametz. The week before Pesach is not the time to stock up on spaghetti. For me, it's always a challenge with bread and cereal. To have enough for sandwiches for my kids' lunches each day, but not so much there will be half a loaf left the day before Pesach. And gauging just the right amount of cereal so the last flake is poured exactly the day before Pesach.

Still, you will have leftover chametz, like vinegar, spices, condiments, alcohol, items that are used in small amounts. Even items that are technically kosher for Pesach, if they have been used during the year, they could have been exposed to chametz and thereby rendered chametz themselves, and so cannot be used during Pesach.

Any nonperishable leftover food should be put in a box and stored separately, or all put together in a cupboard that should remain shut, preferably sealed with a piece of masking tape as well, for the duration of the holiday. You should symbolically sell this food.

By the day before Pesach, your house should be thoroughly cleaned of chametz.

There are, however, a few more steps to take to truly purge it: **Mechirat chametz** and **Bedikat chametz**, which includes the **bitul chametz** (nullification of chametz), and the **bi'ur chametz** (destroying of chametz).

Mechirat Chametz

Unless you are a total whiz at calculating your food consumption, you will still have some chametz in the house come Pesach. Some of it you may choose to give away to friends or charity. But there may be some items you wish to keep (such as your *chametzdig* dishes). In this case, you need to sell them to a non-Jew. There is a special procedure and bill of sale for this called *mechirat chametz*, "selling of chametz." Your rabbi will have forms; there are books with the bill-of-sale form published, and a copy of the form is even available online. This is a formality that most synagogues take care of. It is necessary, because God says, in **Exodus 12:19**, "*. . . There shall be no leaven found in your houses.*" By selling your chametz to a non-Jew, you are no longer in *possession* of the product. You then "buy back" your property when the holiday is over.

There is a commandment that you should not own chametz during Pesach. If a Jewish-owned market did not sell its chametz during the holiday, it would not be considered acceptable to purchase that chametz after the holiday.

The arrangements for the *mechirat chametz* must be made in advance and completed before Pesach begins. For any remnants of chametz that are left, you need to perform a three-part procedure.

Bedikat Chametz

Once the house is thoroughly cleaned and essentially ready, it is time for one last check. *Bedikat chametz* literally means "checking for chametz." It is a ritual that is both symbolic and practical. For Orthodox Jews, it is in fact one last time to examine all the nooks and crannies of your house where crumbs might have fallen. For many, it is merely a symbolic search—you have cleaned your house, now you are symbolically finding the last vestiges of chametz. *Bedikat chametz* is performed on the evening of 14 Nisan, the day before the first seder.

There is a tradition to hide small pieces of bread and to search for them using a candle, feather, and paper bag; some people use a wooden spoon instead of a bag. The candle is to illuminate any dark corners, revealing the chametz. The bag is for keeping the collection of pieces and crumbs that are found. The feather is used to sweep the crumbs into the bag, or onto the wooden spoon. There are some traditions that require ten pieces of bread to be hidden. Why ten? Various interpretations: One draws a connection to Purim, saying the ten represent Haman's ten sons. Another, more lofty interpretation states that the ten represent the ten Kabbalistic attributes of God.

At the beginning of the search, you should say the following blessing,

> *Baruch ata Adonai, Eloheinu melech ha'olam, asher kidshanu b'mitzvotav vitzivanu al bi'ur chametz.*
> Blessed are you, Lord our God, King of the universe, who has sanctified us with his commandments and commanded us to destroy chametz.

(The various statements and blessings relating to the chametz will be found in the beginning of most Haggadot.) After collecting all the chametz, you make a statement that nullifies the chametz still in your house. This does not mean if flour gets into your matzo balls it's okay because you nullified it; this just means if any crumbs are left lying around, it is as if they don't exist.

Earlier I said rules for Pesach were stricter because even an infinitesimal amount of chametz would render an entire dish chametz. While it is true that chametz cannot be nullified *on* Pesach, it can be nullified *before* Pesach, hence the nullification ritual.

When you have finished the search, make this declaration: "Any form of leaven that is in my possession which I have not seen or have not removed, or have no knowledge of, shall be null and disowned as the dust of the earth." This is the **bitul chametz,** the nullification of the chametz.

Finally, keep the crumbs in a safe place; the next morning it is time for the **bi'ur chametz** (destroying the chametz). Literally, *bi'ur* means "destroy" or "burn." Fire is the traditional method for destroying the last bit of chametz, but flushing the crumbs is acceptable as well. There is something satisfyingly symbolic about burning the crumbs, however.

Note that bread crumbs do not really burn that well. This may be why some people wrap the pieces of bread in paper before burning them. You need good kindling and a well-ventilated area that is far from flammable substances to do the *bi'ur chametz*. Again, you make a statement similar but slightly different from the one made upon finding the chametz the night before: "Any form of leaven that is in my possession which I have seen or have not seen, which I have removed or have not removed, shall be null and disowned as the dust of the earth."

Between Meals

From about ten in the morning on the day of the evening of the first seder, we are not supposed to eat chametz (the exact time depends on the time of the sunset, and varies from year to year). We are also not yet supposed to eat matzo—we are supposed to savor the taste only when we do so at the seder. Our lunch on the seder day usually consisted of kosher-for-Passover tuna and yogurt.

Ta'anit Bechorim: Fast of the Firstborn

As the Israelites were preparing to escape from Egypt, God gave them a test of faith— they were to slaughter a lamb and paint their door frames with the blood. As God went through Egypt slaying the firstborn of every family, he would pass over any house with this sign. Further, God says, in **Exodus 13:2,** *"Sanctify unto Me all the first-born, what-soever opens the womb among the children of Israel, both of man and of beast, it is Mine."*

Because the firstborn Israelites were spared, firstborns are obligated to fast on the day before Pesach, from sunset until the seder. However, there is a custom to have a *siyum* celebration that morning. *Siyum* means "conclusion" and refers to when someone completes studying a tractate of Talmud. Such an occasion is worthy of celebration with the community. Therefore, if a firstborn attends a *siyum*, he is obligated to participate in the celebratory meal that follows; the occasion of the *siyum* supercedes the requirement to fast. This has become the normative practice in most communities, and it seems more people observe the *siyum* than the fast.

Some Orthodox rabbis say the fast applies only to males; others say it applies to both males and females. Under Conservative rulings, the fast applies to both males and females.

Most fast days do not have an exemption option. You, personally, may not choose to fast on those days, but according to halacha you are supposed to. There's not an option to finish a Talmud tractate and bypass Tisha B'Av, for example. In *Rite and Reason,* Shmuel Pinchas Gelbard cites three reasons the *siyum* clause is allowed: *Ta'anit Bechorim* is not mentioned in the Talmud, and so is a custom, rather than a rabbinical law.

Also, the fast might weaken someone, making it difficult to fulfill the mitzvot of Pesach properly. Finally, Gelbard writes, "The gentiles had a custom to fast on the day before their holidays. Hence the Rabbis were lenient concerning this fast, so we should not appear to be imitating the gentiles' practice."

However, there are those who advocate observing the fast and not bypassing it. In a comment in Michael Strassfeld's *The Jewish Holidays*, Edward Greenstein writes, "I never attend a *siyyum* to avoid the fast. I am conscious of three reasons. First, I object to the legal loophole of the *siyyum*. It smacks of insincerity and corruption. Torah should be studied for its own sake. Second, I applaud observances that help make us sensitive to the suffering of others, even our enemies, for whom we need special sensitizing. As a firstborn spared, I want to feel for the firstborn of Egypt, who were singled out as victims so that God could make a point. And third, the seder food, that first matzah, tastes extra good following a day of fasting."

The Seder

Pesach is celebrated for eight days (seven days in Israel), but the most significant part of the holiday is the seder. Some Reform Jews and Jews in Israel observe one seder; everywhere else Pesach is celebrated for two nights. Some people question the two-night option, since basically we repeat the entire ritual on the second night. When we lived in Israel and had just one seder, which was at a hotel, I missed our dual-night seders. It gives you the option to share the seder experience with more people.

There are many books that go into great detail on how to conduct a seder, which is beyond the scope of this book on Jewish dietary laws, but I do want to close this chapter with a description of the seder plate.

The Seder Plate

The seder plate, called the **k'arah,** is the symbolic centerpiece of the table. It contains five to six elements, plus the matzo, which are symbolic of the seder and of the Pesach story, which we are obligated to tell this night, as it says in **Exodus 12:24,** *"And you shall observe this thing for an ordinance to you and to your children forever."* The various elements of the seder and the symbolic seder plate developed in part to be entertaining to children—telling children the story of Pesach is part of the commandment. **Exodus 12:26-27** states, *"And it shall come to pass, when your children shall say to you, What is this service to you? And you shall say: 'It is the sacrifice of the Lord's Passover, for He passed over the houses of the children of Israel in Egypt, when He smote the Egyptians, and delivered our houses.' And the people bowed their heads and worshipped."*

Different rabbis have suggested different arrangements of the seder plate over the ages. The most common arrangement of the seder-plate elements is based on one devised by Rabbi Isaac Luria, he of the Tu B'Shvat seder and *Tikkun Leil Shavuot.*

All seder plates have the shankbone, the ***zeroah;*** the egg, ***beitzah; maror,*** bitter herbs; and ***charoset,*** a mixture made from fresh or dried fruit and nuts. The additional two items are ***karpas,*** usually translated as parsley or greens, and ***chazeret,*** usually translated as lettuce, a second bitter herb. The foods used for these categories can vary.

Rabbi Luria's arrangement, while appearing to be a circle, is actually more like a Magen David, a star made with an inverted triangle placed atop another triangle. The *zeroah* is on the upper right, the *beitzah* on the upper left. The *chazeret* forms the point of their upside-down triangle. The *maror* is in the center of the plate, the *karpas* on the lower left, and the *charoset* on the lower right. The point of the upright triangle is beyond the plate—the three matzot that will be used during the seder and that are usually located on a separate plate.

Zeroah is the shankbone of a lamb or, more common in this country, a chicken neck. It represents the lamb the Israelites were commanded to roast that first night of Pesach, back in Egypt. During the days of the Temple, Jews would continue to sacrifice a lamb during Pesach. Since the Temple was destroyed, it is the custom for many communities not to eat roast lamb on Pesach; in some communities, the opposite is true. The *zeroah* literally means "arm," and also represents the strength of God, the outstretched arm that helped save us from the Egyptians, as it says in **Deuteronomy 26:8,** *"And the Lord brought us forth out of Egypt with a mighty hand, and with an outstretched arm, and with great terribleness, and with signs, and with wonders."* The shankbone—or the chicken neck—can figuratively represent a miniature outstretched arm. The Talmud suggests that those who don't eat meat use a roasted beet. Some use a roasted yam, as a play on the word *lamb.* (An elongated yam more closely resembles an arm than a spherical beet, also.)

Beitzah is an egg, preferably roasted or boiled and roasted. Eggs are imbued with much symbolism. The *k'arah* egg represents the festival sacrifice, *korban chagigah,* which was roasted. Eggs are also a symbol of mourning; even though Pesach is a joyous occasion, we remember moments of sadness. The first night of Pesach is the same day of the week as Tisha B'Av, a fast day commemorating the destruction of the Holy Temple. Since the Temple was destroyed, we have been unable to offer sacrifices, and the egg is symbolic of the sacrifice we are unable to offer. The round shape is a symbol of continuity. Eggs are also a symbol of birth and rebirth: Pesach is a spring festival, when the earth is reborn after winter.

The Talmud, in **Pesachim 39a,** mentions five bitter herbs, although the exact translations of three of them are not really clear, which may be why *maror* and *chazeret* are the two that have continued. *Maror* (which has the same root as *mar*, "bitter") is bitter herbs. We eat the bitter herbs twice during the seder, once by itself and once dipped in *charoset*. While many use horseradish for both of these, some use a different kind of *maror* for each mitzvah.

Bitter herbs symbolize various things. They were included in the commandment to eat the slaughtered lamb, in **Exodus 12:8,** *"And they shall eat the meat in that night, roast with fire, and matzos; with bitter herbs they shall eat it."*

The food used for *maror* varies, though the symbolism is similar. The bitter herbs remind us of the bitter time our ancestors had as slaves in Egypt. For some traditions, romaine lettuce is the *maror*. The claim is that it starts out sweet, but becomes more bitter as you chew. This has not been my experience with romaine lettuce, but I appreciate the symbolism, which indicates that initially the Egyptians behaved nicely toward the Israelites; ultimately, their treatment of the Israelites turned bitter.

I grew up with horseradish as the *maror*. We used prepared horseradish, which was colored red with beets. We used to go to Baltimore to do our Pesach shopping, and Baltimore *maror* had a reputation for being truly tear-inducing, sinus-clearingly, mouth-searingly *hot*.

For several years, my family shared a seder with the Bardin family in Washington, D.C. They supplied fresh horseradish from their garden. Horseradish is a root plant. One year, David Bardin gave us a bit of root and told us to plant it. The horseradish has flourished in the past half decade. Long, wide leaves grow almost four feet high, and the root is as pungent as ever.

Chazeret is another kind of bitter herb; not all seder plates have a space for this. Those that do use it for the bitter herb that is eaten with the *charoset*. Seder plates with space for the *chazeret* can use two kinds of bitter herb, but more often, this space on the seder plate is occupied by lettuce.

Charoset represents the bricks and mortar the Israelites were forced to make. When Moses first went to ask Pharaoh to let the Israelites go worship God in the desert, Pharaoh responded by withholding straw from the Israelites, saying they had to find their own to make their quota of bricks. *Charoset*, which literally means "mixture," comes from the same Hebrew root as the word for "clay." Although it is symbolic of an act of suffering for our people, *charoset* has become a sought-after treat of the seder plate. It usually is some sort of sweet, conserve-like mixture made of nuts and fruit. Our tradition, since I followed my grandmother's recipe, was to use apples, walnuts, honey, cinnamon, and Pesach wine. A family friend whose family hailed from Spain would bring his old family recipe *charoset*, made with dates and chestnuts.

Karpas represents the greenery of spring, and literally means "parsley." We always use parsley at our seders. Chassidim use a boiled potato, or sometimes a radish; more likely these were more readily available in the early spring-cum-late-winter of an Eastern European Pesach.

The *karpas* is dipped during the seder. At our seders, we dip the *karpas* in salt water, said to represent the tears shed by our ancestors when they were slaves in Egypt. Some Sephardic Jews use lemon juice or vinegar for the same reason. Some place the salt water on the seder plate; others do not. The salt water also represents the sea, as in the Red Sea that was parted to let the Israelites through during the final leg of their escape from Egypt. I like to think that dipping the parsley also represents the *hyssop,* the plant the Israelites used to dip in blood and then paint their doorposts so God would pass over them.

The Flavors of Pesach

There are certain foods I always associate with Pesach. Yes, matzo balls and chicken soup, and matzo, of course. There were also the foods we would buy only on Pesach. On Pesach I loved to stir up the coffee cake and brownie mixes that came in a box with their own foil pan. Fruit slices, the sugared jelly semicircles, red, orange, yellow, green, with a white band resembling the peel. Candy I'd never touch during the year, but relished on Pesach. My cousin Dea and I used to vie for Barton's seder mints, squares of dark chocolate with a runny peppermint filling.

Certified kosher-for-Pesach foods have expanded tremendously, but still our food choices are limited during this holiday, and restaurants are not an option. Pesach is like a supersanctification of meals because we are triply conscious of what we eat this week, worrying about chametz on top of the other concerns of kashrut.

I feel a connection to other Jews most strongly during Pesach. There is the daily connection of kashrut, but Pesach—a holiday all Jews around the world celebrate at the same time, in any way they choose to celebrate it—always involves rituals, and remembering. Past, present, and future are brought together in the Pesach seder.

A TASTE OF KASHRUT: RECIPES

WHEN I THINK OF JEWISH FOOD, I think of Jewish holidays, as so many of our holidays have favorite foods associated with them. What makes a recipe kosher per se? Look in many kosher cookbooks—the recipes won't seem so different from those in regular cookbooks, at first glance. But then you realize, there are no recipes that call for chicken to be sautéed in butter, for crumbled bacon to be scattered atop a salad, for shrimp to be tossed with pasta. No substitutions are necessary—the recipes can be prepared *as presented* in a kosher kitchen.

Following are recipes I prepare for Shabbat and other holidays, as well as some of my favorites for any occasion.

Challah

Pareve • • • Makes 2 medium loaves of challah

There is something about yeast breads that seems almost magical, the way the dough just swells and rises of its own accord. It's that rising period that makes bread baking seem so time-consuming. Yet I love homemade challah, and the heady aroma that fills the house as it bakes. A bread machine inspired me to make challah on a regular basis, even though there are some very good kosher bakeries nearby.

I developed this recipe for a bread machine, using the dough setting to mix and knead the bread, then taking it out to braid and finish baking in a conventional oven. However, I found that this recipe is flexible, and can be made in a food processor, by hand, or with a standing mixer with a dough hook. I give instructions for each method.

NOTES ON YEAST: Most recipes call for too much yeast, in my opinion, which gives the bread a sour, too yeasty flavor. Most yeast packages contain just over 2½ teaspoons of yeast; this recipe calls for 2 teaspoons. You can use the whole package if you like; I just don't care for the flavor. I buy yeast in a jar and measure it out that way.

So-called instant yeast helps make this an adaptable recipe. Although the packages do not always say this, I have found that you don't need to proof this yeast. You can just add it with the other ingredients, and the bread still rises.

Different rising times yield different textures and flavors. Sometimes I get a late start and let the dough rise only for a couple hours, and the bread will be slightly denser. Other times I let it slow-rise in the refrigerator overnight, and then at room temperature for several hours, which yields an airier bread.

Another bonus of making your own challah is that you can control the richness, the sweetness, the flavors, and the additions. Be creative: Use different sweeteners. Make it more sweet, less sweet, richer with additional eggs; knead in dried cherries, cranberries, apricots, a handful of chopped pecans—whatever your whim. Add herbs, such as rosemary or basil, for an unusual twist, or spices such as cinnamon or cardamom.

I prefer the bread machine dough-mixing option, as it requires the least attention. Put the ingredients in and the machine oversees all the mixing, and does a good job. You can also make the dough the day before and refrigerate it overnight. It continues to rise in the refrigerator, but very slowly. Shape it the next morning, let it rise while you're at work during the day, and put it in the oven as soon as you get home.

> 3 large eggs
>
> 2 teaspoons vanilla extract
>
> 2 tablespoons vegetable oil
>
> 3 tablespoons honey or brown sugar
>
> 3 to 4 cups flour
>
> 1½ teaspoons salt
>
> 2 teaspoons instant yeast
>
> 1 tablespoon poppy seeds or sesame seeds (optional)

FOR ALL METHODS: In a glass measuring cup, beat together the eggs. Add enough water to make 2 cups of liquid. Remove ¼ cup to use for glaze and set aside (keep refrigerated, as you won't need it for several hours).

BREAD MACHINE: The following instructions work with most bread machines. If your bread machine requires a different method for adding the ingredients, follow the manufacturer's instructions.

Add the remaining egg mixture to the bread-machine pan. Add the vanilla, vegetable oil, and honey, if using. Add 2 cups of the flour, then the brown sugar, if using, salt, and 1 more cup flour. Sprinkle the yeast on top.

Set the machine to the Dough setting and start. Check the dough after 5 to 10 minutes. If it seems very sticky, add additional flour, ½ cup at a time. The dough should pull away easily from the sides of the pan.

The Dough cycle usually lasts about 1 hour, but you should let the dough rest and continue to rise for another few hours until doubled in size.

If you are making the challah the day before, remove the dough from the machine and place in a large, lightly oiled bowl. Cover with plastic wrap and refrigerate overnight.

FOOD PROCESSOR: Use the standard blade. Add the remaining egg mixture to the bowl of your food processor. Add the vanilla, vegetable oil, and honey, if using, and process for 20 seconds. Add 2 cups of the flour, then the brown sugar, if using, salt, and 1 more cup flour. Sprinkle the yeast on top. Process using the pulse button, allowing the dough to come together to form a ball. If it seems very sticky, add additional flour, ½ cup at a time. The dough should pull away easily from the sides of the processor bowl.

When the dough forms a ball, you can replace the blade with the plastic dough blade, if you have one; otherwise you can continue to use the processing blade. Knead the dough using the dough blade for 1 to 3 minutes, until it is smooth and elastic.

Remove the dough from the processor bowl. Place it in a large, lightly oiled bowl. Cover with a damp towel and let rise until almost doubled in bulk, about 2 hours.

If you are making the challah the day before, cover the bowl with plastic wrap and refrigerate overnight.

STANDING ELECTRIC MIXER OR BY HAND: Add the remaining egg mixture to a large bowl or the bowl of your standing mixer (the dough is too heavy to use with a handheld mixer). Add the vanilla, vegetable oil, honey or brown sugar, and salt. Mix until blended, about 1 minutes. Add 3 cups flour and the yeast. If using a standing mixer, use the paddle attachment to mix the ingredients together, then switch to the dough hook as the dough begins to come together to form a ball.

If mixing by hand with a wooden spoon, mix until the dough comes together to form a ball.

If the dough is sticky, add additional flour, ½ cup at a time.

When the dough forms a ball, if using an electric mixer, switch to the dough hook. Knead the dough for 7 to 10 minutes, until it is smooth and elastic.

If mixing by hand, remove the dough from the bowl and knead for 7 to 10 minutes, until the dough is smooth and elastic.

Place the dough in a large, lightly oiled bowl. Cover with a damp towel and let rise until almost doubled in bulk, about 2 hours.

If you are making the challah the day before, cover the bowl with plastic wrap and refrigerate overnight.

FOR ALL METHODS: *If you refrigerated the dough, the next morning, remove the dough from the refrigerator. Replace the plastic wrap with a damp towel and let the dough rise in the bowl at room temperature for 1 hour. Continue as instructed.*

After the dough has doubled in size, punch the dough down and divide it into two even sections. Divide each section into the number of pieces you want for braiding the challah. The easiest braid is a three-strand braid, which you braid as you would hair. Let the pieces rest a few minutes—this relaxes the gluten and makes the dough easier to roll out.

Make one loaf at a time. Roll the three pieces into lengths about 18 inches long. Secure the three strands at one end by pinching them together firmly, and braid the strands together. Secure the other end in the same way, by pinching the strands together. Repeat with the second loaf. Place each loaf on a large baking sheet lined with parchment paper. I use a large half-sheet baking pan, and both loaves can fit on the same pan, at an angle.

Cover the loaves with a clean dish towel and let rise 30 to 45 minutes.

About 20 minutes before you plan to bake the challah, preheat the oven to 375°F. Just before baking, brush the challah with the reserved egg mixture. This is what gives challah its golden-brown sheen. Sprinkle each loaf with poppy seeds or sesame seeds, if using.

Bake at 375°F for 20 to 25 minutes, until the loaves are firm and sound hollow when you tap the bottom. They are usually close to ready when the house is filled with the cozy smell of bread baking.

VARIATIONS: Add ½ cup raisins, dried cherries, diced apricots, chopped walnuts, or chopped pecans to the dough.

For a richer challah, use 4 eggs and decrease the water accordingly. You could also add an additional ¼ cup vegetable oil, and an additional ¼ cup sweetener, if you like a sweeter challah. You may need to add additional flour.

For *Yom Tov* challot, divide the dough into two sections, as above, but don't divide the sections. Roll each section into a long rope, thinner at one end than the other. Hold the thick end up slightly, and coil the dough around it to make a round spiral shape. Tuck the thin end in underneath. Follow the same rising, glazing, and baking instructions.

Good challah tends to disappear by Saturday afternoon. But if you do have some left over, it makes terrific French toast for Sunday brunch. It is also an ideal bread to use for bread pudding.

Crunchy Kosher Pickles
Pareve • • • Makes 18 whole pickles

What exactly are "kosher" pickles? According to pickle company glossaries, "kosher" pickles are dill pickles that include garlic in the brine. As to how they got the nomenclature "kosher"? Not entirely clear. Pickles gained popularity in late nineteenth- and early twentieth-century New York, especially on the Lower East Side, where there was an abundance of pickle carts, as well as a dense Jewish population. According to an article in *Kosher Today*, some of the early companies making pickles with garlic emphasized the kashrut of the product, and so the word *kosher* became associated with garlicky dill pickles.

My aunt, Raya Stern, makes pickles that are all the more wonderful because they are so easy to make and don't involve any canning techniques. In the summer, when the farmers' market features bins overflowing with small pickling cucumbers, I make these pickles.

According to my aunt, the pickles will keep for a few weeks, refrigerated, but we usually finish them within the first week. What's fun about these pickles is you can sample them each day as they go from being mildly sour to really sour.

Raya recommends making the pickles in a glass or enameled container. Metal containers can adversely affect the pickles, and the pickling flavor can permeate plastic containers. I now have a large plastic container I use only for pickles (or for things that I want to taste like pickles). Of the spices to use, Raya says: "The amount of spices, garlic, and dill is arbitrary; use more or less to taste."

NOTE: I like the unusual flavor that celery seeds impart to these pickles. If you don't, don't use them.

7½ cups water

¼ cup kosher salt

½ cup white vinegar

2 teaspoons pickling spice or ½ teaspoon each coriander seeds, mustard seeds, celery seeds, and fennel seeds

4 garlic cloves, peeled and cut in half

½ bunch fresh dill

4 pounds fresh pickling cucumbers (about 18 small)

Make the pickles in a glass, enamel, or glazed ceramic container that can hold at least 1 gallon. Wash the container thoroughly before using.

Add water and salt to the container and mix until the salt is completely dissolved. And the vinegar and spices. Mix the solution again. Add the garlic and dill to the brine.

Wash the fresh cucumbers thoroughly in cold running water to remove sand and dirt. Cut off the end tips. Cut into halves or quarters for better brine penetration. Leave smaller cucumbers whole.

Add the cucumbers to the brine. The cucumbers may float, so you should put a glass or ceramic plate on top of them to hold them under the brine. They must be covered with brine to keep from spoiling.

Keep at room temperature for 2 to 3 hours, then refrigerate to keep for longer periods. Raya likes the pickles half-soured, so she starts using them in 1½ days and refrigerates them sooner to slow the souring process.

Sficha

Meat · · · Makes 40 *sficha*

Mimi Mazor is the cataloging and circulation coordinator and cataloging librarian at Hebrew College in Newton, Massachusetts, whose library was essential to my research for this book. Mimi's husband, Baruch, is a Syrian Jew. Mimi, who is Ashkenazic, was intrigued by her mother-in-law Simcha Mizrab's culinary specialties, which were quite different from the foods she knew. Simcha, a mother of ten, was "a meticulous housekeeper and an excellent cook," Mimi says.

Simcha's *sficha* have become a Mazor family mainstay for Shabbat hors d'oeuvres. Squares of flaky pastry are covered with a ground beef and parsley mixture seasoned with pomegranate juice. Simcha made the pastry from scratch, but frozen, pareve puff pastry makes this recipe a breeze to prepare. Pomegranate juice can be found in natural-food stores and kosher markets.

> 1 pound ground beef
> 1 small bunch parsley, ends trimmed, finely minced
> 1 small onion, finely chopped
> ⅛ teaspoon salt
> ⅛ teaspoon freshly ground black pepper
> 3 to 4 tablespoons concentrated pomegranate juice
> One 17.3-ounce box Pepperidge Farm frozen puff pastry sheets,
>   thawed

Place the ground beef in a large bowl. Add the parsley, onion, salt, and pepper. Mix well with a spoon or with your hands. Add 3 tablespoons pomegranate juice. The mixture should come together and form easily into balls. If it seems too dry, add additional pomegranate juice. Set aside.

Preheat the oven to 400°F. Lightly grease two large baking sheets.

There are two sheets of puff pastry in the box. Roll one sheet at a time into a 15- by 12-inch rectangle. Cut each into twenty 3-inch squares. Place the squares on the prepared baking sheets, about ½ to 1 inch apart.

Using your fingers, put approximately 1 tablespoon of the meat mixture on each square. Spread it to the edges, leaving a small space around the edge.

Bake at 400°F for 15 to 20 minutes. The *sficha* are ready when the meat is nicely browned and the edges of the dough are golden.

Mimi says there rarely are leftovers, but if there are, the *sficha* can be refrigerated and reheated.

Sweet-and-Sour Cabbage Salad
Pareve • • • **Serves 6**

This is an easy, tasty make-ahead salad my friend Deb Shapiro makes almost every time friends come over, by popular demand. It actually was given to her by her friend Chhaya Bhatt. "It's an absolutely idiot-proof dish, which is why Chhaya taught it to me," Deb says. It's colorful and crunchy, and sweet and sour, and all kinds of good things. Sometimes for more color, Deb will throw in a shredded carrot. Bear in mind that the dressing needs time to chill. This is a good side salad to make for a Chanukah latke supper.

The Asian noodles to use come in a cellophane package, in a rectangular clump, such as ramen noodles. They are thinner and more delicate than chow mein noodles, but may not always be easy to find.

¼ cup red wine vinegar

½ cup sugar

¾ cup oil

2 tablespoons soy sauce

8 ounces slivered almonds (1 cup)

One 3-ounce package Asian noodles, such as ramen noodles,
   or 2 cups canned Chinese chow mein noodles

1 large head red cabbage, thinly sliced and shredded

4 scallions, whites and part of greens, thinly sliced

Preheat the oven to 350°F.

In a medium saucepan, combine the vinegar, sugar, oil, and soy sauce. Bring to a boil over medium-high heat. Boil for 1 minute, then remove from the heat. Let the dressing cool to room temperature for 10 to 15 minutes, then refrigerate it until chilled.

Toast the slivered almonds and the Asian noodles, if using (do *not* toast the chow mein noodles if you are using those). Put the almonds in a baking pan so they form a single layer. Break up the Asian noodles and scatter them around the almonds. Heat at 350°F for 10 to 15 minutes, until the nuts and the noodles start to turn pale tan. Check after 8 to 10 minutes, when you start to smell a toasty smell. Remove the nuts and noodles when you think they're not quite done, as they burn quickly once they start toasting. Set aside to cool.

In a large bowl, mix together the shredded cabbage and sliced scallions. Add the almonds and toasted noodles.

The dressing thickens as it chills. Stir it, then drizzle it over the cabbage mixture. Mix gently.

Chicken Stock

Meat • • • Makes about 8 cups

It is worth buying a pressure cooker just for making chicken stock alone. Chicken stock takes three or four hours to cook to have a really rich, full-flavored broth. In a pressure cooker, it takes less than an hour, and is as flavorful as the slow-cooked method. I do not salt the stock (kosher chicken is already salty), so I add salt as needed when I use it as a base for other soups. If you plan to eat it plain, the stock benefits from the addition of a little salt.

As you may not have a kosher-for-Pesach pressure cooker, I include directions for both pressure cooker and standard stovetop methods, as this is a soup that can be made throughout the year.

I recommend making chicken stock the day before you're going to use it to make fat removal easier.

For chicken soup, I usually discard the vegetables and chicken used to make the stock, as all their flavor has gone into the soup. Some people like to save these for noshing.

In this recipe, I use a mix of chicken and chicken bones. My butcher sells "chicken frames," which are essentially the bones left behind from the packages of boneless chicken breasts. There is not much meat on the bones, but they make a rich, flavorful stock; upon chilling, it becomes thick and gelatinous.

> 3 pounds chicken and chicken bones, extra fat trimmed and saved for
>   Matzo Balls (see page 207)
> 2 carrots, scrubbed and cut into 1-inch chunks
> 2 celery stalks, cut into 2-inch pieces
> 1 large onion, coarsely chopped
> 1 parsnip, scrubbed and cut into 1-inch chunks
> 4 sprigs parsley
> 10 peppercorns
> 1 bay leaf
> 8 cups water (2 quarts)

PRESSURE COOKER METHOD: Rinse off the chicken. Place it in a pressure cooker with the carrots, celery, onion, parsnip, parsley, peppercorns, and bay leaf. Pour the water over everything. Stir to mix up. Cover, securing the lid, and bring to high pressure over high heat. Reduce the heat to maintain high pressure and cook for 30 minutes. Remove from the heat and let the pressure reduce naturally. This can take 25 to 30 minutes.

When the pressure has dropped, remove the lid, being careful to keep it turned away from you to avoid the steam.

STANDARD STOVETOP METHOD: Rinse off the chicken. Place it in a stockpot with the carrots, celery, onion, parsnip, parsley, peppercorns, and bay leaf. Pour the water over everything. Cover and bring to a boil over high heat. When the mixture first boils, reduce to a simmer and skim off any foam, but do not stir. Cook at a low simmer, without stirring, for 3 to 4 hours. (You could stop cooking after 2 hours, but the stock develops a richer flavor if you cook it longer.)

Let the stock cool slightly, then strain. Refrigerate the stock and remove any congealed fat from the surface after it chills. Store in the refrigerator for up to 3 days, or freeze for up to 3 months.

Chicken Soup with My Mother's Ethereal Matzo Balls

Meat • • • **Serves 6 to 8**

For some people, chicken soup with matzo balls is standard Friday night Shabbat fare. We always have it on Pesach, but not the rest of the year. Some Orthodox, including the Lubavitch, do not eat products made with matzo meal or matzo farfel (called *gebrochts*, "broken" in Yiddish) during Pesach, out of a concern that leavening might take place when the ground matzo is combined with a liquid. But matzo-ball soup on Pesach is a tradition for most Ashkenazic Jews.

This is a time-consuming process, as the matzo balls need time to chill properly and time to cook. Prepare the batter the day before, or early in the morning on the day you want to serve the soup.

I like chicken soup to have tiny pieces of chicken in it, little bursts of flavor that complement the matzo balls. If you prefer larger pieces, cut the chicken accordingly.

> 8 cups Chicken Stock (page 205)
> 1 teaspoon salt or to taste
> 2 carrots, peeled and cut into ⅛-inch circles
> 1 pound boneless, skinless chicken breasts, rinsed and diced

Combine the chicken stock, salt, carrots, and diced chicken in a stockpot. Bring to a simmer and heat, covered, over medium heat until the chicken is cooked through, about 20 minutes. Serve with Matzo Balls (see below).

My Mother's Ethereal Matzo Balls
Meat ◦ ◦ ◦

My mother, Joyce Stern, really does make the best matzo balls (*knaidlach* in Yiddish) I've ever had. They are light, fluffy, yet still substantial, and you always want more, except then you remember that the rest of the meal is coming.

My mother's matzo balls are rich with *schmaltz*, rendered chicken fat, and eggs, which make them light and fluffy. "This time of year you simply forget any worries about cholesterol," my mother says. You can purchase schmaltz at a kosher market, but Mom usually has so much fat left over from preparing chickens for the meal and for the chicken soup, she renders her own. The two important ingredients for flavoring the *knaidlach*, says Mom, are the schmaltz and the chicken stock.

For our family seders, my mother usually at least doubles this recipe.

Schmaltz (Rendered Chicken Fat)

Half a pound of skin and fat yields about 1 cup of schmaltz

Traditionally, schmaltz is made with onions, but my mother makes it with just the chicken skin and fat. You can make a large quantity at one time if you save bits of skin and fat in the freezer whenever you make chicken. Schmaltz will keep in the refrigerator or freezer for several months.

My mother says, "A little bit of skin renders a lot of fat. Some people end up eating the skin, which by now is dark brown and quite shriveled. Doesn't appeal to me, but really appeals to some people." The chicken cracklings are called *grebenes*. Apparently Omi, my grandmother, ate grebenes with gusto.

Chicken skin and chicken fat

Fry the skin and fat over medium heat in a frying pan. The fat will melt and sizzle off the skin. It should take 10 to 20 minutes. Watch carefully so it does not burn. Remove the skin and pour the melted fat into a glass bowl or jar. Let cool, then refrigerate or freeze.

Matzo Balls

Makes 16 matzo balls; serves 8

To make these vegetarian, use oil instead of schmaltz and vegetable stock or water instead of chicken stock. Increase the salt to 1 teaspoon.

¼ cup schmaltz (see above), melted and cooled (if it is too hot, it will cook
   the eggs)

4 eggs, lightly beaten

1 cup matzo meal

¾ teaspoon salt

¼ cup chicken stock

Stir together the melted schmaltz and eggs.

Stir together the matzo meal and salt in a separate bowl.

Stir the egg mixture into the matzo-meal mixture. Add the chicken stock. The batter should be thick, not runny, like cookie dough. If it is too thin, add additional matzo meal.

Cover the bowl and refrigerate for 1 full hour or longer. ("I usually refrigerate the batter for a good hour and a half," Mom says. "The longer chilling time makes the matzo balls more feathery. If you refrigerate for less than an hour, you'll get hard matzo balls," she advises. "You can even refrigerate the batter overnight.")

When you are ready to cook the matzo balls, bring 4 quarts water mixed with 2 teaspoons salt to a boil over high heat. ("Try to avoid an aluminum pot. It seems to impart an off flavor," Mom says. "Stick to enamel or stainless steel.")

If you are doubling the recipe and have two large pots, heat salted water in both. Matzo balls take a long time to cook, but they take even longer if they are too crowded together. ("If you put too many in the pot," Mom says, "then the sides of the matzo balls will be in contact with each other instead of with the water.") The matzo balls will almost double in size as they cook.

When the water boils, remove the matzo-ball mixture from the refrigerator. Using a teaspoon, scoop out the batter and use your hands to roll it into a ball shape. ("You want to work quickly," Mom says. "Because you want them to be cold and solid when they go into the water. If you spend too much time trying to shape it, it will be counterproductive—when you put it in the pot if it's too warm, pieces will break off and float away. Don't be fussy about the shape.") Immediately put the matzo ball into the water, which should be between a simmer and a rolling boil. There is enough batter to make 16 matzo balls.

Cover the pot and simmer 1 hour.

After 1 hour, remove a matzo ball with a slotted spoon and cut it in half to test for doneness. The ball should be of a uniform consistency and color. It should be a pale yellow. If the center is darker, it is not fully cooked. If the matzo balls are not yet done, cook another 20 minutes and check again.

When they are finished cooking, remove the matzo balls, place in bowls of hot chicken soup, and serve.

If making ahead, drain the matzo balls well and store in the soup you will be serving. The soup further enriches the flavor of the matzo balls.

NOTE: Mom says she never cooks the matzo balls in the soup because they would dilute the flavor of the soup.

Do not cook the matzo balls more than 1 day in advance. If you make them 1 day in advance, store them in the soup. Reheat the soup and matzo balls together, but do not boil. You don't want to cook the matzo balls any further.

Vegetable Stock

Pareve • • • Makes 3 quarts

Our Shabbat meals are usually vegetarian. Vegetarian soups can be made with water, but I find they taste richer if you use vegetable stock. I make a lot and freeze it to have on hand. I tend to discard the vegetables after making stock, as they have little flavor left. In a pressure cooker, the stock is ready in about 30 minutes; the standard stovetop method takes about 90 minutes.

1 pound mushrooms, halved
2 ounces dried mushrooms

4 large carrots, scrubbed and cut into thirds

4 fist-sized potatoes, scrubbed and cut into quarters

12 dried tomatoes

2 medium onions, quartered

5 sprigs parsley

12 cups water (3 quarts)

PRESSURE COOKER METHOD: Place all ingredients in the pressure cooker. Cover, securing the lid, and bring to high pressure over high heat. Reduce the heat to maintain high pressure and cook for 12 minutes. Remove from the heat and let the pressure reduce naturally for 10 minutes, then quick-release the pressure.

When the pressure has dropped, remove the lid, being careful to keep it turned away from you to avoid the steam.

STANDARD STOVETOP METHOD: Place all ingredients in a stockpot. Cover and bring to a boil. Reduce the heat and simmer for 1 hour, or until the potatoes and carrots are pierceable with the point of a knife. Remove from the heat.

Let the stock cool slightly, then strain, pressing gently on the vegetables to release any liquid. Discard the vegetables. Use the stock immediately or store in the refrigerator for up to 4 days. Vegetable stock may be frozen for up to 2 months.

Red Lentil Soup

Pareve • • • Serves 8

I make this hearty soup as a first course for Shabbat dinner with enough leftover that I can have it for lunch the next few days. The soup cooks very quickly in a pressure cooker, but lentils, unlike other legumes, cook relatively quickly, too, so the standard stovetop method doesn't take that long.

Seitan, also called "wheat meat," as it's made from wheat gluten, is high in protein and low in fat. I like the texture it adds to the soup. You could also add a 10-ounce package of frozen spinach, thawed and drained.

> **2 quarts vegetable broth**
>
> **One 28-ounce can diced tomatoes**
>
> **½ cup red wine (optional)**
>
> **3 carrots, peeled, cut in half lengthwise and cut into thin slices**
>
> **2 cups red lentils, rinsed**
>
> **One 8-ounce package seitan, drained if in liquid and diced (optional)**

Put the broth, tomatoes, and wine, if using, in a large pot or pressure cooker and heat over high heat. Add the carrots and the red lentils. Continue to heat while you add the seitan.

If you are using a pressure cooker, cover, secure the lid, and bring to high pressure over high heat. Reduce the heat to maintain pressure and cook 8 minutes. Quick-release the pressure.

If you are cooking with a standard stovetop pot, cover and bring to a boil. Reduce the heat to a simmer and cook until the lentils are done, 30 to 40 minutes. Lentils are done when they are soft all the way through, without any give at the center.

Chilled Cucumber–Yogurt Soup

Dairy • • • **Serves 8**

When I lived in Israel virtually every restaurant that served soup had cold cucumber soup on their menu from about March through November. Because it's refreshing and amazingly easy to make, I prepare it throughout the summer. Many recipes include minced garlic; I find the garlicky taste lingers longer than I'd like, so I don't use it.

How you prepare the cucumbers can make the soup very different in feel. I've pureed the mixture with an immersion blender or in the food processor, I've grated or shredded the cucumbers, used them with and without the skin. I prefer the cucumbers diced, with the skin on, when I can get unwaxed organic cucumbers at the farmers' market.

Use whatever fresh herbs you have on hand. I always use mint, but sometimes add basil or parsley.

> **One 32-ounce container nonfat yogurt**
>
> **1 yogurt container of water**
>
> **1 teaspoon salt**
>
> **2 English cucumbers or 5 pickling cucumbers, peeled if desired, cut in half lengthwise, seeded, and diced (about 4 cups diced cucumber)**
>
> **2 tablespoons chopped mint**
>
> **Freshly ground black pepper to taste**
>
> **Additional mint leaves for garnish**

Stir the yogurt until smooth in a large bowl. Add the water and stir until smooth. Stir in the salt. Add the cucumbers and mint. Chill until ready to serve. You may need to restir the soup, as the yogurt and water separate a little. Serve garnished with a mint leaf.

Sliced Potato–Onion Kugel

Pareve • • • **Serves 6 to 8**

Potato kugel (*kugel* means "pudding") is a Shabbat tradition. Traditional potato kugel is made with grated or ground potatoes, mixed with eggs. I prefer the more potatoey flavor and texture of this version, made with sliced potatoes and no eggs. The starch from the potatoes holds it together naturally. The recipe can be made without olive oil, but it adds a palate-pleasing richness.

> 3 pounds Russet or baking potatoes, peeled and sliced into ⅛-inch-thick rounds
>
> 1 medium onion, halved and thinly sliced
>
> 2 tablespoons olive oil
>
> 1 teaspoon salt
>
> Freshly ground black pepper to taste
>
> 1 cup vegetable stock or ¾ cup water mixed with ¼ cup white wine
>
> Extra oil for the pan

Preheat the oven to 400°F. Oil a 9- by 13-inch baking pan.

Place one-third of the potato slices in a single layer, with the edges overlapping slightly, in the prepared pan. Spread half the onions on top. Drizzle with 2 teaspoons of the olive oil and sprinkle with salt and pepper, if desired.

Cover this with a second layer of potatoes, starting at the opposite end of the pan from the first layer, again overlapping the edges slightly. You should have one-third of the potatoes left.

Cover this layer with the remaining onions, another 2 teaspoons olive oil, salt, and pepper. Place the remaining potatoes on top of this onion layer in the same manner. Drizzle the top with the remaining 2 teaspoons olive oil, and sprinkle with salt and pepper.

Pour the vegetable stock or wine-water mixture over the potatoes. Cover the pan with aluminum foil.

Bake at 400°F for 30 minutes. Remove the aluminum foil and bake for an additional 15 minutes, until the edges of the potatoes are golden and the center can be pierced easily with the point of a knife.

VARIATION: Sage goes very well with potatoes. Sprinkle 1 teaspoon minced fresh sage or ½ teaspoon dried sage with the salt and pepper on each layer of potatoes (using a total of 1 tablespoon minced fresh or 1½ teaspoons dried sage).

Rosemary Sweet–Potato Kugel

Pareve • • • **Serves 6 to 8**

Every once in a while, regular potato kugel seems just a little bit *too* omnipresent. Then I feel in the mood for sweet potatoes. Too often, the natural sweetness of sweet potatoes gets exaggerated with the additions of sugar and sweet spices such as cinnamon. While those preparations are fine, I think cooking sweet potatoes with savory herbs yields a more complex side dish.

3 pounds sweet potatoes, peeled and sliced into ⅛-inch rounds
1 tablespoon dried rosemary or 2 tablespoons minced fresh rosemary
  leaves
1 tablespoon olive oil
Extra oil for the pan

Preheat the oven to 375°F. Oil a 9- by 13-inch baking pan.

Layer one-third of the sweet potatoes in the prepared pan, overlapping slightly. Sprinkle with 1 teaspoon of the dried rosemary, or 2 teaspoons of the fresh, and drizzle with 1 teaspoon of the olive oil.

Make a second layer of overlapping sweet-potato slices, starting at the opposite end of the pan from where you began the first layer. Sprinkle with 1 teaspoon dried rosemary, or 2 teaspoons fresh, and drizzle with another teaspoon olive oil.

Make a third layer of overlapping slices, using the remaining sweet potatoes, starting at the opposite end of the pan from where you began the second layer. Sprinkle with the remaining 1 teaspoon dried rosemary, or 2 teaspoons fresh, and drizzle with the remaining 1 teaspoon olive oil.

Bake, uncovered, at 375°F for 30 to 45 minutes. Check after 30 minutes. The edges should be turning light brown. The kugel is ready when the sweet potatoes can be pierced easily with the point of a knife.

Classic Lokchen Kugel
Dairy • • • Serves 8

Barbara Model is a fabulous cook and the usual caterer for our shul. Often she will serve lokshen (noodle) kugel, which she credits to her mother, Annie Model. She was kind enough to share the recipe. "My mother's kugel is loved by all that have sat at her table," Barbara says. "Her proudest story is that she was asked repeatedly to make it at her brother's for a Fifth Avenue crowd in New York. I've been making it for years. It is a classic that always receives compliments and recipe requests." This cheesecake-like kugel seems particularly appropriate for Shavuot.

    1 pound medium egg noodles
    ¼ cup salted butter, melted
    5 eggs
    1 pound cottage cheese

2 cups sour cream

1 cup milk

½ cup sugar

1 teaspoon vanilla extract

1 cup crushed cornflakes for top (optional)

Extra butter for the pan

Preheat the oven to 350°F. Lightly butter a 9- by 13-inch baking pan.

Boil 2 quarts of water mixed with 2 teaspoons salt in a large pot. When the water boils, cook the egg noodles according to the package instructions, until al dente, still slightly chewy at the center. Drain and toss with the melted butter. Set aside.

Beat the eggs in a large bowl. Add the cottage cheese, sour cream, milk, sugar, and vanilla. Mix until well blended. Add the noodles to the cheese mixture and mix well.

Pour into the prepared pan. Top with crushed cornflakes, if desired.

Bake at 350°F for 1 hour, until golden brown.

Fluffy Pesach Vegetable Kugels

Pareve • • • Makes 30 to 42 individual kugels

Pesach is a family get-together holiday, and our family alternates Pesach seders between my Stern family in Washington, D.C., and my husband Jeffrey's Robbins family in New England. During the first dozen years of our marriage, seders with the Robbinses were held at the home of Auntie Judy and Uncle Arthur in Providence, Rhode Island. There I discovered new-to-me traditions, such as the hard-boiled-egg course, for which a shelled hard-boiled egg is served in a small bowl of salt water. The meal invariably included Judy's delectable vegetable kugels, which we sometimes called vegetable muffins, since they are baked in a muffin tin.

Over the years, all the "kids" have gotten married and started their own families. A few years ago Judy and Arthur sold their house, so our Robbins seders are now with Jeffrey's parents, Donald and Esther, in Cambridge. My father-in-law made sure to get the vegetable kugel recipe from Judy to carry on this very important culinary tradition.

Judy will not take credit for the recipe, however. Mrs. Eleanor Bohnen, wife of Temple Emanuel's Rabbi Eli Bohnen, created the recipe a few decades ago. "She was an outstanding cook," Judy says. "And she always shared her recipes." These vegetable kugels were in such demand that Mrs. Bohnen typed up the recipe, with precise instructions. "They are a *patchke* and a half to make," Judy admits. But well worth it. Enough so that Judy makes these vegetable kugels throughout the year.

> **2 cups matzo farfel (do not use crumbled matzo; packaged farfel pieces are more uniform in size)**
> **2 cups cold water**
> **2 tablespoons vegetable oil plus ⅓ cup vegetable oil**
> **2 medium onions, finely diced**
> **2 medium carrots, peeled and grated**
> **3 medium celery stalks, finely diced**
> **1 medium green pepper, finely diced**
> **2 medium potatoes, peeled, grated, and drained of excess liquid**
> **2 tablespoons sugar**
> **1 teaspoon salt or to taste**
> **½ teaspoon freshly ground black pepper or to taste**
> **1 tablespoon finely chopped fresh parsley**
> **6 eggs**
> **Extra oil for individual muffin units**

Soak the farfel in a large bowl filled with cold water for 1 hour. Drain off the excess water in a colander, but do not press it out.

Prepare the muffin tins. This recipe makes 30 to 42 individual muffins, depending on how much you fill each individual tin. They are easier to release from the pan if you use nonstick muffin tins, but you'll need a lot of tins (not everyone has four kosher-for-Pesach nonstick muffin tins). You can use disposable aluminum muffin tins; just make sure they are well oiled. Even nonstick tins should be oiled—Mrs. Bohnen recommends ⅛ teaspoon oil per nonstick tin. Disposables may need more.

If you are serving a lot of food, make the larger number of muffins by filling each tin halfway; people can always have seconds.

So, prepare your muffin tins accordingly and preheat the oven to 375°F.

Heat 2 tablespoons oil over medium heat in a large frying pan. Sauté the onions until they begin to be translucent, about 5 minutes. Add the carrots, celery, and green pepper. Sauté only until tender-crisp, about 5 minutes. Do not overcook or the vegetables will be too soggy when they bake. Scrape the vegetables into a large bowl and let cool for 10 to 15 minutes, so the eggs won't cook when you add them.

Add the potatoes, ⅓ cup oil, sugar, salt, pepper, and parsley to the vegetable mixture.

While the vegetables cool, prepare the eggs. Break 4 eggs into a small bowl or glass measuring cup. Separate the remaining 2 eggs. Add the yolks to the whole eggs and beat together. Stir the egg mixture into the vegetables. Fold in the drained farfel.

Beat the egg whites until stiff but not dry in a separate bowl. Fold the egg whites into the vegetable mixture.

Fill the prepared muffin tins, halfway if you want 42 smaller muffins, almost to the top if you want 30 larger muffins. Bake at 375°F for 20 to 30 minutes, until the muffins are slightly puffed and starting to brown on top. The smaller muffins cook more quickly; check after 20 minutes. Cool in the pan for 10 minutes before serving.

You can prepare the vegetable kugels a few days in advance. If so, underbake them slightly and refrigerate. When ready to serve, warm them up in a 375°F oven for 15 minutes.

To freeze, remove the kugels from the muffin tins. Place on a cookie sheet and let them freeze until solid, 60 to 90 minutes. When frozen, put the kugels in a plastic bag. To reheat, put a metal cooling rack on a cookie sheet and put the kugels on this, which keeps them from getting soggy as they reheat. Reheat at 375°F for 15 to 20 minutes.

Perfect Potato Latkes

Pareve • • • Makes about sixty 3-inch latkes

In our house, Chanukah means latkes, potato pancakes. All five of us love latkes. What's not to like about potatoes fried in oil? We always have them at least once on Chanukah; often more, as our kids clamor for them. Over the past decade, my husband, Jeffrey, became our household's chief latkemaker, in part, I think, in response to my tendency to try to make them a little healthier. "Lots of oil is key," he'll declare as I attempt to demonstrate that you can make "perfectly good" latkes with only a thin film of oil or, even worse, with cooking spray instead of oil. I have to admit that, while a minimal amount of oil does make "perfectly good" latkes, a substantial amount of oil makes perfect latkes.

After all, frying is the point on Chanukah. The holiday commemorates the miracle of the oil in the Holy Temple, so we celebrate by eating foods fried in oil.

When we make latkes, we don't mess around. Sure, you can have them as a side dish. But since they are an infrequent treat, for at least one night of Chanukah (more often two), our family has a latke supper, with maybe a salad on the side. We enjoy them as a dairy meal, topped with sour cream (or yogurt, for those of us who are fat-conscious), as well as home-made applesauce. We also tend to have extended family over during Chanukah, so this recipe makes a lot. Leftovers (and there are not a lot) can be reheated in the toaster oven.

While latkes taste best fresh out of the pan, we all like to eat together as a family. Jeffrey will make several batches, keeping them warm in the oven, separated by paper towels. Then we bring out the platters and dig in.

NOTE: You may not use the entire bottle of vegetable oil, but it's a good idea to have enough around just in case.

One 32-ounce bottle safflower or canola oil

10 pounds potatoes (we use a mix of Russet and Yukon Gold)

2 onions

6 eggs, lightly beaten

1 tablespoon salt or to taste

¼ cup flour or matzo meal

Heat two large frying pans over medium heat. Add oil to a depth of ¼ inch. Let the oil heat over low heat as you mix the latkes.

Wash and scrub the potatoes if you want to keep the skins on, or peel them. Grate the potatoes. This is easiest to do in a food processor, but can also be done with a hand grater. Grate the onions and mix with the potatoes in a large bowl. In a separate bowl lightly beat the eggs and salt. Add to the potatoes and mix thoroughly. Sprinkle the flour over the mixture and mix in.

Turn the heat under the oil to medium. The oil is ready when a bit of potato dropped in it sizzles. Use a ⅓-cup measuring cup to scoop up the batter. Drop it into the hot oil and flatten with the back of a spatula.

Cook the latkes until golden brown on one side, about 4 to 5 minutes, then flip over and cook the second side until golden, another 3 to 4 minutes. When ready, remove to a plate covered with a layer of paper towels to absorb the oil. Serve immediately or keep warm in a low oven (200°F) until ready to serve.

Serve with bowls of sour cream (or plain yogurt) and applesauce.

Applesauce

Pareve • • • Makes 6 to 9 cups of applesauce, depending on the size of your apples

Applesauce has become the expected accompaniment to potato latkes. It is not sacrilege (since it's not an issue of kashrut, after all) to admit that I don't see the appeal. My daughter concurs, but the rest of my family smothers the pancakes with applesauce and relishes every bite.

We live in New England, famed for its apples, and often go apple picking in the fall. The thing about apple picking is, you always pick *way* more apples than you could ever possibly eat. So you have to figure out various ways to preserve them, such as in pies and crumbles. And applesauce, which freezes and is the easiest to make.

A most useful tool for making applesauce is a Foley Food Mill. This is a sort of pan with a holed, angled bottom and a metal plate that pushes cooked food through those holes as you turn a handle. These food mills are inexpensive and available in hardware and kitchen supply stores. The beauty of using a food mill is, you don't need to peel or core the apples because the skin and seeds are strained out as you turn the handle. Homemade applesauce is so tasty, you'll find a food mill is a worthwhile investment. Since you'll only use it for fruit, it can stay pareve.

If you do not have a food mill, core the apples. You can leave the skins on for color; they will remain behind when you press the apples through the colander, or you can peel them.

Use your favorite apples or a variety of apples for a more complex flavor. I prefer unsweetened applesauce, but you can sweeten it to taste. Add sugar gradually, a tablespoon at a time, to avoid oversweetening. If you use cider or apple juice instead of water, that will add some sweetness.

> **12 apples, washed and cut in quarters**
> **½ cup water, apple juice, or apple cider**
> **Sugar to taste**

Place the apples and water, juice, or cider in a large pot. Heat over medium-low heat, covered. Stir the apples every 4 or 5 minutes to avoid scorching. If the pan seems dry, add more liquid. Cook the apples until soft, and until you can cut the apples with a spoon, about 20 minutes.

Remove from the heat. Set the Foley Food Mill over a large bowl. Add the apples, a couple of cups at a time, to the food mill, and mill into the bowl. Alternately, press the apples through a colander, using the back of a large spoon.

Taste the applesauce for sweetness and add sugar, if desired. Store, refrigerated, for up to 1 week; it can be frozen for up to 3 months. The frozen sauce will be slightly thinner, but still very good.

Carrot Coins

Pareve • • • **Serves 6**

Carrots have various symbolic meanings for Rosh Hashanah. In this recipe, they're sliced into rounds, resembling coins, to symbolize prosperity, and are cooked in vinegar and honey to highlight their natural sweetness. I like the Rosh Hashanah apple connection of cider vinegar, but you could experiment with different kinds of vinegar. These can be made very quickly in a pressure cooker; it takes a little longer in a standard stovetop pan. Do not overcook. Carrots should be tender, yet still slightly firm to the touch—pierceable with a fork but not mushy.

¾ **cup water**

2 **tablespoons cider vinegar**

1 **tablespoon honey**

About 4 **pounds carrots, peeled and sliced into** ⅛-**inch rounds to yield**
   about 3 cups

⅓ **cup minced fresh parsley**

Mix together the water, vinegar, and honey in a measuring cup. Mix until the honey is dissolved.

PRESSURE COOKER METHOD: Put the sliced carrots in the steamer container of your pressure cooker. Pour the vinegar mixture over the carrots.

Lock the lid in place. Over high heat, bring to high pressure. Reduce the heat to maintain the pressure and cook for 1 minute. Turn off the heat and allow the pressure to reduce naturally. When the pressure is down, transfer the carrots, drained, to a serving bowl. Toss with the parsley.

STOVETOP METHOD: Put the sliced carrots in a medium saucepan. Add the vinegar mixture and stir to coat the carrots.

Over high heat, bring the liquid to a boil. Reduce the heat to a low simmer and cover the pan. Cook 15 minutes, stirring occasionally. If the liquid starts to evaporate, add a few more tablespoons of water. Cook until the carrots are tender, but still slightly firm. Drain the carrots and transfer to a serving bowl. Toss with the parsley.

May be served hot, room temperature, or cold.

Roasted Roots

Pareve • • • **Serves 4**

Beets, especially those of late autumn, have a sweet earthiness and brilliant color that brighten any meal. The magenta from the beets stains the sweet potatoes and carrots, which makes for a cheerful, colorful dish to have on your plate during the gray days of winter. Roasting enhances the sweetness of these vegetables, and they need little more than a touch of olive oil and salt for flavor.

1 tablespoon olive oil plus 1 teaspoon olive oil

1 bunch beets (4 to 6 medium beets)

4 carrots

1 sweet potato

¼ teaspoon salt or to taste

Preheat the oven to 400°F. Line a baking sheet with heavy-duty aluminum foil (this makes cleanup infinitely easier). Pour 1 tablespoon olive oil onto the foil and use a bit of paper towel or a pastry brush to spread it around the pan.

Trim the ends from the beets and peel them. Cut the beets into ½-inch chunks and place on the prepared sheet. Trim the ends from the carrots and peel them. Cut the carrots in half lengthwise, then cut each half into 1-inch pieces and place on the prepared pan. Stir them around in the pan to coat with oil.

Bake the beets and carrots at 400°F for 15 minutes while you prepare the sweet potato. The sweet potato takes less time to cook, so you will add it later. Peel the sweet potato and cut into 1-inch chunks. Toss with the remaining 1 teaspoon olive oil and add to the baking pan.

Bake for another 30 to 45 minutes, until the vegetables can easily be pierced with the point of a knife. Put the vegetables in a serving bowl and toss gently with the salt.

Butternut Squash Puree

Pareve • • • Serves 4 to 6

This is a mainstay for autumn Shabbat dinners. It is both the easiest squash preparation and the one I like best. There's no peeling or chopping. I put the squash in the oven and it roasts as I prepare everything else. You can use the same technique with other squash, but I prefer the smooth sweetness of butternut.

> 1 large butternut squash (about 2 pounds)
> 1 tablespoon olive oil
> 1 apple, peeled, cut in half, and cored
> 1 onion, cut in half

Preheat the oven to 400°F. Line a baking sheet with heavy-duty aluminum foil (this makes cleanup infinitely easier). Pour the olive oil onto the foil and use a bit of paper towel or a pastry brush to spread it around.

Wash the outside of the squash. Cut off the stem and cut the squash in half lengthwise, as evenly as possible. Scoop out the seeds and discard. Place an apple half in one seed cavity and an onion half in the other. Place the squash, cut side down, on the baking sheet. Put the remaining onion half and apple half elsewhere on the baking sheet.

Bake at 400°F for 45 to 60 minutes, until the aroma of roasting squash fills the kitchen and the squash can easily be pierced with a knife point.

Remove the squash from the oven and let it cool on the pan for at least 15 minutes, so you don't burn your hands when handling it.

Scoop the soft flesh into a bowl. Add the apple and onion, which should both be very soft. With a fork or a potato masher, blend the apple, onion, and squash together. For a smoother puree, use a food processor. Keep in a warm oven (200°F) until ready to serve. May also be served at room temperature.

Roasted Green Beans

Pareve • • • Serves 6 to 8

This recipe was inspired by one in Mollie Katzen's *Still Life with Menu*, and has become our standard green-vegetable dish for Thanksgiving for nearly a decade. It's good served hot, cold, at room temperature, the day it's made, the day after it's made—it's a very forgiving recipe. Plus, it's easy. Green beans are available almost throughout the year, too.

> 1 tablespoon olive oil
> 2 pounds green beans, ends trimmed
> 1 large onion, quartered and sliced
> ½ teaspoon salt
> 2 tablespoons balsamic vinegar

Preheat the oven to 400°F. Line a baking sheet with heavy-duty aluminum foil (this makes cleanup infinitely easier). Pour the olive oil onto the foil and use a bit of paper towel or a pastry brush to spread it around. Add the green beans and onions and stir to coat with oil. Sprinkle the salt over the beans and stir to distribute.

Bake at 400°F for 45 to 60 minutes, until the onions are soft and begin to caramelize. Stir every 20 minutes. When the beans are done, remove from the oven. Put the beans in a serving bowl. Add the balsamic vinegar and stir. Serve warm, cold, or at room temperature.

Matzo-Vegetable Stuffing

Meat • • • Serves 6

Our Aunt Judy Robbins adapted this recipe from a dog-eared Passover recipe booklet. Her daughter Alisa now makes it for her seders. Judy prefers to use broken matzo for the stuffing, as opposed to matzo farfel, because she says it gives the stuffing more texture. The recipe, as is, is enough for a 4- to 5-pound chicken; triple it for an 18- to 20-pound turkey.

½ cup vegetable shortening or schmaltz (see Matzo Balls, page 207)

¾ cup minced onions

1 cup diced celery

1 cup diced mushrooms

10 matzos, finely broken

1 teaspoon salt (reduce to ½ teaspoon if using salted broth)

¼ teaspoon freshly ground black pepper

1 tablespoon paprika

1 egg, lightly beaten

Two 10.75-ounce cans condensed chicken broth *or*
   2½ cups homemade Chicken Stock (page 205)

Melt the vegetable shortening or schmaltz in a large frying pan over medium heat. Add the onions and sauté until translucent, 7 to 9 minutes. Add the celery and mushrooms and continue to sauté until the mushrooms give off much of their liquid. Add the broken matzos and stir to toast slightly. Remove from the heat and transfer to a bowl. Stir in the salt, pepper, and paprika.

In a large bowl mix together the lightly beaten egg and the chicken broth. Stir into the matzo mixture.

Stuff into the cavity of a chicken or turkey. If there is extra, bake it along with the chicken in a lightly greased baking pan covered with aluminum foil.

Apple-Pear Charoset

Pareve   Makes about 5 cups

Charoset is one of those dishes I absolutely love and can't get enough of during the seders. And every year when I make it, I resolve not to wait a whole year before trying it again. Yet, a year flies by once more before I enjoy the sweet, juicy, crunchy combination of apples and walnuts. Somehow, reserving charoset just for Pesach makes it more special.

On the seder plate, charoset represents the bricks and mortar our ancestors had to mix when they were slaves in Egypt. Despite its somber symbolism, charoset has come to mean something happier in the seder, a mixture that softens the intensity of bitter herbs. Ashkenazic charoset tends to be apple-based, and that is the charoset we always make, while Sephardic charoset can be made from a variety of dried fruits and nuts.

NOTE: If grating by hand, it is easier to leave the apples and pears whole and to grate up to the core, which gives you something to hold on to. If you are using a food processor, core the apples and pears.

> 6 apples, preferably Gala, Fuji, or Braeburn, peeled
> 3 ripe pears, peeled
> 1½ cups chopped or ground walnuts
> 1 to 3 tablespoons honey
> 2 to 4 tablespoons sweet kiddush wine, such as Manischewitz

Grate the apples and pears together into a large bowl. Mix with the walnuts. Add 1 tablespoon honey and 2 tablespoons wine and taste. Add more honey and wine to make it sweeter or tarter, according to what you like.

Refrigerate, covered, until ready to serve.

Chilled Herb–Baked Salmon

Pareve • • • Serves 8 to 10

Cold salmon, usually poached, has become an almost de facto tradition for *Yom Tov* and Shabbat lunches, since salmon tastes good both hot and cold. I've enjoyed many "a nice piece of fish," as my grandmother-in-law, Bubbe Robbins, used to say, but one of the best was made by Naava Frank and Gregg Stern at a Shabbat-Shavuot luncheon. It was a cold, rainy Shavuot that year, despite it being early June, a typical New England unpredictable spring. But the salmon was cheerful, a large, long fillet, pale pink and decorated with yellow rounds of lemon, beckoning like little suns. It was delicious, perfectly cooked, and there was plenty of it, so I helped myself to seconds and asked for the recipe. Salmon, Naava says, is Gregg's specialty.

Unlike most cold salmon preparations, this fish is *not* poached. Rather, it is baked. The result is a moist, tender, flavorful fish. Get the freshest fish possible. Frozen fish will not taste as good.

¼ cup extra virgin olive oil

1 tablespoon dried dill

1 teaspoon dried oregano

1 teaspoon dried thyme

Dash cayenne

1 teaspoon paprika

½ teaspoon salt or to taste

¼ teaspoon freshly ground pepper or to taste

One 4-pound salmon fillet

Two lemons, skin scrubbed, thinly cut into
    ¹⁄₁₆- to ⅛-inch slices

Extra oil for the pan

Preheat the oven to 350°F. Lightly oil a 9- by 13-inch baking pan.

Mix together the dill, oregano, thyme, cayenne, paprika, salt, and pepper in a small bowl. Rinse the fish, pat it dry, and drizzle both sides with olive oil, rubbing it in with your fingers ("Really work it in," Gregg says). Place the fish in the pan, skin side down. Sprinkle the top with the herb mixture. Place the lemon slices over the herbs on the salmon. Place any extra slices next to the fish in the pan.

Bake at 350°F for 40 to 50 minutes, until the center of the salmon is opaque. Let cool to room temperature, then chill in the refrigerator overnight. May also be served warm.

Spiced Fish Stew
Pareve • • • **Serves 8**

Lorna Sass's pressure cooker cookbooks are what really inspired me to give pressure cookers a try, and their value in the kitchen for a busy mom is repeatedly confirmed for me. Fish actually does not need pressure cooking, as it cooks in minutes. But the vegetables in this stew cook much faster when the pressure is on.

Sass's *The Pressured Cook* has a seafood recipe—definitely not kosher—but some of the elements intrigued me. I like this stew because it is an easy one-dish meal—complete with starches, orange vegetables, green vegetables, protein. And it makes good leftovers, so I make a big pot and have it for lunch or supper for the next few days.

2 bunches Swiss chard

1 tablespoon olive oil

2 teaspoons cumin seeds

1 cup chopped onions

½ teaspoon paprika

½ teaspoon celery seeds

¼ teaspoon mace

½ teaspoon ground coriander

¼ teaspoon saffron

1 pound Yukon Gold potatoes, peeled and cut into 1-inch pieces

1½ pounds butternut squash, peeled, seeds removed, and cut into 1-inch pieces

One 28-ounce can diced tomatoes

2 cups Vegetable Stock (page 210)

1 cup white wine

2 pounds firm white fish such as halibut, rinsed and cut into 1-inch pieces

Lime wedges

Prepare the Swiss chard. Wash thoroughly to eliminate all sand. Trim the ends. Separate the leaves from the stems. Chop the stems into ½-inch pieces and set aside. Chop the leaves into 1- to 2-inch pieces and set aside, separate from the stems.

BOTH METHODS: Heat the oil in the pressure cooker or stockpot. Add the cumin seeds, stir for 30 seconds, and then add the onions. Sauté for 2 minutes, then sprinkle in the paprika, celery seeds, mace, and coriander. Crumble in the saffron. Stir to coat the onions with the spices.

Add the chopped chard stems, still stirring over medium-high heat. Add the potatoes and butternut squash, and stir gently. Add the tomatoes, stock, and wine.

If using a pressure cooker, lock the lid in place and bring to high pressure over high heat. Cook for 3 minutes. Turn off the heat. Quick-release the pressure. Remove the lid, tilting it away from you to avoid any steam.

If using a stockpot, cover the pot, bring liquids to a boil, and then simmer on low heat for 30 to 40 minutes, until the potatoes and squash are tender enough to be pierced with the tip of a knife.

EITHER METHOD: Bring the stew to a simmer when the potatoes are done, and add the Swiss chard and fish. Simmer over medium-low heat for 4 to 5 minutes, until the fish is opaque and done and the chard is cooked through.

Serve in wide bowls plain or with rice garnished with a lime wedge.

New England Fessenjen
Meat   •••   Serves 6 to 8

Fessenjen is a traditional Persian dish. Meat or poultry, either ground and formed into balls or kept in pieces, is cooked slowly in a sauce that includes pomegranate juice or pomegranate molasses and a generous helping of ground walnuts. Pomegranate juice is available at kosher markets and in natural-food stores, but it is not always easy to find. In this recipe, cranberry juice makes an intriguing alternative, pairing those all-American ingredients turkey and cranberries. This recipe was inspired by one created by Copeland Marks, prolific documenter of exotic cuisines, in his book *Sephardic Cooking*. The fruit gives it a sweet-and-tangy flavor that makes it feel particularly appropriate for Sukkot.

I make this dish using a slow cooker, usually for Shabbat dinner on Friday night. I do the prep work in the morning, and it is ready in time as Shabbat begins.

MEATBALLS

1 pound ground turkey, half light and half dark meat

1 medium onion, grated

½ teaspoon salt

¼ teaspoon freshly ground black pepper

1½ teaspoons grated fresh ginger

1 tablespoon vegetable oil

SAUCE

1 tablespoon olive oil, if needed

2 cups chopped onions (about 2 medium onions)

½ cup long-grain white rice, preferably basmati

½ cup walnuts, toasted and ground

½ teaspoon turmeric

¼ teaspoon ground cardamom

¼ teaspoon ground cloves

½ teaspoon ground ginger

½ teaspoon ground cinnamon

½ teaspoon salt

One 6-once can tomato paste

2 cups cranberry juice (*not* unsweetened)

1 cup water

1 teaspoon honey

½ cup dried apricots (about 16)

½ cup dried cranberries

Mix together the ground turkey, grated onion, salt, pepper, and fresh ginger. Form into 1-inch balls; you should have about 48 meatballs.

Heat the oil in a large skillet over medium heat. Add one-third of the meatballs and cook briefly on all sides, so they hold their shape firmly, about 3 minutes. Remove to a plate and repeat with the remaining meatballs. Set aside.

In the same pan, add 1 additional tablespoon oil, if necessary. Add the onions and sauté for 5 to 7 minutes, until they begin to soften. Add the rice and stir to mix with the onions, then add the walnuts and mix. Add the turmeric, cardamom, cloves, ground ginger, cinnamon, and salt, and stir to coat the onion mixture with the spices. Pour the onion mixture into a slow cooker.

In a medium bowl, stir together the tomato paste, cranberry juice, water, and honey. Pour into the slow cooker and mix with the onion mixture.

Add the meatballs and stir gently to distribute them evenly. Drop the apricots and the cranberries over the surface of the sauce.

Place the lid on the cooker and cook on Low for 6 to 7 hours. There will be a lot of sauce, which will thicken as it cooks. Serve with rice.

Slow-Roasted Savory Brisket

Meat   Serves 8 to 10

My mother-in-law, Esther Robbins, is a terrific cook, especially when it comes to meat and chicken. She has certain signature dishes, and brisket is one of them. It is her Pesach specialty, always requested.

Brisket is one of those ubiquitous Pesach entrées that few seem to do well. Brisket is a tough cut of meat; the problem, Esther says, is people don't cook it long enough. Unlike chicken, which dries out if you cook it too long, brisket becomes more tender. Esther always gets single-cut brisket because it's leaner. "The double cut is so fatty," she says. "It's horrible."

Another key to successful brisket is to make it the day before you plan to serve it. In addition to it tasting better the next day, letting the brisket chill overnight in the refrigerator allows the fat to congeal so you can remove it easily. It is also much easier to slice the brisket when it is cold. If you try to slice it while it is still warm, it will fall apart into a stringy mess. Slice it while it is cool, and then warm it up for serving, as instructed.

6 to 7 pounds single-cut brisket

3 garlic cloves, peeled and minced or grated

1½ inches fresh ginger, peeled and minced or grated

Freshly ground black pepper to taste

2 tablespoons dried thyme

2 tablespoons dried marjoram

2 tablespoons dried oregano

4 to 5 good-sized onions, finely chopped by hand or in a food processor

4 celery stalks, finely chopped by hand or in a food processor

2 cups ketchup

¼ cup honey

¼ cup sweet-and-sour sauce

½ cup red wine

2 pounds baby carrots

8 small red-skinned potatoes, scrubbed and cut in half

Preheat the oven to 450°F.

Rinse and pat dry the brisket. Rub the garlic, ginger, pepper, thyme, marjoram, and oregano over the entire surface of the meat. Place half the onions and celery in a large roasting pan. Put the brisket on top and put the remaining onions and celery on the top and sides of the brisket.

Cook the brisket, uncovered, at 450°F for 30 minutes. This will brown the surface of the meat and help seal in the flavors as it slow-roasts later. After 30 minutes, remove the brisket from the oven and lower the heat to 325°F.

While the meat roasts, prepare the sauce. Combine the ketchup, honey, sweet-and-sour sauce, and red wine in a bowl, and mix until blended.

Scatter the baby carrots and potato halves around the brisket. Pour the prepared sauce over the meat and vegetables. Cover the entire pan with aluminum foil. (Esther says you can use a roasting-pan lid as well, but foil is easier and provides a better seal.)

Cook for 3 to 6 hours. The standard rule is 30 minutes per pound, but the brisket benefits from longer cooking. The meat, when ready, should be brown and a little caramelized. Stick a fork or knife point into the meat. If it is ready, it will almost fall apart. If it is not ready, check again after 45 minutes.

When ready, remove from the oven. Let the brisket cool to room temperature, in the pan. When cool, put in refrigerator overnight.

The next day, preheat the oven to 350°F.

Remove the pan from the refrigerator. Remove the brisket to a cutting board and cut into 12 to 14 slices.

Skim any congealed fat from the pan and discard. Put the slices, overlapping, back in the pan. Cover and cook 40 minutes, until the meat and vegetables are heated through.

Serve the slices with the carrots and potatoes. Spoon the gravy that forms from the sauce and juices in the pan on top of each slice.

Lemon-Scented Roast Chicken

Meat • • • Serves 4

My friend Elizabeth Sternberg trained as a professional chef before becoming the Combined Jewish Philanthropies' Director of Housing for People with Disabilities. A meal at her house is always a treat. "Chicken is my favorite food," she told me and rattled off a list of chicken recipes she makes regularly. Her favorite is a simple roast chicken. "I prefer a whole chicken; I think it cooks better," she says. "It seems like there's more flavor when you roast chicken, it's the right consistency. And I like carving it."

One 4-pound whole chicken, rinsed and patted dry
2 tablespoons olive oil
4 garlic cloves, peeled and finely minced
Zest and juice from 1 lemon; save lemon halves
2 teaspoons dried rosemary
½ cup minced fresh parsley

Preheat the oven to 375°F. Remove any excess fat from the chicken and discard (or save for making schmaltz). Remove the neck and giblets from the cavity, if they're there. Put the squeezed lemon halves in the cavity of the chicken.

Combine the olive oil, garlic, lemon zest and lemon juice, rosemary, and parsley, and mix well. Lift the skin and cover the back and front of the chicken with the parsley mixture, slipping it between the skin and the meat.

Tie the drumsticks together. This helps the chicken cook more evenly. Place the chicken on a rack in a roasting pan, legs down. Bake at 375°F for 30 minutes. After 30 minutes, rotate the bird so that the legs face up. Continue roasting for 45 to 60 more minutes, until the skin begins to brown and the juices run clear when you pierce the thigh.

Remove from the oven, let stand for 15 minutes, and then carve and serve.

Hearty Beef Cholent

Meat • • • **Serves 6**

Cholent has become a classic Shabbat afternoon dish. It cooks at a low heat for a long time (10 to 20 or more hours), and is usually a heavy, hearty, meaty stew. It evolved as a Shabbat afternoon meal because it could be put in a low oven or kept warm over a low burner, and would cook overnight, yielding a warm meat dish for the celebratory Shabbat afternoon lunch. Cholent is not exactly a light lunch—more a stick-to-your-ribs winter dish, traditionally made with barley, beans, potatoes, and meat. Lima beans are usual, but Great Northern beans cook better in a slow cooker. I developed this recipe for an article I wrote for *The Boston Globe* several years ago.

1¼ cups Great Northern or navy beans, soaked overnight

2 pounds potatoes (about 4 medium), peeled and cut into
   1-inch chunks

½ cup pearl barley

15 garlic cloves, peeled

2 teaspoons paprika

1 teaspoon salt

½ teaspoon freshly ground pepper

1½ pounds lean beef, cut into 6 pieces

2 medium onions, chopped

6 cups beef broth or Chicken Stock (page 205)
   (if you use canned broth, reduce the salt to ¼ teaspoon)

Drain the beans and place in the slow cooker. Top with the potato chunks and barley. Distribute the garlic around the pot.

In a small bowl, mix together the paprika, salt, and pepper, and sprinkle a small amount on all sides of each piece of meat. Sprinkle the remaining spice mixture over the ingredients in the slow cooker.

Heat a skillet over medium-high heat. Brown the meat for a few minutes on all sides and set aside. Sauté the onions in the same pan, until slightly softened, about 3 minutes.

Add the onions to the cooker and place the meat chunks on top. Pour the broth over the mixture and cook 16 to 20 hours on Low.

Mushroom-Bean Vegan Cholent

Pareve • **Serves 6 to 8**

This delicious vegan cholent is famous at our shul in Cambridge, Temple Beth Shalom. Gabriel Kaptchuk and his father, Ted, make it annually for a Shabbat kiddush in honor of our nonagenarian Reb Moshe Holcer. On Friday afternoon, Ted and Gabriel fill several slow cookers in the synagogue kitchen, making enough cholent to feed more than one hundred congregants Shabbat lunch the next day.

This cholent is simultaneously hearty and light, richly flavored with a variety of mushrooms, beans, and vegetables.

Ted and Gabriel are cooks who never keep track of measurements; as Ted says, "The cholent works no matter what mish-mash of ingredients go into the pot." But those of us who wish to re-create the dish need something a little more precise. Our shul's caterer and superb cook, Barbara Model, spoke with the Kaptchuks and developed a recipe based on theirs with exact measurements. She makes her version on the stovetop; the Kaptchuks make theirs in a slow cooker.

This recipe is a blend of their efforts. I like the ease of a slow cooker and the reproduceable results of precise measurements. Notable differences: The Kaptchuks are very generous with oil—using almost twice as much as called for here. Barbara also adds paprika to her version.

NOTE: The beans need to soak overnight. Ted prefers to include dried lima beans, "the larger the better."

6 tablespoons olive oil, divided

2½ cups chopped onions

1¼ cups assorted dried beans (white and red kidney beans, navy beans, fava, lima, etc.), soaked overnight in 1 quart water

1½ cups barley

1 dried shiitake mushroom (Ted says more than 1 shiitake mushroom makes the cholent taste too "Chinese")

6 assorted dried mushrooms (Ted recommends dried Polish mushrooms; porcini also work well)

4 garlic cloves, peeled and thinly sliced

3 tablespoons sesame oil, divided

1½ teaspoons dried dill or 6 sprigs fresh dill, chopped

½ cup chopped fresh parsley

1 cup chopped collard greens

2 cups fresh white mushrooms, lightly washed, stems trimmed, cut into quarters

1 portobello mushroom, cut in half and cut into ¼-inch slices

6 small white potatoes, peeled and cut in half

1 celery stalk, sliced into 1-inch pieces

2 carrots, peeled and cut into ½-inch pieces

1 parsnip, peeled and cut into ½-inch pieces

6 to 8 cups water mixed with 1 teaspoon salt, or 6 to 8 cups vegetable stock (see page 210)

Place 1 tablespoon olive oil in the bottom of the slow cooker. Tilt to coat the bottom.

Place half the onions in the cooker.

Drain and rinse the beans. Put half the beans on top of the onions, then half the barley. Scatter the dried mushrooms and garlic slices on top. Drizzle with 1 tablespoon sesame oil and 1 tablespoon olive oil.

Place the remaining beans, then the remaining barley, then the remaining onions in the cooker. Sprinkle with the dill and parsley.

Add the collard greens, white mushrooms, portobello mushroom, potatoes, celery, carrots, and parsnip. Drizzle with the remaining 4 tablespoons olive oil and 2 tablespoons sesame oil.

Pour the salted water or vegetable stock over everything. The liquid should fill the cooker almost to the top.

Put the lid on the cooker and cook on Low for 12 to 14 hours.

Enchilada Lasagna
Dairy • • • **Serves 6 to 8**

Not exactly a traditional Jewish dish, but it is an easy one to throw together from packaged goods. Further, it is one that two out of three of my children will eat—and even ask for seconds.

3 cups prepared salsa, divided

12 corn tortillas

1½ cups grated Cheddar cheese

Two 15-ounce cans kidney beans, drained and rinsed

Two 15-ounce cans pinto beans, drained and rinsed

1 cup cottage cheese

Oil for the pan

Preheat the oven to 350°F. Lightly oil a 9- by 13-inch or 10- by 15-inch baking pan.

Put 1 cup of the salsa on a plate. Dip each tortilla in the salsa so the tortilla is coated. Stack the tortillas up as you dip them.

Place six tortillas in the pan, covering the bottom. The tortillas will overlap. Pour any salsa remaining on the plate on top of the tortillas in the pan. Set the remaining six tortillas aside, stacked. Sprinkle ½ cup of the grated cheese over the tortillas.

Mix together the kidney beans, pinto beans, 1½ cups of the salsa, and the cottage cheese in a large bowl. Spoon the bean mixture on top of the tortillas in the baking pan and smooth. Sprinkle ½ cup grated cheese on top of the bean mixture.

Cover the beans with the remaining tortillas, overlapping to cover the entire surface. Pour the remaining ½ cup salsa on top of the tortillas. Sprinkle the remaining ½ cup grated cheese on top.

Bake at 350°F for 30 minutes, until the cheese on top is bubbling. Remove from the oven and keep warm on a *blech,* hot plate, or in a low oven until ready to serve.

Gingered-Tomato Chickpeas

Pareve • • • **Serves 6**

Yamuna Devi's *The Art of Indian Vegetarian Cooking* is a wealth of information and inspiration. Many recipes are time-consuming to prepare, with several exotic spices. I happen to have exotic spices on hand, since we live near an Indian market, but I've adapted this recipe so that it can be made with spices found on supermarket shelves.

Devi's original recipe called for chickpeas cooked from scratch; I use canned chickpeas for convenience. This dish is quick, easy, and popular in my family. Sometimes I double the recipe to have leftovers for lunches all week.

1 tablespoon oil

½ teaspoon black or yellow mustard seeds

1½ teaspoons cumin seeds

1 tablespoon minced fresh ginger

One 28-ounce can diced tomatoes

One 14.5-ounce can tomato puree

½ teaspoon salt

¼ teaspoon ground allspice

1½ teaspoons ground coriander

1 teaspoon turmeric

½ teaspoon ground cinnamon

Three 15-ounce cans chickpeas, drained and rinsed in warm water

Heat the oil in a large pot over medium heat. Add mustard seeds, cumin seeds, and ginger, and sauté for less than a minute. Avoid burning the seeds. Add the diced tomatoes, tomato puree, salt, allspice, coriander, turmeric, and cinnamon. Heat for a few minutes, then add the chickpeas. Bring the mixture to a boil, then simmer gently for about 10 minutes, stirring occasionally.

Serve with brown rice.

Carrot-Almond Torte with Apple-Apricot Compote

Pareve • • • Makes 10 to 12 servings

My policy for Pesach desserts is no matzo meal, no milk, no margarine. No matzo meal because I want a dessert that would taste good throughout the year, not one that tastes kosher for Pesach. No milk because I am usually making desserts for the seder, which tends to be a meat meal. No margarine because I don't care for its flavor. I prefer not to make a recipe that calls for butter, substituting margarine, so I'll use one calling for oil or one with no added fat.

This recipe meets those qualifications. I adapted it from *New Kosher Cuisine for All Seasons,* a cookbook of holiday menus put together by my kids' Solomon Schechter Day School of Greater Boston, edited by Ivy Feuerstadt and Melinda Strauss. The recipe in the book, submitted by Judy Zomer, is called Carrot Cake for Pesach, but I feel this is such a delicious cake, it deserves a more elegant, year-round name. The cake rises as it bakes, then falls as it cools. The result is moist, nutty, and surprisingly light.

I created the fruit compote to go with it for an impressive finish. For the compote, use Gala apples, if possible, or a pie apple such as Cortland. They hold their shape when cooked.

6 eggs, separated

1 cup sugar

1¼ cups finely grated carrots

1 cup almonds, finely ground

1 teaspoon lemon juice

1 teaspoon ground cinnamon

1 tablespoon sliced almonds (optional)

Oil for the pan

Apple-Apricot Compote (recipe follows)

Preheat the oven to 350°F and grease a 9- or 10-inch springform pan.

Beat the egg yolks with ½ cup sugar in a large bowl until thick and pale. Add the carrots, ground almonds, lemon juice, and cinnamon. Mix well.

In a separate large bowl, beat the egg whites until soft peaks form. Gradually add the remaining ½ cup sugar while beating and continue beating until stiff peaks form. Do not overbeat.

Fold one-quarter of the egg-white mixture into the carrot mixture to lighten it, then gently fold in the remaining egg whites.

Pour the batter into the prepared pan and smooth the top. If desired, sprinkle with the sliced almonds.

Bake at 350°F for 45 to 55 minutes, until lightly browned and a tester inserted in the center comes out clean.

Cool the pan on a wire rack. The torte will sink significantly as it cools. Let cool at least 30 minutes before removing the sides of the springform pan.

To serve, cut the torte into wedges. Top each slice with Apple-Apricot Compote.

Apple-Apricot Compote
Makes about 2 cups

1 tablespoon lemon juice

1 tablespoon honey

½ cup orange juice

½ cup apple juice

1 teaspoon ground cinnamon

2 apples, preferably Gala, peeled, cut in half, cored,
   and thinly sliced

12 dried apricots, cut into quarters

Combine the lemon juice, honey, orange juice, apple juice, and cinnamon in a medium saucepan and stir to combine. Add the apples and apricots, and stir to coat with juice. Place over medium-high heat and bring to a boil. Reduce the heat to a simmer and cook until the apples are just barely tender, 3 to 4 minutes. Watch carefully—you don't want the slices to turn into mush. Remove from the heat. The compote may be made in advance and refrigerated; reheat before serving.

Honey Cake

Pareve • • • Makes two 9- by 5-inch loaves; serves 12 to 16

Honey cake is a Rosh Hashanah tradition but, as much as I love cake, I was never that fond of it until I enjoyed a Rosh Hashanah kiddush at my friend Elizabeth Sternberg's house. There was a buffet of desserts, including a platter with something that Elizabeth called honey cake, though it looked and tasted quite different from what I thought of as honey cake, as it was studded with nuts and dried fruit. This cake has a pleasing complexity of flavors—honey, orange, spices—and textures from a variety of nuts and fruits. Elizabeth's mother, Diane Diamond Sternberg, has been making this cake since Elizabeth was young.

You may notice that the cake has no fat or eggs added—this is not a mistake!

> 3 cups all-purpose flour
>
> 1 teaspoon ground cinnamon
>
> ⅛ teaspoon ground cloves
>
> ½ teaspoon ground nutmeg
>
> 1 teaspoon baking soda
>
> 1¾ cups honey
>
> 1½ cups orange juice
>
> ½ cup pistachios
>
> ½ cup chopped walnuts
>
> ½ cup raisins, dried cherries, or dried cranberries
>
> ½ cup dried apricots, roughly chopped
>
> ¼ cup slivered almonds
>
> Oil for the pans

Preheat the oven to 350°F. Grease two 9- by 5-inch loaf pans.

Sift the flour, cinnamon, cloves, nutmeg, and baking soda into a large bowl.

Mix the honey and orange juice in a separate bowl until blended. Add the pistachios and walnuts.

Add the nut and honey mixture to the dry ingredients, and mix well. Stir in the raisins and apricots. Do not overmix.

Divide the batter between the two pans. Sprinkle the top of each with the slivered almonds.

Put the pans in the oven and reduce the temperature to 325°F.

Bake for 1 hour and 45 minutes. Test for doneness after 90 minutes with a skewer or toothpick. If it comes out dry, then the cakes are done.

Cool the cakes on a rack for 30 minutes and loosen the sides before unmolding.

Honey Layer Cake with Caramelized Apples
Dairy • • • Makes 12 servings

My son Eitan's birthday is in April, and it seems every other year he has to make do with a kosher-for-Pesach cake—so I try to come up with creative, non-*Pesachdig*-tasting variations. However, one year when his birthday was *not* during Pesach, he was very precise as to the kind of cake he wanted: a honey-flavored layer cake, with honey-flavored frosting between the layers, topped with apples sautéed with butter and brown sugar. No spices. I like a culinary challenge. We also have lots of September birthdays in our family, and the flavor combination of this cake seems perfect for Rosh Hashanah.

This recipe is quite different from both the preceding recipe and from traditional honey cakes, which I usually find have a gingerbread flavor. Ironically, it was inspired by a maple-gingerbread recipe by Susan Purdy in *The Perfect Cake*. Use a flavorful honey, as this cake really tastes like the honey you use. The only additional flavorings are vanilla—no spices—and butter. You can use margarine or oil to make it pareve but I don't recommend it, as the butter contributes to the flavor.

1 large egg

1 cup honey

1 cup plain yogurt, stirred until smooth

¼ cup unsalted butter, melted and cooled

1 teaspoon vanilla extract

2⅓ cups all-purpose flour

½ teaspoon baking powder

1 teaspoon baking soda

¼ teaspoon salt

Oil for the pans

Preheat the oven to 350°F. Spray or lightly grease two 8-inch round cake pans.

Combine the egg, honey, yogurt, melted butter, and vanilla in a large bowl. Using an electric mixer, beat on medium speed until well blended.

Put the flour, baking powder, baking soda, and salt in a sifter. Sift half the flour into the honey mixture. On low speed, blend until fully incorporated. Sift in the remaining flour and blend in until smooth.

Divide the batter into the prepared pans. Bake at 350°F for 25 to 30 minutes, until pale gold in color and a tester inserted into the center of the cakes comes out clean.

Cool in the pans for 20 minutes, then remove and cool on racks.

When fully cool, spread Honey Cream Frosting between the layers and on the top of the cake (not on the sides). To serve, slice into wedges and put on individual plates. Top each slice with a spoonful of Caramelized Apples.

Honey Cream Frosting

The tang of the cream cheese offsets the sweetness of the honey. It's important to sift the confectioners' sugar, otherwise the frosting will be lumpy and no amount of beating will smooth out those sugar lumps.

8 ounces cream cheese, at room temperature

2 tablespoons salted butter, at room temperature

Pinch salt

3 tablespoons honey

1½ cup sifted confectioners' sugar

Cream together the cream cheese, butter, and salt until smooth, using an electric mixer or a wooden spoon. Blend in the honey, then the confectioners' sugar. The frosting should be of an easily spreadable consistency. If it seems too thin, add additional sifted confectioners' sugar, 1 tablespoon at a time.

Caramelized Apples

I prefer to use Pink Lady or Gala apples for this recipe, as they hold their shape well and have a tangy flavor that complements the honey in the cake.

2 tablespoons salted butter

3 apples, peeled, cored, and cut into ½-inch chunks

¼ cup light brown sugar

Melt the butter over medium heat in a medium saucepan. Add the apples and sauté for 2 minutes. Sprinkle the brown sugar over the apples. Bring to a simmer, then lower the heat, and simmer over low heat for 5 to 10 minutes, until the apples are softened but still hold their shape. Serve warm; the compote may be reheated.

Chocolate Pudding Cake

Pareve or Dairy • • • Serves 8 to 10

When I was growing up, my mother would make chocolate pudding cake for Shabbat or as a special-occasion dessert. I always thought it was so cool: You start with a normal-looking cake batter, then do the odd thing of pouring water all over it so that it looks like you've just ruined it. While it bakes, it turns into a toothsome chocolaty cake with a pudding-like sauce underneath. The sauce is thick but liquidy when hot from the oven; when it cools, the sauce becomes more like a pudding. This has become one of my daughter Shoshanna's favorite desserts.

This recipe makes two cakes, enough for our family plus guests. We often have it for Shabbat dessert. If we're having a dairy meal, I'll make it with melted butter. (And it's good topped with ice cream.) For a meat meal, I'll make it with oil. If there are no nut allergies to worry about, I like walnut oil. Otherwise I use a flavorless oil such as safflower.

Make sure to use two pans. Do *not* combine the batter into one large pan, as the center will not cook properly.

$2\frac{1}{2}$ **cups all-purpose flour**

$\frac{1}{2}$ **cup cocoa**

2 tablespoons baking powder

$1\frac{1}{2}$ **teaspoons salt**

$2\frac{1}{2}$ **cups light brown sugar**

$1\frac{1}{2}$ **cups water**

6 tablespoons melted unsalted butter or oil

1 tablespoon vanilla extract

Oil for the dishes

TOPPING

$\frac{1}{2}$ **cup light brown sugar**

$2\frac{1}{2}$ **cups hot water**

Preheat the oven to 350°F. Grease two large (2-quart) soufflé dishes or two 9-inch square or round cake pans with high edges.

Sift together the flour, cocoa, baking powder, and salt into a large bowl. Mix in the brown sugar. Add the water, melted butter or oil, and vanilla, and mix until smooth.

Divide the batter between the two prepared pans.

Sprinkle the batter in each pan with ¼ cup brown sugar for the topping. Pour 1¼ cups hot water over the batter in each pan. It will look like you are messing up the cakes, but magic chemistry happens while they bake.

Bake at 350°F for 30 to 45 minutes. The batter will rise and form into a smooth-topped cake. It should be firm to the touch. A toothpick or cake tester inserted partway into the cake should come out clean. If you stick it in all the way to the bottom, you will pick up some of the sauce, which is underneath the cake. Serve warm or at room temperature.

Rum Pecan Pie

Pareve • • • Makes two 9-inch pies; serves 16 polite people, and 12 who really love pecan pie

My aunt, Raya Stern, makes this pecan pie every year for Thanksgiving. She developed it with a dual purpose in mind: It's nondairy so it could be pareve, and my cousin Dea, who had developed an allergy to dairy, could eat it. She also was allergic to legumes, so Raya included a margarine that had no soy oil in it. Make sure the margarine for the crust comes straight from the refrigerator and is cold—*not* room temperature.

PASTRY CRUST
2 cups all-purpose flour, plus more for rolling out the dough
1 teaspoon salt

⅔ cup cold pareve corn oil margarine

6 to 8 tablespoons ice water

Extra oil or margarine for the pan

Lightly grease two 9-inch pie pans.

Measure the flour and salt into a large bowl. Cut the margarine into the flour with a pastry mixer or two knives. Add the water 1 tablespoon at a time, pushing the mixture together with a fork. Use a little less water than you really need to get it to stick together—it goes from crumbly to too sticky in a few teaspoons.

Divide the dough in half. Flatten each half into a disk. Wrap one disk in plastic wrap and refrigerate while you roll out the other half on a floured surface. (Pastry dough is the opposite of bread dough—you want to handle it as minimally as possible so as not to develop the gluten, which makes a tougher crust.) Roll the dough of one disk into a circle large enough to fit a 9-inch pie pan.

Lift the dough carefully and place it in one of the prepared pans. Refrigerate while you roll out the second disk of dough and fit it into the second pie pan. Refrigerate both shells while you prepare the pecan filling.

PECAN FILLING
½ cup pareve corn oil margarine

1 cup light brown sugar

1 cup white sugar

½ cup light corn syrup

½ cup dark corn syrup

6 large eggs

2 tablespoons rum

3 cups pecans

Preheat the oven to 350°F.

Put the margarine, brown sugar, and white sugar into a large bowl, and beat until combined using an electric mixer set on medium-high speed. Add the light and dark corn syrups, and beat in. Add the eggs one at a time and beat until thoroughly incorporated. With the mixer running, add the rum.

Using a spatula, fold in the pecans. Divide the mixture between the two pie shells. Bake at 350°F for 30 to 40 minutes, until the center of the pie looks almost firm.

Let cool to room temperature before serving.

Chocolate-Flecked Meringues

Pareve • • • Makes about 6 dozen 1½-inch kisses

Meringues are ideal for Pesach; they tastes like cookies, not like they're missing something. For my kids, meringues are not just a Pesach dessert. They love them throughout the year, and meringues are my son Gabriel's most requested cookie. They are wonderfully simple to make, and however many I make, there are rarely leftovers. I make them bite-sized, and they are so light and crispy, it's easy to pop many into your mouth without realizing they're disappearing.

My kids like them with and without the chocolate chips. Sometimes, if I'm making them plain, I'll use a vanilla bean instead of vanilla extract for an added depth of flavor. I've sometimes also added 1 tablespoon of fresh chopped mint leaves.

I grind the chocolate chips for two reasons. First, it makes for a more delicate cookie, with the chocolate spread throughout, instead of sinking to the bottom as the cookie bakes, which happens with whole chocolate chips. Second, it makes it easier to form the cookies using the plastic bag technique described in the recipe.

The recipe may be halved, but these cookies store well in an airtight container.

NOTES: If you make these on a rainy or humid day, the meringues will not stay crisp. They're still good, but will be sticky and chewy instead of light and crispy.

I use two half-sheet baking pans, which are larger than standard cookie sheets, so you can fit all the batter into two pans. If you have smaller baking sheets, you may need to use three pans.

¾ cup chocolate chips

¼ teaspoon salt

4 large egg whites

1 cup sugar

1 teaspoon vanilla extract

Preheat the oven to 300°F. Line two or three baking sheets (see headnote) with parchment paper. Set the racks in the oven to divide it into thirds.

Partially grind the chocolate chips in a food processor until they consist of smaller chips and ground chocolate. Set aside.

Sprinkle the salt over the egg whites in a large mixing bowl. Using an electric mixer (use the whisk attachment if you are using a standing mixer), beat the egg whites on medium speed for 1 minute. Change to high speed and continue beating until soft peaks form. Continue beating and gradually add the sugar. Once all the sugar has been incorporated, add the vanilla and continue beating just until it is incorporated. The egg whites should be smooth, but not dry, and satiny white. Add the semiground chocolate chips and mix for about 10 seconds.

You can drop the batter on the prepared baking sheets using a teaspoon, but the easiest and quickest way to form meringues is using a plastic bag and piping them. If you have a pastry bag, use that. Otherwise, scrape the batter into a large plastic bag. (I use a large zipper-top plastic bag.) Seal the top, then snip a corner at the bottom of the bag, leaving an opening that is about ½ inch across. Hold the bag near the top and squeeze the batter out through this hole into kiss-shaped rounds about 1 inch to 1½ inches across. Allow ½ to 1 inch between cookies. You can fit about 36 to 40 meringues on a large baking sheet.

Bake two sheets at a time at 300°F for 20 to 25 minutes, until the cookies are firm. To test, remove one cookie from the sheet (the bottom will probably stick regardless if it is ready or not). Put it in the freezer for 1 minute, then remove it. If it is chewy, the meringues should cook for a few more minutes. If it is crispy, it is ready.

The meringues will continue to firm up as they cool. Let cool on the pans for at least 10 minutes, otherwise the bottoms will stick to the parchment. Remove and store in an airtight container.

Hamantashen Trio
Pareve or Dairy

Ah, hamantashen. I collect recipes for this three-cornered Purim pastry, and try different doughs every year. My absolute favorite, a dairy dough, is made with cream cheese, which is what my mother used.

I use my cousin Ittamar Weissbrem's dough when I'm making hamantashen with my kids; it's more cookielike, and more forgiving. This dough can be made with butter or margarine. Since I prefer not to cook with margarine, when I want to make a pareve dough, I use Esty Oppenheimer's Persian hamantashen pastry, which calls for oil. It also has the advantage of being ready to use immediately, as it doesn't need to chill.

For hamantashen fillings, anything goes. My cousin Dea Haupt says, "It's a good way to use up all those jars of jam and jelly that only have a tablespoon left—that's generally how I flavor my hamantashen." In our house, we all have different preferences. My son Gabriel likes small chocolate peanut butter cups. Eitan is fond of lemon curd or raspberry jam, while Shoshanna likes chocolate chips and bits of white chocolate. I'm partial to marmalade mixed with a little bit of ground coffee beans, while my husband, Jeffrey, prefers traditional poppy seed.

I offer a trio of hamantashen pastries and a trio of fillings.

Hamantashen Pastry

Cream Cheese Pastry

Dairy • • • Makes 3 to 4 dozen hamantashen, depending on the size

This dough is slightly tangy and bakes into a tender, flaky pastry. It is a dough more for grown-ups than children, as it is not very sweet. It is my personal favorite. The dough should be chilled several hours.

This dough can be tricky to work with—getting the corners to stay sealed is a perpetual challenge. No matter how tightly I pinch those edges together, half the hamantashen open into misshapen circles while they bake. Refrigerating the formed hamantashen for 20 minutes before baking does help, if you have the time or space to do that. Regardless of appearances, they taste great.

½ cup unsalted butter, at room temperature

4 ounces cream cheese, at room temperature

2 tablespoons sugar

1 teaspoon vanilla extract

1 cup all-purpose flour

Pinch salt

Cream together the butter and cream cheese until light and fluffy using an electric mixer. Add the sugar and vanilla and mix well. Add the flour and salt and mix just until combined. The dough should come together, and should not be sticky.

Chill the dough, preferably overnight.

Roll and form the hamantashen as described on page 261.

Oznei Haman Pastry

Dairy or Pareve • • • Makes 6 to 7 dozen hamantashen,
depending on the size

My father's cousin Ittamar Weissbrem, who lives in Israel, loves to cook. Every Purim he makes dozens of *oznei haman*, as hamantashen are called in Hebrew, and fills them with poppy-seed filling. This is my American adaptation of his recipe. The dough is more workable if you refrigerate it, but Ittamar admits that he does not always do this.

2½ cups all-purpose flour

½ cup sugar

½ teaspoon baking powder

¼ teaspoon salt

½ cup unsalted butter or margarine, cut into small chunks

1 teaspoon vanilla extract

3 eggs, lightly beaten

Combine the flour, sugar, baking powder, and salt in a large bowl. Add the butter or margarine. If you have a standing mixer, use the paddle attachment to blend in the butter; otherwise, do so by hand or with a pastry knife. The mixture should be crumbly, the texture of cornmeal. Add the vanilla and work it in.

Add two-thirds of the beaten eggs. The dough should come together as a ball. If is too dry, add more egg; if too wet, add additional flour. When it comes together into a cohesive ball, not sticky, flatten it into a disk, wrap in plastic wrap or wax paper, and refrigerate for 1 hour, until firm.

Roll and form the hamantashen as described on page 261.

Persian Hamantashen Pastry

Pareve • • • Makes 6 to 7 dozen hamantashen, depending on the size

Esty Oppenheimer, native of Israel and babysitter for my friend Heather Zacker, was born on Purim and is named for Queen Esther. (Her brother, also born on Purim, is named Mordechai.) Naturally, hamantashen are a specialty for Esty. She estimates that she makes at least 100 hamantashen each year for the *mishloach manot* packages she gives to friends and family.

Esty's parents immigrated to Israel from Iran, so there is an Iranian element to the fillings she prepares (coconut-cherry, sesame). This recipe is made with orange juice and oil.

This dough has the advantage of not needing to chill. It's ready to use immediately.

3 cups all-purpose flour

½ cup sugar

1½ teaspoons baking powder

1½ teaspoons baking soda

¾ teaspoon salt

2 eggs

¼ cup orange juice

½ cup vegetable oil

In a large bowl, mix together the flour, sugar, baking powder, baking soda, and salt.

In a separate bowl, lightly beat together the eggs, orange juice, and vegetable oil. Add to the flour mixture and mix until the dough comes together in a ball. The dough should not be sticky. If it is, add additional flour.

Roll and form the hamantashen (see page 261).

Hamantashen Fillings

Coconut-Cherry Filling

Pareve or Dairy • • • Makes 1½ cups filling

1 cup shredded coconut

1 cup sour cherry jam

1 tablespoon sugar

2 teaspoons melted butter (optional)

Toast the coconut. Heat in a skillet over medium heat. Watch carefully. The coconut will begin to brown in a couple of minutes. Stir for a few seconds, then remove from the heat.

Stir together the jam, coconut, sugar, and butter, if using, in a small bowl. The filling will keep for several weeks in the refrigerator.

Sesame Filling

Pareve • • • Makes 1¾ cups filling

½ cup sesame seeds

1 cup raspberry or strawberry jam

1 cup crushed almonds

Toast the sesame seeds. Heat them in a skillet over medium-high heat. Watch carefully. The seeds will not appear to cook at all for several minutes, then will suddenly start browning. When the seeds begin to brown, lower the heat and stir for a few more seconds. When more seeds than not appear toasted, remove from the heat.

Stir together the jam, almonds, and toasted sesame seeds in a small bowl. The filling will keep for several weeks in the refrigerator.

Poppy-Seed Filling

Pareve • • • Makes 1½ cups filling

Our cousin Ittamar's hamantashen specialty is poppy-seed filling. "I like a lot of poppy seeds," he says, "so I grind my own." He usually doubles this recipe.

You do not need to grind the poppy seeds, but it gives the filling a more intense flavor. Ittamar uses small white raisins available in Israel. I prefer to use currants.

½ cup water

1 cup sugar

2 tablespoons honey

¼ cup lemon juice

1 cup poppy seeds, ground in a blender or food processor

½ cup small currants or golden raisins

1 tablespoon grated lemon zest

Put the water, sugar, and honey in a medium saucepan. Place over medium-high heat and stir until the sugar is dissolved.

Add the lemon juice, poppy seeds, and currants or raisins. Bring to a near boil and simmer for 1 minute.

Remove from the heat and stir in the lemon zest. Let the mixture cool to room temperature before using. The filling will keep for up to 1 week in the refrigerator.

ASSEMBLING THE HAMANTASHEN: Preheat the oven to 350°F. Line two baking sheets with parchment paper or lightly grease the pans.

On a lightly floured surface, roll out your choice of dough. The dough should be rolled about ⅛ inch thick. Cut into circles using a cookie cutter or a glass. I prefer smaller cookies, and cut 2- or 3-inch circles. If you are making these for a lot of *mishloach manot* packages, you can make the cookies smaller.

Fill with 1 to 1½ teaspoons of filling. Fold part of the circle over in three places, to form the traditional triangle shape. Pinch the corners together firmly. If you have space in your refrigerator, and time to spare, refrigerate the formed hamantashen for 20 minutes before baking (especially if using the cream cheese pastry, as that has a tendency to open as it bakes).

The cookies do not spread much as they bake, so you can place them ½ to 1 inch apart. Because they take time to prepare, I usually put one tray in the oven while I am working on the second.

Bake for 15 to 20 minutes at 350°F, until light brown at the edges. Remove the hamantashen from the baking sheets and cool on wire racks.

SOURCES

THIS BOOK SERVES as an overview and general introduction to kashrut and some of the Jewish dietary laws and traditions related to Shabbat, Pesach, and the other holidays. But there are many books that go into great depth on all aspects of what I have covered here. There is always more information on a given topic, always more to learn.

Books are invaluable resources. And today the Internet is one, too. While many websites come and go, there are those that seem to be here for the duration, are updated regularly, and provide a wealth of information not found in books alone. The Internet offers links to people as well—some of the scholars and rabbinic authorities I was able to speak with I found through articles posted on the Web. I offer below the best sources I have found in the written word, both printed on paper and on computer screens. I realize not everyone has access to the Internet at home, but libraries offer the service, and it can be extremely useful to those seeking more information.

Note, however, that the Web is a very dynamic place, and Internet addresses can disappear or change without notice.

Kashrut Supervising Agencies

Kashrus Magazine is a publication that reports on concerns relevant to keeping kosher. They publish an annual Kosher Supervision Guide. As of January 2004, the guide listed more than 620 kashrut symbols and supervising agencies worldwide, with more than 450 in the United States and Canada. That is a lot, and not all may be reliable; while the magazine does confirm all the technical information about a company, they do not verify the credentials of the listed agencies. Some organizations are small, while some agencies may consist of an individual rabbi, as I discussed in the introduction. There are also many local organizations that may supervise your local restaurant or bakery, and thus be familiar to you, and therefore reliable. If you have a question about a supervising agency, check with your rabbi or with one of the larger agencies.

The four largest supervising agencies are the following:

The Orthodox Union
11 Broadway
New York, NY 10004
(212) 563-4000
Fax: (212) 564-9058
email: *info@ou.org*
www.ou.org, www.ou.org/kosher/

Many useful articles are on their website, but finding them is not always easy. Once you do, they are definitely worthwhile. You can call or e-mail with questions, and there are very helpful people. However, the organization is very large, so sometimes it may take a few days to get a response.

Kof-K Supervisor Organization
201 The Plaza
Teaneck, NJ 07666
(201) 837-0500
www.kof-k.com
Some useful information; not nearly as detailed as the other three sites.

Star-K Kosher Certification
11 Warren Road
Baltimore, MD 21208-5234
(410) 484-4110
Fax: (410) 653-9294
www.star-k.com

Very well done website, the easiest and most comprehensive to use. Their publication, much of which is available online, is *Kashrut Kurrents*. You can also call with kashrut questions, usually with quick responses.

OK Kosher Certification
391 Troy Avenue
Brooklyn, NY 11213
(718) 756-7500
Fax: (718) 756-7503
www.okkosher.com

Well done website with many useful articles. Their publication is *Kosher Spirit* (*www.kosherspirit.com*). It used to be called *Jewish Homemaker* (*www.homemaker.org*); archives are available online. You can also call with kashrut questions, and are likely find someone who will answer fairly soon.

There are other large American certifiers, although they tend to be oriented more toward local (as in city or state) companies and products. One with a worthwhile website is that of the Chicago Rabbinical Council, *www.crcweb.org*.

There are over a hundred certifiers internationally. A few have websites with useful and interesting information that give a perspective of kashrut observance abroad. Notable foreign websites include the following:

Australia—New South Wales (NSW) Kashrut Authority *www.ka.org.au*

Canada—MK Vaad Hair or Jewish Community Council of Montreal *www.mk.ca*

England—London Beit Din *www.kosher.org.uk*

Mexico—Kosher Maguén David (KMD) *www.kosher.com.mx* Kashrut explained in Spanish, with listings of kosher establishments and products in Mexico

South Africa—Union of Orthodox Synagogues of South Africa (UOS) *www.uos.co.za*

Kashrut Sources

Books

The Laws of Kashrus by Rabbi Binyomin Forst (Mesorah Publications, Ltd.; The ArtScroll Series, 1993, 2002). Truly detailed information on all the technical elements of kashrut, such as *basar b'chalav* issues, with references to primary sources. Very useful if you want extremely in-depth information.

Keeping Kosher: A Diet for the Soul by Samuel H. Dresner and David M. Pollock (United Synagogue of Conservative Judaism Commission on Jewish Education, 2000, 1982, 1966, 1959). Fourth edition of the Conservative movement's publication on kashrut. Good general information.

Kashruth: A comprehensive background and reference guide to the principles of Kashruth by Rabbi Yacov Lipschuz (Mesorah Publications, Ltd.; The ArtScroll Series, 1988). Detailed information about kosher foods, including additives and preservatives. No index.

Periodicals

There are several periodicals that address issues of kashrut. The kashrut supervising agencies mentioned earlier have regular publications, as do most of the Jewish movements. Following are a couple more periodicals:

Kashrus Magazine
P.O. Box 204
Brooklyn, NY 11204
(718) 336-8544
Fax: (718) 336-8550
www.kashrusmagazine.com

Kashrus Magazine has been published since 1980 under the editorship of Rabbi Yosef Wikler. The magazine is published five times a year, and includes an indispensable annual Kosher Supervision Guide—no one else produces such a comprehensive list. They also publish *Kashrus Monthly*, usually a one-page listing of twenty to thirty updates on kosher food products, such as mislabeling, certification changes, and so on.

Their website is updated sporadically, but it includes a useful sample listing of supervising agencies and magazine articles.

Kosher Today

P.O. Box 1451

Lowell, MA 01853

(212) 868-2960 or (978) 256-6490

www.koshertodaymagazine.com

They have an online weekly newsletter, which is very timely, as well as a monthly print publication, which is less so but useful nonetheless. Very informative articles about the international kosher food industry. The newsletters are published by Integrated Marketing Events & Expositions, a company that sponsors Kosher Fest, an annual industry trade show (*www.kosherfest.com*).

Websites

Kosher Quest

www.kosherquest.org

Very detailed Orthodox site on kashrut, with frequent kashrut updates. Includes an online version of the in-print book *Is It Kosher?: Encyclopedia of Kosher Foods Facts & Fallacies* by Rabbi E. Eidlitz.

www.kashrut.com

Scharf Associates

P.O. Box 50

Sharon, MA 02067

(781) 784-6890

Fax: (781) 784-6890

email: *ajms@kashrut.com*

A thorough clearinghouse site on kashrut-related issues maintained by the very knowledgeable Arlene J. Mathes-Scharf.

www.chelm.org

This is a personal website on kashrut maintained by Steven Ross Weintraub. Although it is not updated regularly, the information is not time-sensitive. Very informative and accurate.

Chowhound's Kosher Message Board

www.chowhound.com/boards/kosher/kosher.html

Chowhound is a message board of opinions on food-related matters. This one is dedicated to kashrut, and enables you to get unofficial answers to kosher questions, such as what are good sources for kosher wine and where are reasonably priced places to stay for Pesach.

Go Kosher

bhtech.net/temp/Go_Kosher/

5 Lamont Court

Brooklyn, NY 11225

1-888-GO-KOSHER

(718) 773-7340

email: *lebovic@mindspring.com*

A business that, for a fee, will help kasher your home

"Ask the Rabbi" Sites

Several websites include an "Ask the Rabbi" section, where you can ask a rabbinical expert questions on kashrut and other Jewish-related issues. They also include a searchable archive of questions and answers. Sample questions include "Is calcium carbonate a dairy ingredient?" (No) and "If a food item is labeled 'non-dairy,' is that the same as pareve?" (No—it might contain animal-based additives).

The best sites I've found include the following:

www.jewish.com

Useful, somewhat clunky (as in slow to respond), site with questions and answers on Jewish rituals, including kashrut. Contributors include Orthodox, Conservative, and Reform rabbis—an unusual clearinghouse.

www.halacha.net

A general information site of rabbis and scholars who will answer any questions you may have on Jewish topics, from an Orthodox perspective. Includes an archive and Q&As.

www.ohr.edu

Succinct information about holidays and kashrut.

www.askmoses.com

The perspective here is generally Orthodox. Available in five languages: English, Hebrew, Russian, Spanish, and French.

Jewish Movements

Orthodox

The Orthodox Union

See page 264. The OU is one of the largest Orthodox organizations, as well as being a kashrut supervising organization.

The Orthodox Union Network

www.yerushalayim.net

A comprehensive, reasonably up-to-date list of links to Jewish sites operated by the Orthodox Union.

National Council of Young Israel (NCYI)

3 West 16th Street
New York, NY 10011
(212) 929-1525 or (800) 617-NCYI
Fax: (212) 727-9526
email: *ncyi@youngisrael.org*
www.youngisrael.org

Represents roughly 150 Orthodox congregations in the United States and Canada. A guide to affiliated synagogues.

Chabad-Lubavitch in Cyberspace

www.lubavitch.com

Chabad is the outreach arm of the Lubavitch Chassidim. Includes links to all Chabad Houses around the world. Chabad is active in encouraging all Jews to be more observant, and will help you kasher your kitchen. They are helpful, but some find their tactics strong and almost proselytizing.

Conservative

The Rabbinical Assembly

3080 Broadway
New York, NY 10027
(212) 280-6000
email: *rabassembly@jtsa.edu*
www.rabassembly.org
Site for Conservative rabbis, with links to other Conservative sites

Jewish Theological Seminary

3080 Broadway
New York, NY 10027
(212) 678-8000
www.jtsa.edu and *www.learn.jtsa.edu*
The main Conservative rabbinical school, with much information on Conservative Judaism.

Second site has a series of educational articles on Jewish issues.

The United Synagogue of Conservative Judaism

The Rapaport House
155 Fifth Avenue
New York, NY 10010-6802
(212) 533-7800
Fax: (212) 353-9439
email: *info@uscj.org*

www.uscj.org

The umbrella organization for the Conservative movement. Includes information on Solomon Schechter Day Schools, Jewish publications, and many other resources.

Mercaz USA
155 Fifth Avenue
New York, NY 10010
(212) 533-7800 × 2016
Fax: (212) 533-2601
email: *info@mercazusa.org*
www.mercazusa.org
"The Zionist membership organization of the Conservative Movement."

Women's League for Conservative Judaism
475 Riverside Drive, Suite 820
New York, NY 10115
(212) 870-1260 or (800) 628-5083
Fax: (212) 870-1261
email: *womensleague@wlcj.org*
www.wlcj.org

The Federation of Jewish Men's Clubs Inc.
475 Riverside Drive, Suite 832
New York, NY 10115
(212) 749-8100 or (800) 288-FJMC
Fax: (212) 316-4271
International@JMC.org
www.fjmc.org

Reform

Hebrew Union College
3101 Clifton Avenue
Cincinnati, OH 45220
(513) 221-1875
Fax: (513) 221-1847
www.huc.edu
The Reform movement has rabbinical schools in several locations, in addition to the above address. The website will link you to them all, as well as to other schools and sites affiliated with the Reform movement.

Central Conference of American Rabbis
355 Lexington Avenue
New York, NY 10017
(212) 972-3636
email: *info@ccarnet.org*
www.ccarnet.org
The rabbinical organization for the Reform movement. Includes links to Reform platform and Responsa.

Union for Reform Judaism
633 Third Avenue
New York, NY 10017-6778
(212) 650-4000
www.uahc.org
The umbrella organization for Reform synagogues in America.

Reconstructionist

Jewish Reconstructionist Federation
7804 Montgomery Avenue, Suite 9
Elkins Park, PA 19027
(215) 782-8500

Fax: (215) 782-8805
email: *info@jrf.org*
www.jrf.org
General information on the Reconstructionist movement, with essays and links to other sites. Publishes *Reconstructionism Today*, some of which is available online.

Reconstructionist Rabbinical College
1299 Church Road
Wyncote, PA 19095-6143
(215) 576-0800
Fax: (215) 576-6143
www.rrc.edu
The Reconstructionist rabbinical school.

Jewish Cooking

Cookbooks

I have, shall we say, *many* cookbooks. And many Jewish cookbooks. I recommend the following:

Jewish Cooking in America (Alfred A. Knopf, 1994, 1998); *The Jewish Holiday Kitchen* (Schocken Books, 1988); and *The Foods of Israel Today* (Alfred A. Knopf, 2001), all by Joan Nathan. I love Nathan's books. They have great, varied recipes and are incredibly informative. The first book offers a fascinating account of American Jewish culinary history. The second is one of the quintessential Jewish holiday cookbooks. And the third is a wonderful survey of Israeli Jewish cuisine.

The New Jewish Holiday Cookbook by Gloria Kaufer Greene (Times Books, 1985, 1999). One of my favorite Jewish holiday cookbooks. Green has an accessible, informative writing style, and the recipes are both familiar and different as well as varied, with information on holiday customs.

The Sephardic Kitchen (HarperCollins Publishers, 1996) and *Yiddish Cuisine* (Jason Aronson, 1993) by Rabbi Robert Sternberg. Well-written accounts of two very different types of Jewish cooking.

New Kosher Cuisine for All Seasons, edited by Ivy Feurstadt and Melinda Strauss (Ten Speed Press, 1993). A publication of recipes from the Solomon Schechter Day

School of Greater Boston (where my kids go), and an enjoyable collection of holiday menus.

The Book of Jewish Food by Claudia Roden (Alfred A. Knopf, 1996), a collection of 800-plus recipes, with historical information, both Sephardic and Ashkenazic.

Spice and Spirit: The Complete Kosher Jewish Cookbook edited by Esther S. Blau (Lubavitch Women's Cookbook Publications, 1997). Truly a wealth of kosher recipes, with information on holidays and kashrut, from a Lubavitch perspective.

The World of Jewish Cooking (Simon & Schuster, 1996) by Gil Marks. Marks writes frequently on Jewish food for several publications, and the book is filled with more than 500 recipes, plus interesting tidbits of information on all kinds of Jewish cooking.

Web Recipe Sources

www.jewishfood-list.com
Detailed exchange of recipes organized by type of food and by holiday

www.jewish-food.org
Plethora of Jewish recipes

www.cyber-kitchen.com/rfcj
Tons of recipes, many organized by holiday, including smaller holidays such as Tu B'Shvat

Kosher Restaurants and Markets

Areas where there are the largest concentrations of Jewish populations are the areas that have the greatest number of kosher restaurants. Manhattan, for example, has 188 kosher restaurants, according to a reliable website database search.

Restaurants change frequently, so it is worth getting the most recent edition of *The Jewish Travel Guide*. It's published annually by Jewish Chronicle Publications in London, distributed by Bloch Publishing in the United States. It is not always easy to find, but it is the best hard-copy guide.

You can also check Jewish Community Centers. J.C.C.s often have a kosher dining option, albeit usually cafeteria style.

The best resources for kosher sources is the Web, although not everything is updated regularly. There are several websites that claim to be Kosher Restaurant Guides; many I checked were out of date. However, there are two that, at least based on a local search, are updated frequently and seemed to list only open restaurants.

The website *www.shamash.org/kosher* has a database of kosher restaurants around the world, as well as city and state listings. The guide includes pertinent information such as address, phone, hours, website, as well as information on who supervises the restaurant, whether it's meat or dairy; occasionally, there are reviews.

The website *www.kosherdelight.com* is also up to date and includes the same pertinent information. This site also offers a guide to local kosher markets, caterers, synagogues, and supervisory organizations.

Kosher Food Sources

There are several sources for kosher food by mail and on the Internet. Ideally, for kosher meat, you'll probably want to buy it fresh at a local butcher. But sometimes that may not be an option, and mail-order is an alternative. The following are a few options. Because food-oriented establishments are ever-changing, it is a good idea to call or e-mail before placing an order.

www.mykoshermarket.com
www.kosherkingdomonline.com
www.aviglatt.com
www.koshercornucopia.com
www.koshermania.com
www.kosher.com

Kosher venison and bison are not available at all kosher butchers, but they are available by mail:

Musicon, Inc.
385 Scotchtown Road
Goshen, NY 10924
(845) 294-6378
Fax: (516) 239-8915
email: *norman@koshervenison.com*
www.koshervenison.com

www.kosherbison.com
(928) 395-1049

Miscellaneous Jewish Information

Websites

Soc.Culture.Jewish Newsgroups
www.scjfaq.org/faq
Incredibly detailed overview on all things Jewish. Excellent, informative site, though sometimes hard to find. Seems to exist in various incarnations simultaneously.

Shamash: The Jewish Network
www.shamash.org
Frequently updated source of Jewish information, with many good links, including links to specialized mailing lists.

www.jewishencyclopedia.com
The 1906 Jewish Encyclopedia, online, complete with graphics. Fascinating material. Useful, too.

Judaism 101
www.jewfaq.org
An unbelievably thorough and incredibly well-written and researched website exploring all aspects of Judaism. Copy is written by law librarian Tracey Rich, who de-

scribes herself as "just a traditional, observant Jew who has put in a lot of research." I'll say. This is one of the best, most objective, agendaless, and useful sites on Judaism I have seen.

www.akhlah.com
A child-oriented website offering an introduction to various aspects of Judaism from an Orthodox perspective, including an outline of the *melachot* of Shabbat, an introduction to the Hebrew alphabet, and a summary of each book of the Torah. All accompanied by cheerful, colorful graphics. Good for kids and for novices. *Akhlah* is slang for "cool" or "groovy."

www.hebcal.com
A useful guide to the Hebrew calendar. Will convert any date from Hebrew to Gregorian calendars, or vice versa.

National Center for the Hebrew Language
www.ivrit.org
I use various transliterated Hebrew words in this book. Knowing and understanding Hebrew brings an added dimension to prayers and to understanding the Torah. This site is a good resource as an introduction to Hebrew.

Jewish Virtual Library
www.us-israel.org
A virtual online encyclopedia of information on Jewish topics, ranging from kashrut to the holidays to who's who in Jewish history. Some factual information may need to be verified at other sources, but it is a very useful overview reference.

New Jersey Region United Synagogue of Conservative Judaism
www.uscj.org/njersey/bracha12.html
A list of fifty-two common blessings and when to say them, in Hebrew, English transliteration of the Hebrew, and English. The site offers other information as well, but I find it most useful for the *brachot*.

Ohr Torah Stone

www.ohrtorah.org.il

The website for Rabbi Shlomo Riskin, in Israel. Much useful information on the holidays and other Jewish concerns.

www.wikipedia.org

An online encyclopedia with a useful section on Kashrut and Jewish issues.

Jewish Heritage Online Magazine

www.jhom.com

An online magazine with several well-researched articles. Especially worthwhile are their articles on holidays.

Bible and Halacha Information

Books

The Stone Edition Tanach, edited by Rabbi Nosson Scherman (Mesorah Publications, The ArtScroll Series, 1996, 2000). A terrific edition of the Tanach, all under one cover.

The Schottenstein Edition Talmud Bavli (Mesorah Publications, The ArtScroll Series). A beautiful edition of the Talmud, in English and Hebrew, wonderfully cross-referenced. Comes in two sizes. Not all the books of the Talmud are available in English yet, but they have only a few more to go. A worthwhile addition to any Jewish library.

Back to the Sources: Reading the Classic Jewish Texts, edited by Barry W. Holtz (Summit Books, 1984). A useful guide to Jewish texts.

Websites

Mechon Mamre

12 Hayyim Vital Street
Jerusalem, Israel
972-2-652-1906

email: *home@mechon-mamre.org*`

www.mechon-mamre.org

General information about texts. The best part of this site is the online Hebrew-English Tanach. They use a 1917 JPS translation.

Project Genesis

www.torah.org

An invaluable site, with commentary by Orthodox rabbis from all over and all kinds of halachic issues, including kashrut, the weekly Torah portion, and the holidays. Extremely useful for those who want in-depth insights.

www.ucalgary.ca/~elsegal/index.html

A site maintained by Professor Eliezer Segal, Department of Religious Studies, University of Calgary. The site can be a little buggy, but the content makes it worthwhile. Segal has articles on Jewish topics ranging from "Tshlonet" to "The Huppah: From Eden to Today" that are thoroughly researched and informative. Includes a comprehensive guide to the various Orthodox movements.

Rashi Yomi

www.rashiyomi.com

This is an amazing resource site maintained by Dr. Russell Jay Hendel. You can look up any verse in the Torah (the Five Books) and find the accompanying Rashi commentary, in English.

Sichos in English

www.sichosinenglish.org

Includes several very detailed online publications on religious matters, such as cooking on Shabbat and other holiday observances.

Jewish Law

www.jlaw.com

Gets into the halachic and legal technicalities of Jewish law, including information on State Kosher Consumer Protection Laws.

BIBLIOGRAPHY

Abrahams, Israel. *Festival Studies*. Philadelphia: Julius H. Greenstone, 1906.

Alpert, Rebecca T., and Jacob J. Staub. *Exploring Judaism: A Reconstructionist Approach*. New York: The Reconstructionist Press, 2000, 1985.

Angel, Gilda. *Sephardic Holiday Cooking*. Mount Vernon, NY: Decalogue Books, 1986.

Bachman, Ramona. *Simply Kosher: Exotic Food from Around the World*. Jerusalem, Israel: Gefen Publishing House, 1994.

Barras, Rabbi Hyman J. *Minchas Chai "Gift of Life."* Bronx, NY: Waldon Press, 1974.

Berman, Jeremiah J. *Shehitah: A Study in the Cultural and Social Life of the Jewish People*. New York: Bloch Publishing Co., Inc., 1941.

Berman, Louis A. *Vegetarianism & the Jewish Tradition*. New York: Ktav Publishing House, 1982.

Birnbaum, Philip, editor. *Maimonides' Mishneh Torah (Yad Hazakah), abridged*. New York: Hebrew Publishing Co., 1967, 1944.

Blau, Esther S., editor-in-chief, Lubavitch Women's Organization—Junior Division. *The Spice and Spirit of Kosher-Jewish Cooking*. New York: Bloch Publishing Co., Inc., 1977.

Blau, Esther S., editor-in-chief, Tzirrel Deitsch, and Cherna Light. *Spice and Spirit: The Complete Kosher Jewish Cookbook*. New York: Lubavitch Women's Cookbook Publications, 1997.

Central Council of Jewish Religious Education in the United Kingdom and Eire. *The Book of Kashrut*. Great Britain: The Central Council of Jewish Religious Education in the United Kingdom and Eire, 1948 (na).

Cohen, Noah J. *Tsa'ar Ba'ale Hayim: The Prevention of Cruelty to Animals: Its Bases, Development and Legislation in Hebrew Literature*. Jerusalem, Israel; New York: Feldheim Publishers, 1976, 1959.

Cohn, Rabbi Jacob. *The Royal Table: An Outline of the Dietary Laws of Israel*. New York: Bloch Publishing Co., Inc., 1936.

Cooper, John. *Eat and Be Satisfied: A Social History of Jewish Food*. Northvale, NJ; Jerusalem, Israel: Jason Aronson, Inc., 1993.

Donin, Rabbi Hayim Halevy. *To Be a Jew: A Guide to Jewish Observance in Contemporary Life*. New York: Basic Books, 1991, 1972.

Dresner, Samuel H., and David M. Pollock. *Keeping Kosher: A Diet for the Soul: Revised Edition of the Jewish Dietary Laws and A Guide to Observance*. New York: United Synagogue of Conservative Judaism Commission on Jewish Education, 2000, 1982, 1966, 1959.

Dresner, Samuel H., Seymour Siegel, and David M. Pollock. *The Jewish Dietary Laws, Revised and Expanded Edition: "Their Meaning for Our Time" by Dresner, "A Guide to Observance" by Siegel and Pollock*. New York: United Synagogue Commission on Jewish Education, 1982, 1966, 1959.

Duschinsky, C. *May a Woman Act as a Shoheteth? Reprinted from The Gaster Anniversary Volume, edited by B. Schindler and A. Marmorstein*. London: Taylor's Foreign Press, 1937.

Epstein, Rabbi Dr. Isidore, translator. *Babylonian Talmud, Seder Kodashim, Hullin I*. London: Soncino Press, 1948.

——. *Babylonian Talmud, Seder Kodashim, Hullin II*. London: Soncino Press, 1948.

Forst, Rabbi Binyomin. *The Laws of Kashrus: A Comprehensive Exposition of Their Underlying Concepts and Applications*. Brooklyn, NY: Mesorah Publications, Ltd.; The Artscroll Series, 2002, 2000, 1993.

Freedman, Seymour E. *The Book of Kashruth: A Treasury of Kosher Facts & Frauds*. New York: Bloch Publishing Co., Inc., 1970.

Friedland, Susan R. *Shabbat Shalom: Recipes and Menus for the Sabbath*. New York: Little, Brown and Company, 1999.

Friedlander, Gerald. *Laws and Customs of Israel*. London: Shapiro, Vallentine and Co., 1924.

Ganzfried, Solomon. *Code of Jewish Law, Volume III (Kitzur Schulchan Aruch)*. Translated by Rabbi Dovid Oratz. New York: Star Hebrew Book Company/Hebrew Publishing Company, 1927.

Gastwirt, Harold P. *Fraud, Corruption, and Holiness: The Controversies Over the Supervision of Jewish Dietary Practice in New York City 1881–1940*. Port Washington, NY: National University Publications Kennikat Press, 1974.

Gelbard, Shmuel Pinchas. *Rite and Reason: 1050 Jewish Customs and Their Sources*. Translated by R. Nachman Bulman. Petach Tikvah, Israel: Mifal Rashi Publishing, 1998.

Greenburg, Betty D., and Althea O. Silverman. *The Jewish Home Beautiful*. New York: The Women's League of the United Synagogue of America, 1950, 1941.

Greenburg, Blu. *How to Run a Traditional Jewish Household*. New York: Fireside, 1983.

Gross, Rabbi Sholom Yehuda. *Encyclopedia of Kashruth: Vol. IV: Kosher for Long Life*. Brooklyn, NY: Mosad Brucha Tova, 1980.

Grunfeld, Dayan Dr. I. *The Jewish Dietary Laws, Volume One: Dietary Laws Regarding Forbidden and Permitted Foods, with Particular Reference to Meat and Meat Products*. London/Jerusalem/New York: Soncino Press, 1972.

———. *The Jewish Dietary Laws, Volume Two: Dietary Laws Regarding Plants and Vegetables, with Particular Reference to the Produce of the Holy Land*. London/Jerusalem/New York: Soncino Press, 1972.

Halperin, Rabbi Levi Yitzchak. *Kashrut and the Modern Kitchen*. Translated by Samuel Jaffe. Jerusalem, Israel: Feldheim & the Institute for Science and Halacha, 1994.

———. *Shabbat and the Modern Kitchen: Electrical and Electronic Devices on Shabbat*. Translated by Rabbi Dovid Oratz. Jerusalem, Israel: Gefen Publishing House, 1986.

Isaacs, Ronald H. *Every Person's Guide to Purim*. Northvale, NJ; Jerusalem, Israel: Jason Aronson, Inc., 2000.

Kahan, Rabbi Israel Meir. *The Dispersed of Israel*. New York: Aaron Kagan/Torath Chofetz Chaim Publications, 1951.

Kaplan, Aryeh. *Sabbath: Day of Eternity*. New York: National Conference of Synagogue Youth/Union of Orthodox Jewish Congregations of America, 1984, 1974.

Kashrus Division, Student Organization of Yeshiva, Rabbi Isaac Elchanan Theological Seminary. *A Guide to Kashrus and Yom Tov*. New York: Yeshiva University (na).

Katz, Jacob. *The "Shabbes Goy"/Goi shel Shabat: A Study in Halakhic Flexibility*. Translated by Yoel Lerner. Philadelphia: The Jewish Publication Society, 1989.

Klagsbrun, Francine. *The Fourth Commandment: Remember the Sabbath Day*. New York: Harmony Books, 2002.

Klein, Isaac. *A Guide to Jewish Religious Practice*. New York; Jerusalem, Israel: The Jewish Theological Seminary of America, 1992, 1979.

———. *Responsa and Halakhic Studies*. Jersey City, NJ: KTAV Publishing House, 1975.

Lamm, Norman. *The Sabbath: Model for a Theory of Leisure*. New York: Jewish Education Committee of New York, 1969.

Levi, Shonie B., and Sylvia R. Kaplan. *Guide for the Jewish Homemaker*. Translated by Herbert Danby. New York: Schocken Books and Farrar Straus and Company, 1971, 1964, 1959.

Levin, S. I., and Edward A. Boyden. *The Kosher Code of the Orthodox Jew: Being a literal translation of that portion of the sixteenth-century codification of the Babylonian Talmud which describes such deficiencies as render animals unfit for food (Hilkot Terefor, Shulhan Aruk); to which is appended a discussion of talmudic anatomy in the light of the science of its day and of the present time*. Minneapolis, MN: University of Minnesota Press, 1940.

Levinger, I. M. *Shechita in the Light of the Year 2000: Critical Review of the Scientific Aspects of Methods of Slaughter and Shechita*. Jerusalem, Israel: Machon Maskil L'David, Mifalei Torah Vehoraah, Machon of Kashruth, 1995.

Lewin, Rabbi Isaac, Rabbi Michael L. Munk, and Rabbi Jeremiah J. Berman. *Religious Freedom: The Right to Practice Shehitah*. New York: Research Institute for Post-War Problems of Religious Jewry, 1946.

Lipschuz, Rabbi Yacov. *Kashruth: A Comprehensive Background and Reference Guide to the Principles of Kashruth*. Brooklyn, NY: Mesorah Publications, Ltd.; The Artscroll Series, 1988.

Maimonides. *Code of Maimonides Book Ten, The Book of Cleanness*. Translated by Hyman E. Glodin. New Haven, CT: Yale University Press, 1954.

———. *Mishneh Torah, The Book of Knowledge: Edited According to the Bodleian (Oxford) Codes with Introduction, Biblical and Talmudical References*. Translated by Moses Hyamson. Jerusalem, Israel: Boys Town Jerusalem Publishers, 1965.

Manischewitz Co. *Tempting Kosher Dishes: Prepared from World-Famous Manischewitz's Matzo Products.* Cincinnati, OH: B. Manischewitz Co., 1930.

Munk, Michael L. and Eli, editors, and I. M. Levinger. *Shechita.* Brooklyn, NY; Jerusalem, Israel: Gur Aryeh Institute for Advanced Jewish Scholarship, Feldheim Distributors, 1976.

Olitzky, Kerry M. *Preparing Your Home for Passover: A Guide for Spiritual Readiness.* Philadelphia: The Jewish Publication Society, 2002.

Plaut, W. Gunther, editor, Central Conference of American Rabbis. *A Shabbat Manual/Tadrich L'Shabbat.* New York: Ktav Publishing House, 1972.

Rabbinical Assembly. *Proceedings of the Committee on Jewish Law and Standards of the Conservative Movement 1980–1985.* New York: The Rabbinical Assembly, 1988.

Reider, Freda. *The Hallah Book.* Jersey City, NJ: KTAV Publishing House, 1987.

Rosenberg, Stuart E. *The Search for Jewish Identity in America.* Garden City, NY: Anchor Books/Doubleday, 1965, 1964.

Rudavsky, David. *Modern Jewish Religious Movements: A History of Emancipation and Adjustment.* New York: Behrman House, 1979, 1967.

Schauss, Hayyim. *The Jewish Festivals.* New York: Schocken Books and the Union of American Hebrew Congregations, 1962, 1938.

Schloff, Linda Mack. *And Prairie Dogs Weren't Kosher: Jewish Women in the Upper Midwest Since 1855.* Saint Paul, MN: Minnesota Historical Society, 1996.

Schwartz, Richard H., Ph.D. *Judaism and Vegetarianism.* New York: Lantern Books, 2001.

Segal, Samuel M. *The Sabbath Book.* New York: Behrman's Jewish Book House, 1942.

Sheinkopf, Rabbi David I. *Gelatin in Jewish Law: An Exposition of the Halakhah Pertaining to the Use of Inedible Animal Parts as Sources for Kosher Food.* New York: Bloch Publishing Co., Inc., 1982.

Steingroot, Ira. *Keeping Passover: Everything You Need to Know to Bring the Ancient Tradition to Life and Create Your Own Passover Celebration.* San Francisco, CA: CollinsSanFrancisco, 1995.

Vainstein, Yaacov. *The Cycle of the Jewish Year: A Study of the Festivals and of Selections from the Liturgy.* Jerusalem, Israel: The Department for Torah Education and Culture in the Diaspora, the World Zionist Organization, 1964.

Washofsky, Mark. *Jewish Living: A Guide to Contemporary Reform Practice.* New York: UAHC Press, 2001.

Weinreich, Max. *Geshikhte Fun Der Yidisher Shprakh: History of the Yiddish Language*. New York: Workman's Circle, 1973.

Welfeld, Irving. *Why Kosher?: An Anthology of Answers*. Northvale, NJ; Jerusalem, Israel: Jason Aronson, Inc., 1996.

Wolff, Eliezer. *Keeping Kosher in a Nonkosher World*. Brooklyn, NY: Shmuel Wolff, 1989.

Wolfson, Dr. Ron. *The Shabbat Seder: The Art of Jewish Living, a Project of the Federation of Jewish Men's Clubs and the University of Judaism*. Woodstock, VT: Jewish Lights Publishing, 1996, 1985.

INDEX

Shabbat meal preparation and, 124, 125, 127, 186

blenders:

    kashering of, 98, 184

    see also immersion blenders

blood:

    shechita and, 34, 35, 36–37

    spots in eggs, 58–59

    Torah prohibition against consumption of, 21, 28–29

bones, 75

Brachot, 145

bread, 65–66

    Orthodox halacha on, 54, 66

    see also challah

bread machines, kashering of, 99

brisket, slow-roasted savory, 236–37

butternut squash puree, 226

cabbage salad, sweet-and-sour, 203–4

cabinets, kashering of, 89, 182

cake:

    chocolate pudding, 251–52

    honey, 247–48

    honey layer, with caramelized apples, 248–50

candles, lighting of:

    on Chanukah, 154

    for Shabbat, 119, 125, 130, 154

capon, 57

carmine, 76

Caro, Joseph, 5, 102

carrot(s):

    -almond torte with apple-apricot compote, 245–47

    coins, 143, 223–24

    in roasted roots, 224–25

    on Rosh Hashanah, 143

casein, 77–78

castoreum, 76

caviar, 63, 64

chagim, see holidays

chalav stam (neutral milk), 60

chalav Yisrael (milk of Israel), 59, 60, 61

chalef (slaughterer's knife), 34, 37

challah, 196–200

    for Rosh Hashanah, 140

    separating of, 66–68, 129

    for Shabbat, 129

chametz, 173–75

    checking for, *see bedikat chametz*

    commandment against consumption of, 173, 174

    definition of, 173–74, 175

    destroying of, *see bi'ur chametz*

    selling of, *see mechirat chametz*

Chanukah, 134, 152–56

    candlelighting on, 154

    culinary traditions of, 154–55

    gift giving on, 155–56

    menorah (*chanukiah*) for, 154

    story of, 153

charoset:

    apple-pear, 229

    on seder plate, 192, 193

Chassidism, 8, 13, 82, 157

chazara (returning), 122, 125–26

chazeret (bitter herb), 192

Cheddar cheese, in enchilada lasagna, 242–43

cheese:

    as Chanukah food, 155

    kosher, 61–62

    see also dairy; *specific cheeses*

chegavim (grasshopper species), eating of, 28

fish: (*continued*)
   selection of, 64–65
   stew, spiced, 232–33
flatware, metal, kashering of, 104–5, 186
flood, biblical, omnivorous diet acceptable
    after, 20, 21
fluffy Pesach vegetable kugels, 217–20
foie gras, 57–58
Food and Drug Administration (FDA), 43
   ingredient label regulations and, 41
food processors, kashering of, 98, 184
foulares, 164
Fraud, Corruption, and Holiness (Gastwirt),
    43, 44
frosting, honey cream, for honey layer cake
    with caramelized apples, 250
Frutas, Las (Fruticas), 157
frying pans, kashering of, 106

gebrochts, 179–80
Gedaliah ben Ahikam, 144
gelatin, Orthodox vs. Conservative rulings on,
    74–76
Gemara, 4–5
   see also Talmud
Genesis, Book of, 115, 119, 141, 160
   dietary stipulations in, 20–21, 22, 28, 168
   as prehistory of Jewish people, 171
   Shabbat and, 113–14, 116
genetically modified organisms (GMOs),
    72
ginger(ed):
   fresh, in slow-roasted savory brisket,
    236–37
   -tomato chickpeas, 244
glassware, kashering of, 102–3, 186

glatt kosher, 35
glycerides, mono- or di-, 76–77
glycerine (glycerol), 77
glycine, 77
Golinkin, David, 178
grains:
   chadash and *yahsan,* 73
   chametz yielding, 174
   considered kitniyot, 175–76, 177
   in making matzos, 179
   see also specific grains
grape juice, matzo made with, 179
grapes, 70–72
   on Tu B'Shvat, 159
green beans, roasted, 227
Greenspan, Ari, 27, 28
Greenstein, Edward, 190
griddles, kashering of, 101, 185
grills, outdoor, kashering of, 101, 185
Guide to Jewish Practice, A (Teutsch), 10
Guide to Jewish Religious Practice, A (Klein),
    8, 113, 155
Guide to the Perplexed (Rambam), 11

hag'alah, 103–6
Haggadah, 170
hakafot, 152
halacha, 6
   information on, 278–79
halibut, in spiced fish stew, 232–33
hamantashen:
   fillings, 163, 164, 260–62
   origin and name of, 163
   pastry, 257–59
   trio, 256–62
Havdalah, 119, 120, 128, 130–31

hearty beef cholent, 239–40

Hebrew language, 18, 19

hechshers (kosher certification):
  food sales boosted by, 44, 48
  generic K, 46
  ingredient kosher vs., 3, 40–42
  mashgiach and, 47–48
  obtaining of, 46–49
  Pesach and, 174–75, 178, 181–82
  symbols in, 42, 44, 45–46
  verifying of, 46

Heinemann, Moshe, 62

herb-baked salmon, chilled, 230–31

Heschel, Abraham Joshua, 118–19

History of the Yiddish Language (Weinreich), 49

holidays (*chagim*):
  kashrut and, 132–69
  seasonal tie-in of, 133
  Three Pilgrimage Festivals (*Shloshet Haregalim*), *see* Pesach; Shavuot; Sukkot
  Torah description of, 134, 135, 136, 137, 139, 144, 145, 147, 150, 151, 165–66, 167, 171–72, 173, 179, 182, 187, 189, 190–91, 192
  types of, 134–37
  see also specific holidays

honey, 22
  in apple-pear *charoset*, 229
  cake, 247–48
  layer cake with caramelized apples, 248–50
  on Rosh Hashanah, 140–41
  in slow-roasted savory brisket, 236–37

Horayot, 141

horseradish, 192

Hoshanah Rabbah, 134, 139, 151

How to Run a Traditional Jewish Household (Greenberg), 136, 155

immersion blenders, kashering of, 98–99, 185

ingredient kosher, 88
  additives and, 41
  FDA labeling regulations and, 41
  keeping hechsher kosher vs., 3, 40–42

inosinic acid (inosinate), 77

insects, kosher, 27–28

Isaiah, Book of:
  fasting in, 144
  Shabbat in, 116, 121

Israel:
  kitniyot in, 177, 178
  produce from, 68, 71, 72, 157
  Purim in, 165
  Yom Tov holidays as celebrated in Diaspora vs., 136

Isserles, Moses, 5, 102, 176

Jacob, angel wrestling with, 22

Jeremiah, Book of, 144

Jewish calendar, 132–34
  Gregorian calendar vs., 132–33
  as lunisolar, 133
  months in, 133, 134, 136, 161
  years in, 133–34, 161

Jewish Dietary Laws, The (Grunfeld), 11, 20, 29, 70

Jewish Encyclopedia, 37

Jewish Festivals, The (Shauss), 155–56

Jewish Holidays, The (Strassfeld), 190

Jewish Living (Washofsky), 112

Jewish Travel Guide, The, 274–75

New Jewish Holiday Cookbook, The (Greene), 163
Noah, 20, 21, 115, 168
noodles:
    Asian, in sweet-and-sour cabbage salad, 203–4
    egg, in classic lokchen kugel, 216–17
Numbers, Book of, 107, 169
    holidays mentioned in, 139

oils, 74
OK (circle K) certification, 44
oleic acid, 77
olives, on Tu B'Shvat, 159
Omer HaTnufah, 166
onion-potato kugel, sliced, 214–15
orange juice:
    in apple-apricot compote, 246–47
    in honey cake, 247–48
Orejas de Haman, 163
orlah, 72, 157
Orthodox Judaism, 7–8, 44
    Kashrut in, 3, 8, 10, 13–14, 25, 45, 50,
        53–55, 56, 60, 62, 63, 65, 66–67, 68, 70,
        72, 73, 74–76, 77, 79, 80, 82, 88, 89, 90,
        91, 93, 94, 95, 97, 98, 99, 101, 102,
        103, 104, 105, 106, 107, 108–9, 113
    Pesach rulings of, 176, 179–80, 183, 184,
        186, 189
    Shabbat observances of, 112, 113, 126, 127
    women's and men's roles in, 8, 152
    Yom Tov cooking in, 137
Orthodox Union (OU), 8, 44
ostriches, 25
OU certification, 42, 44
ovens:
    kashering of, 94, 184
    in Shabbat cooking, 126

oxystearin, 77
oznei haman, 163
    hamantashen pastry, 258

pans, kashering of, 106–7, 186
pareve, 49, 50, 86
parsley:
    in carrot coins, 223–24
    in lemon-scented roast chicken, 238
    on seder plate (*karpas*), 193
    in *sficha,* 202–3
pastry, hamantashen, 257–59
pear-apple charoset, 229
pecan(s):
    in challah variation, 200
    rum pie, 252–54
pepsin, 77
perfect potato latkes, 220–21
Persian hamantashen pastry, 259
Pesach, 133, 137, 165, 170–94
    cooking restrictions on, 173
    names of, 172
    as Pilgrimage Festival, 38, 147, 166
    purchasing food for, 181–82
    seder for, *see* seder, Pesach
    significance of, 170, 171, 172–73
    Song of Songs read on, 161
    story of, 171–72
    stricter level of kashrut observance during,
        174
    as supersanctification of meals,
        193–94
    Ta'anit Bechorim (Fast of the Firstborn)
        and, 189–90
    in Torah, 134, 166, 171–72, 173, 179, 182,
        187, 189, 190–91, 192
pesach, 172

Song of Songs, Pesach reading of, 161

soup:

chicken, with my mother's ethereal matzo balls, 206–7

chicken stock, 205–6

chilled cucumber–yogurt, 213

red lentil, 212

vegetable stock, 210–11

sour cream, in classic lokchen kugel, 216–17

squash (*karah*):

butternut squash puree, 226

as symbolic Rosh Hashanah food, 141, 142

Star-K Certification, 35, 42, 45

Starr, David, 8, 14, 109

stearic acid, 77

Steigman, Dovid, 33

Sternberg, Robert, 142–43, 163

stew, spiced fish, 232–33

stock:

chicken, 205–6

vegetable, 210–11

strawberry jam, in hamantashen sesame filling, 260

stuffing, matzo-vegetable, 228

sturgeon, 63, 64, 76

sufganiot (jelly doughnuts), 155

sukkah (Sukkot booth):

building and decorating of, 147–50, 170

schach for, 148, 149

Sukkot, 38, 133, 137, 139, 147–51, 170

Arba Minim (Four Species) on, 150–51

culinary traditions of, 151

Ecclesiastes read on, 161

food preparation restrictions on, 147

as Pilgrimage Festival, 38, 147

in Torah, 134, 147, 150

sweet-and-sour cabbage salad, 203–4

sweet potato:

in roasted roots, 224–25

-rosemary kugel, 215–16

swordfish, 63

Ta'anit Bechorim (Fast of the Firstborn), 135

siyum loophole and, 190

Ta'anit Ester (Fast of Esther), 134, 135, 162

tables, Pesach covering of, 183

tahor (ritually clean), 19

tallit (prayer shawl), 18

Talmud, 4, 5, 6, 7, 15, 141–42, 159

Chanukah in, 154

on deaths of Rabbi Akiva's students, 166

on first month of the year, 134

and laws of kashrut, 18, 26, 29, 31–32, *33, 34*, 39, 50, 53, 57, 59, 61, 63, 75, 83, 85

New Year days described in, 156–57

on Pesach, 170, 174, 176, 178, 191, 192

on Purim, 163

Shabbat and, 120, 121, 124

siyum and, 189, 190

on Tishri, 134, 139

on Yom Kippur, 145

tamei (ritually impure), 19–20

Tanach (Bible), 4, 5, 278–79

other holidays in, 134, 135, 136, 137, 139, 144, 145, 147, 150, 151, 156, 161, 165–66, 167, 171–72, 173, 179, 182, 187, 189, 190–91, 192

Shabbat in, 113–18

tefillin (phylacteries), 18

Teflon, 106

Temple, Holy (*Beit Hamikdash*), 147, 153–54, 165–66, 167, 168, 169, 191

Ten Commandments, 5, 20, 38, 115, 167

Tendler, Moshe, 63